THE ART OF LIFE

THE ART OF LIFE

ON LIVING, LOVE AND DEATH

Edited by Jonathan Rutherford

Lawrence & Wishart
LONDON

Lawrence and Wishart Limited
99a Wallis Road
London
E9 5LN

First published 2000

British Library Cataloguing in Publication Data.
A catalogue record for this book is available from the
British Library

ISBN 0 85315 906 8

Text setting Derek Doyle and Associates, Liverpool
Printed and bound by Redwood Books, Trowbridge

CONTENTS

Preface   7

Introduction: Mere Life   9
Jonathan Rutherford

The Sacred Life   19
Madeleine Bunting

Zombie Categories   35
Interview with Ulrich Beck

Re-thinking Work   52
Suzanne Franks

The Art of Life   63
Jonathan Rutherford

No Place Like home   79
Roshi Naidoo

Friendship   89
Ray Pahl

On Being Alone   115
Wendy Wheeler

Masculinity: A Risky Path to Take?   135
Michael Kenny and Nick Stevenson

Authority   152
Rachel Thomson

Living with Death   164
Brian Heaphy

Being Alive   183
Interview with Adam Phillips

Shopping Around for a Place to Stay   197
Zygmunt Bauman

Notes on Contributors   220

Acknowledgements   223

Poems

Nina Cassian   *Temptation*   18

Jacek Podsiadlo   *Grass Accepts*   107
                    Don't Leave Me   108

Stephen Knight   *The Stepfather*   109
                    A British Summer   110

Anna Robinson   *Love Poem*   111
                    My Name Is ...   112

Bo Carpelan   (untitled)   128
                    (untitled)   129

Frances Angela   *1999*   130
                    16th June 1999   131

Jackie Kay   *Fiction*   133

Brian Patten   *April Morning Walk*   176
                    The Armada   177

Jaan Kaplinski   (untitled)   178
                    (untitled)   179

Mimi Khalvati   *Gooseberries*   180
                    Middle Age   181
                    Youthing   183

PREFACE

This book is about the ethics of living. It's about how we might invent new ways of speaking about relationships 'between people'. It considers friendship, identity, belonging, virtue, being alone, being alive, death, love, and the sacred.

We are living through a cultural revolution in which the relationships between the local and the global, the political and the ethical, the public and the private are being transformed. In consequence our beliefs and moral values, and our personal experiences and attitudes, are in a state of flux. The old religious authorities and political ideologies which once promised to sustain us through life have been discredited. We find ourselves alone in a society in which we are continually having to make judgements and choices affecting our life course.

The majority of us in the West may no longer fear hunger or destitution, but there are now new dreads of loneliness, failure, insecurity and disenchantment. Wealth and success are no guarantees of happiness. Depression, stress, poverty, no work and over-work, all take their toll on the quality of our lives. Politicians assiduously promote a version of modernity which defines progress in terms of instrumental competence rather than human well being. Their preference tends to be for the imposition of conformity over diversity, for control rather than innovation and creativity, and for organisational efficiency rather human sympathy: school pupils will learn more, nurses will care more efficiently, workers will work harder. Individuals are valued by their market success or productive usefulness. This reflects an ideology of modernisation which is driven by technological imperatives, not by democracy; by the market, not society.

In reaction to this version of modernity, there has been a resurgence of popular interest in spirituality, objects and spaces of the sacred, and new practices of identity and collectivity. In a culture of individualism and privacy we need a recognition of our mutual interdependence. People can live without ideology, but, as the Polish philosopher Leszek

Kolakowski has said, they cannot live without beliefs and shared values. We need to win back an ideal of modernity which is about democracy, personal self-fulfilment and collective well being. The Art of Life is intended as a small step in that direction.

Jonathan Rutherford
February 2000

INTRODUCTION: MERE LIFE

Jonathan Rutherford

This morning I wrote out a list of what I have to do at work – the phone calls I must make, the individuals I have to speak to, the photo-copying to be done, the book to return to the library and the book I must borrow. Divided by a line across the page, I have written the shopping I intend to get after work: milk, margarine, butter, potatoes, vegetables, biscuits, cereals. Sometimes I pin a small piece of paper above my desk at home which lists the lists I must make for the coming week. It is a practice which I imagine will somehow settle and order the future. At least it sets it out task by unforgotten task.

This has been an era of lists – the best ever films, the top one hundred records, the sexiest men, the best dressed women, the build-ing of the century, the twelve step AA programme, the *Cosmopolitan* lists of dos and don'ts in sex, life and love. In an age of uncertainty lists make us feel secure by ordering the contingent and making it compre-hensible and manageable.

The past three decades have witnessed an increasing preoccupation with identity, an attempt to give ourselves meaning and representation by creating an itinerary of our lives. We endeavour to fasten ourselves in a narrative of memory. The past is excavated to elicit the continuity of our selves, our languages and cultures, a desire to leave nothing to chance, to thwart the vicissitudes of life and evade mortality: do not forget, remember this, remember me. Comfort in the past, together with unease with the present, has led to nostalgia and an anxious attempt to evade the turbulence of modernity. And yet identity is something more than solace in the face of an insecure future. Nietzsche argued that self-knowledge is self-creation. Richard Rorty describes identity making as an ethical practice of 'changing the way we talk, and therefore changing what we want to do and what we think we are'.[1] Identity-making is a process of coming to know

9

oneself. It does involve looking to the past, not simply to secure oneself within a safe narrative, but to discover the causes that have made us. Moreover, history connects us as individuals not just to our own personal pasts, but to the social past. It demands we make interpretations of our life experiences. And in identity-making we are also agents of history: we draw on the past, imagine the future and transform the present. 'That is what the modern search is for: where to go next', writes Theodore Zeldin in *An Intimate History of Humanity*: 'The stones of history need to be reused to construct roads which lead to where one wants to go'.

Where do we want to go? How are we to live and what are the things that matter to us which will provide us with our guiding principles? In the affluent parts of the world, we have today an historically unprecedented level of choice, affluence, mobility. Perversely this is our problem. We live with a crisis of choice in a society of secular individualism in which collective ideals expressing social solidarity and values have been dissipated. After two millennia the answer of institutionalised religion to the need for community – the dictats of a monotheistic faith or belief in the omnipotent authority of god – have, for many, come and gone. The sociologist Emile Durkheim described sacred things as being collective ideals which have fixed themselves on material objects, ideas and representations awakened in us by the spectacle of society. But this description suggests a traditional and homogeneous culture, and a relatively unchanging society, in which each individual knew their place. The Reformation began modernity's transformation of this kind of society. The Protestant revolution of the seventeenth century abstracted religion from people's everyday lives. The meaning of life was no longer fixed, but became a task of individual self-reflection and the examination and interpretation of god's word. The sacred gradually came to reside in the mind rather than the body and community. By the end of the eighteenth century there was a growing belief that individuals were endowed with a moral sense. Morality was not simply the edict of ecclesiastical authority or the calculation of divine reward or punishment; it was a voice within. The growth of this individualism raised the question of what were the bonds which held people together in society.

During this period the Romantic poets began to redefine the idea of the sacred. For them the ineffable quality of human existence was the sublime, an intimation of something which exists beyond words and which accounts for the mystery of human life. It was a representation of the individual yearning for life and connection to something more than the self. Today we are left, like Mathew Arnold, listening to the melancholy roar of the receding tide of the sea of faith. In Arnold's poem 'Dover Beach', written in 1851, he concludes: 'And here we are as on a darkling plain/ Swept with confused alarms of struggle and flight,/Where ignorant armies clash by night.' For him the substitute for the loss of religious community, and the protection it offered from nihilism and arbitrary violence, is love and culture: a deep and abiding belief in the goodness of other human beings, and the expression of this faith in the finest works of art and literature. But that belief too, in our democratic age, is viewed with suspicion, as a tattered and dated example of the imposition of class cultural authority.

We can literally see our world today, in the image of earth taken from space. Globalisation has compressed space and time; tourism colonises regions of the earth once inaccessible and remote from the west; media industries lift cultures from their localities and standardise them. But all this seeing on our part does not guarantee our understanding, or even our recognition of other people different from ourselves. The paradox of globalisation is that it has encouraged our defensive concern for the local, the familiar and intimate. In contemporary post-industrial societies we shun grand narratives, global schemes, moral absolutes and big ideas, and instead have turned inward, into our selves. We eschew political parties and public ideologies. Social commentators have lamented this preoccupation with personal life and self-fulfilment as a form of narcissism encouraged by the desire for personal gain and transient satisfaction. Modern capitalism and mass entertainment, they argue, have created a solipsistic world of consumerism which promotes style over substance, image over content. Popular culture is commodified and meaningless and individuals have become rootless and caught in a spiral of transient commitments and failed obligations

This is too simplistic a description of modern western life. It is true that there is widespread cynicism about parliamentary democracy, particularly amongst the younger generation, and that notions of the public good have tended to be displaced by the ideology of individual choice. It is also true that capitalism has extended commodification into increasing areas of social life and culture, just as Marx foresaw over one hundred years ago. The sociological fact of individualisation and privatisation is largely a consequence of the resurgence of neo-liberal capitalism. But this phenomenon is also shaped by people's resistance to capitalism's utilitarianism and its instrumental concern with ends over means. The current turn to the self does not have to be read simply as a retreat from civic virtue or as a defeat for democracy, by morally indifferent individuals. The quest for personal fulfilment – to be true to one's own self - can be viewed as a re-evaluation of moral and political purpose, and a search for what an ethics of living might be. Contrary to what the knockers of modern culture say, this ethic of self-fulfilment cannot be reduced to self-indulgence or egotism. The development of personal consciousness or spiritual beliefs requires emotional and moral labour. Identity is not a discrete individualistic undertaking; it is dialogical: each of us requires social recognition or we are nothing. Our preoccupation with personal relationships cannot be explained simply in terms of the narrowing of our political and social horizons: such reflection is crucial for self-discovery and self-confirmation. The ethic of self-fulfilment has its own implicit morality – the right of everyone to achieve their own unique way of being human. To ignore the needs of others is to fail to live with in its own terms, which require that difference must be recognised and acknowledged. Such an ethic is thus the prerequisite for the consolidation of the values of feminism and gay liberation, and the countering of racism and inequality. Despite the erosion of representative democracy, the spirit and impetus of the democratic revolution inaugurated in the 1960s golden era of consumer capitalism has extended itself into the spheres of culture, family life and personal relationships, as new forms of ethical practice.

This cultural revolution in the sphere of the personal has seen a shift away from morality as an over-arching and universal system of rules and obligations, to more local, negotiated, forms of ethics, a style in keeping with the Stoic philosophers of Ancient Greece and their injunction to 'spend your whole life learning how to live'. 'The precept of the "care of the self"', wrote Michel Foucault, 'was, for the Greeks, one of the main principles of cities, one of the main rules for social and personal conduct and for the art of life'.[2] Today, moral authority and its injunctions can no longer be simply imposed on individuals without challenge or negotiation. Increasing numbers of the population are generating their own ethics in relation to their sexuality, health, bodies and outlook on life. However, new ethical practices and forms of spirituality do not simply replace the more traditional moral systems; they critically engage with them, and in the process adapt and transform them. We are not witnessing the decline of morality, but its burgeoning and pluralisation toward more hybrid, dialogic forms of ethical pragmatism.

On the whole, politicians schooled in the ways of a prescriptive and authoritarian discourse of governance don't understand how to respond to what is happening; nor do they have the political and linguistic means to engage with it in a constructive way. And yet concern with an ethics of the self has been a defining characteristic of modernity. With the rise of individualism in the sixteenth century, criticism of religious and moral authority has been instigated in a growing belief in the importance of the self. 'Finding myself quite empty, with nothing to write about', wrote Michel de Montaigne in his *Essays* published in 1580, ' I offered my self to myself as theme and subject matter.' Montaigne's concern with the care of the self led him to recognise the importance of everyday life. In his essay 'To philosophise is to learn how to die', he argues that the chief aim in life is pleasure: 'Even in virtue our ultimate aim ... is pleasure', he writes, adding, 'we ought to have given virtue the more favourable, noble and natural name of pleasure'. It is an approach in which the management of the self is integral to the ethical consideration of the individual relationship to authority and society. Montaigne, under the nose of the Vatican censor, initiated the challenge to a monadic moral order and its association of value with ascetic denial and dutiful obedience. Virtue is not to be found in an external law or deity, it grows out of the pleasure we discover in being with ourselves, and with those we love and befriend. The fact that we strive to live for ourselves does not mean that we do not also live for others. Just as equally those who live for nobody are not necessarily living for themselves.

The problem we face today is a crisis of moral and cultural leadership. Public political authority is held in contempt. This makes it difficult to distinguish between the private ethic of self-realisation – which has been the driving motor of the democratic revolution – and a public ethic of mutual accommodation which has cruelly suffered from the obsession with neo-liberal ideology shared by the Conservatives and New Labour. A new democratic settlement between the individual and society must maximise the ethical autonomy of the individual within a recovered notion of the public good. That requires a revival of democracy. Such a politics must ask how we are to live together, and how we are to recognise the needs of others and accept our responsibility for them.

This is a question we can apply to those who are poor and excluded – marginal people, exceptions to those of us who are decently fed and housed, and incorporated into the civic order and cultural life of society. Such people have no voice, no language to represent themselves politically and culturally. And yet it is these people – the exception which proves the rule – who are central to the exercise of political power. They represent life laid bare, life without the art. In the face of their powerlessness and dispossession they can only claim to be human, and that they deserve to live as we do. But their claim that they have value simply because they are alive is the weakest one people can make to others when they have no civic status, no cultural identity, and no political or juridical authority. They exist, so to speak, outside the walls of the city, in a realm where moral and legal obligations wane and power and violence take precedence. 'Is man no more than this', laments Shakespeare's mad King Lear. Cast out on the heath, stripped of the robes of office, Lear reflects on his demise. 'Thou art the thing itself; unaccommodated man is no more but such a poor, bare forked animal as thou art'.

It is this 'simple living body' which is excluded from the public discourse of politics; yet its absence forms the nucleus from which political power is built. Michel Foucault has taught us to pay attention to how forms of governance in schools, factories, hospitals and prisons subject the body to disciplinary practices. He has described how biological life itself is the site upon which sovereign power is exercised. In the concluding part of *The History of Sexuality: An Introduction* he writes: 'For a long time, one of the characteristic privileges of sovereign power was the right to decide life and death'. Such absolutism is no longer a general feature of politics in liberal democracies and yet the hierarchical evaluation and gradation of human life around gender, race and class continues to be a powerful dynamic of European societies. Its presence can also be detected in debates around the uses of gene technology, the rationing of health care and the patenting of DNA.

What is it we talk about when we talk about life? In his essay 'Critique of Violence', Walter Benjamin addresses this question in his discussion of the role of sovereign violence in juridical law-making.[3] Violence, he argues, is an integral element of law making. In the moment a law is instated violence is not deposed; a law does not become an end immune and independent from violence. Rather, it is one which is intimately and necessarily bound up with it. Benjamin, in his attempt to understand the nature of juridical power over the individual, tries to conceptualise this relationship. To do so he must define what is the bearer of the link between violence and the law.[4] He describes this bearer as 'mere life', a portend of Foucault's idea of the 'simple living body'. Mere life is the human being stripped of his or her social existence – the accoutrements of identity and civic status – such that they are excluded from the category of 'Man'. 'Mere life' is Lear's 'unaccommodated man' who is without recourse to the law and the codes of civility.

Benjamin's essay was written in 1921 before the rise of Nazism and yet it is prescient of the barbarism to come. In one disturbing paragraph he asks us to question the supposition (he calls it dogma) that human life is sacred. To illustrate his point, he puts forward the argument of those who oppose revolutionary violence and the killing of oppressors: 'We profess that higher even than the happiness and justice of existence stands existence itself'. It is a proposition which Benjamin argues is false and ignoble if existence is to mean nothing other than mere life. And yet the proposition contains 'a mighty truth' if it means that the non-existence of human beings is something more terrible than the 'not-yet-attained condition of the just man'. We can never 'live' as human beings if we are simply reduced to mere life. We cannot, it seems, claim the right to justice, goodness, mercy simply by dint of our bodies' being alive. Such social discourses cease to operate on the terrain of mere life. It is here, in this exclusion from social and moral discourses, that sovereign power operates. There is no sacredness in the human vulnerable to violence from other humans. What then distinguishes us from plants and animal life? Benjamin has no answer. He suggests that we might track down the source of this dogma of the sacredness of human life. What we will find is the 'last mistaken attempt of the weakened western tradition' to seek out the mystery of god. In less than a decade the Nazis placed mere life at the heart of their rule. What had been excluded became central to a literal politics of life and death. Jews and whole ethnic groups and populations were killed with impunity.

We live today with the moral ideal of authenticity. Each of us has an original way of being human, and we try to live this, and be true to ourselves. This ethic of self-fulfilment celebrates the idea of life as an expression of our desire for freedom. And yet we have failed to question what we mean by life - it possesses an ambiguous meaning, which is reflected in the word sacred. The latin term *sacer* means consecrated and sacred, but it also means infamous or detestable. What we tend to claim as our life are its social aspects. What we tend to exclude is mere life, the biological breath, heartbeat and brain activity of our bodies.

To be reduced to a state of mere life is to be denied the right to the social aspects of life, which give human existence legitimacy, and make it purposeful. A celebratory affirmation of life is thus insufficient because it fails to address the question of its relationship to politics.

Similarly, an ethic of self-fulfilment which is based on self consciousness is not enough. When we seek knowledge in order to find meaning in ourselves we grasp at words and language. To understand something we draw it in and make it our own. What is other to the self and becomes known is reduced to being the same. Being thus becomes the affirmation of the same. Difference is erased. This failure to accept the indisputability of the other has been the principle weakness of Romanticism and more recent forms of holism and eco-consciousness. It is a failure whose origins lie in Hegel's dialectic of recognition, which structures the self and other as a relationship of domination and struggle. Only through the domination of the Other can an individual achieve an identity (self-knowledge, self-preservation and self-mastery).

For the philosopher Emmanuel Levinas this antagonism is a consequence of our emphasis on self-consciousness – the ambitions of the ego. He argues that from the outset of one's life there is an ethical dimension involved in the encounter with the other: 'One comes not into the world but into question.'[5] When one acquires language and says 'I' and comes into being, one has to respond to one's right to one's own existence. Being in the world displaces others, and usurps their space. Levinas is concerned with the effect he will have on others. This concern for the other originates anterior to self-consciousness in an 'unrepresentable past'. He wants to establish an ethics which acknowledges our indefinable and yet unavoidable responsibility for the Other. To do so he reaches for a metaphysical description. We are, he claims, responsible for our neighbour, 'for the other man, for the stranger or sojourner, to which nothing in the rigorously ontological order binds me – nothing in the order of the thing, of the something, of number or causality'(p84). Levinas insists on the sanctity of the other and my responsibility for him or her. The ethical is the condition of our existence whatever our individual worth or worthlessness. 'It is in the laying down by the ego of its sovereignty ... that we find ethics and also probably the very spirituality of the soul, but most certainly the question of the meaning of being, that is, its appeal for justification'(p85).

Levinas's ethics is a defence of mere life, drawing it within the orbit of our moral responsibility to others. His mix of Jewish humanism and metaphysics resembles the language of the Tao. But it provides an important caveat to the belief in the interconnectedness of life. His insistence upon an ethics of living recognises the contingent nature of life and provides for a pragmatism and politics which can address the incommensurability of the other and of difference. Thus, being is not the same as the self, but is self in dialogue with the other. The question of philosophy, says Levinas, is not 'why being rather than nothing?'; rather, it is 'how being justifies itself'(p86). The art of life is to accept doubt and uncertainty. To recognise our fallibility and the messiness of human affairs, in the knowledge that there are no final solutions to our predicament, no foregone conclusions, or moral absolutes. Perhaps a contemporary image of the sacred might be the image of the earth taken from space, the beautiful fragile, solitary, blue and green globe amidst the dust and ash of the solar system. Here we are alone in this together, for better or worse, with nothing more, but most important nothing less than, our own humanity.

NOTES

1. Richard Rorty, 'The Contingency of Language', in *Contingency, Irony and Solidarity*, Cambridge University Press 1989, p20.
2. Michel Foucault, 'Technologies of the Self', in *Ethics Essential Works 1*, edited by Paul Rabinow, Allen Lane, The Penguin Press, p226. See also Michel Foucault, *The Care of the Self: The History of Sexuality Volume Three*, Allen Lane, The Penguin Press, 1988.
3. Walter Benjamin, 'Critique of Violence', in *One Way Street and Other Writings*, Verso 1985.
4. For a fascinating and thought provoking analysis of the relationship between mere life and political power read Giorgio Agamben, *Homo Sacer: Sovereign Power and Bare Life*, trans. Daniel Heller-Roazen, Stanford University Press, 1998.
5. Emmanuel Levinas, 'Ethics as first Philosophy', in *The Levinas Reader*, ed. Seán Hand, Blackwell 1996, p81.

Temptation

Call yourself alive? Look, I promise you
that for the first time you'll feel your pores opening
like fish mouths, and you'll actually be able to hear
your blood surging through all those lanes,
and you'll feel light gliding across the cornea
like the train of a dress. For the first time
you'll be aware of gravity
like a thorn in your heel,
and your shoulder blades will ache for want of wings.
Call yourself alive? I promise you
you'll be deafened by dust falling on the furniture,
you'll feel your eyebrows turning to two gashes,
and every memory you have – will begin
at Genesis.

Nina Cassian

THE SACRED LIFE

Madeleine Bunting

One of the most extraordinary social revolutions in the fifty years since
the second world war has been the decline of institutional religion in
Western Europe. If current rates of decline continue, there will be no
Methodists in the UK by the middle of the next century. Every year
fifty thousand Catholics in England and Wales give up going to Sunday
mass. The declining number of vocations to the priesthood in France,
once regarded as the elder daughter of the Catholic church, is leaving
parishes empty. Seminaries are closing in Ireland, the country which
once exported a surplus of priests to serve all over the world – for lack
of candidates. This revolution is extraordinary because of the pace of
the decline, and because the absence of a collective religious narrative
makes contemporary Western Europe, historically and anthropologi-
cally, a strange new experiment in human culture. After all, institutional religion is thriving in virtually every other part of the globe,
including America, where 90 per cent of the population still regularly
attend church. Every previous society has developed and lived by a
religious tradition which explained the place of the individual and
community in the cosmos, and ordered relations between people
(particularly over reproduction) and with the environment. Rituals
expressed and reinforced the tradition. In many cultures, this tradition
was maintained and interpreted by priests or elders who acquired great
authority from their position. But in Western Europe, shared beliefs,
ritual and religious hierarchies are all in the process of being swept
away.

The statistics paint a clear picture of decline, but the common conclusion drawn from them – that this is a process of secularisation – appears
to be profoundly wrong. Polls in the UK consistently indicate that the
vast majority of people (over 70 per cent) say they believe in God. Many
admit to praying even if they never go in a church or synagogue. My

argument is that there is no decline in religiosity, defined as a yearning for, and fascination in, spirituality, but that it has largely moved outside of the institutions of faith. Millions of people are, individually or in small groups, separately fumbling towards a new formulation of faith which can become hugely powerful in their lives. This movement is happening all over the West; ten years ago, it was on the margins; now it is seeping into and beginning to influence the mainstream. But I say people are 'fumbling' towards this new formulation, because this quest, at present, is having to negotiate huge obstacles.

The first and most obvious of these obstacles is a powerfully propagated and seductive materialism. Consumer capitalism thrives on and ruthlessly exploits our insecurities; it offers illusory choices and manipulates our desire for liberation and happiness, all in the name of selling more trainers and more perfume, more goods we never knew we needed. What makes consumerism so pernicious is that it is self-fuelling; indeed, many of us are in some degree of addiction without even being aware of it. Television, which unquestioningly promotes its values, dominates most homes; we have allowed it to intrude into the most private, intimate areas of our life, and most of us have to some extent internalised the values it propagates. Consumer capitalism is a hugely powerful ideology which, in its expanding global reach, and in its ability to absorb and corrupt any challenge to it, has far outstripped its competitors (such as communism). To reject such an ideology requires a struggle to resist consumerism's false promises, and the way it undermines our own autonomy, and to hold true to intimations of an integrity, liberation and happiness. Not an easy task.

It is not made easier by the second obstacle in this quest for a new formulation of faith: the lack of a common language. This is one of the main reasons why much of the faith which exists outside church has become a very private, individual matter, which has sometimes prompted the conclusion that religion has been privatised. Language enables people to share experience, but at present it doesn't exist; people find it hard to express their faith and are isolated. For example, how many people would happily stand up in their office and declare they were 'religious'? And what would their colleagues understand by that? – that they went to church/mosque/synagogue regularly, had a clearly defined set of beliefs and lived their lives by them. Just thinking through the scenario reveals how religious language is still inextricably linked to the traditional institutionalised faiths. At the same time, the universal 'spiritual' language of liberation, happiness, peace of mind, harmony, found in all world religions, has been hijacked and trivialised by consumerism; cars and tampax offer liberation, insurance policies bring peace of mind, and harmony is a hair spray.

THE LANGUAGE OF FAITH

This new faith lies, incipient, inchoate and often under-developed, all around us; it simply requires a shift of perception to recognise what we are looking at. To achieve that, one needs, above all, to redefine the language. I want to look at six words, and, by considering their dictionary definitions, illustrate what we have lost the power to express, what we need to recapture and how that is already happening. The words are: religion, devotion, sacred, holy, spirit and life.

'Religion' is defined in the Oxford Concise Dictionary as: '*1) belief in a superhuman controlling power especially in a personal God entitled to obedience and worship. 2) expression of this in worship. 3) a thing that one is devoted to*'. It comes from the Latin *religio*, meaning 'obligation, bond, reverence'. This definition is monotheistic, which rules out a swathe of belief systems, most notably Buddhism, as religions. It summarises the relationship with God as 'obedience and worship', thus speaking to a severe image, of the God with a white beard wagging his finger variety. It's hard to tally this common image of God with the first commandment God gave Moses: 'you shalt love the Lord your God with all your heart and with all your power'. How is it that Western Christianity replaced love with obedience as the defining characteristic of our relationship with God? Given our much prized personal freedom from external authority, it is not surprising that a religion primarily conceived of in terms of obedience loses its followers. But in turning our backs on the external authority figure, we have also lost sight of other elements bundled into this dictionary definition.

'Devotion' is placed after obedience and worship as a central activity of religion. 'Devote' is defined as '*to apply or give over (resources or oneself) to a particular activity purpose or* person'. Devotion is neutral, you can be devoted to whisky or cocaine as readily as to God, but within a religious tradition, the important point is that devotion is giving of yourself; it requires putting the object of devotion above your own self interests. Another point to pause over is that the three meanings of the Latin term *religio* are vital preoccupations of contemporary culture: *obligation* raises the whole issue of responsibility and its relationship to individual freedom; *bond* relates to belonging and identity within communities, nations and the cosmos; closely related, *reverence*, refers to how those bonds inspire deep emotion of awe, respect – towards others, towards the planet – and order behaviour accordingly.

'Sacred' is an even more unfashionable word than religion, and it is not hard to see why, given how closely associated with the practices and rituals of institutionalised religion it has become. Its definition is: '*1) exclusively dedicated or appropriated to a god or to some religious purpose. 2) made holy by religious association. 3) connected with religion. 4) safeguarded or required by religion, reverence or tradition.*' But there are some important points about this word which we have lost sight of; the sacred is something to be safeguarded and protected, and that can be done by religion, reverence or tradition. The term sacred means that something is made holy.

'Holy' is another unfashionable word with a lot of pejorative associations. Holy is defined as '*morally, spiritually excellent and perfect*'. Interestingly, this dictionary has a hazy grasp of theology: equating holiness with being perfect is incompatible with Judaic-Christian or Islamic thinking. But the definition conveys something of a sense of 'holiness' as it is now commonly understood – as morally puritanical, life-denying piety and impossible perfection. Yet the fascinating point about 'holy' is that it is closely related to 'whole' in the Germanic from which it derives. Here we have a glimpse of an entirely different understanding of holiness – as someone or something whole. '*Whole is unbroken, intact, not less than all there is of, complete in itself.*' This is a concept which increasingly intrigues contemporary culture; being emotionally 'centred' and 'holistic' living are two examples of a search for completeness.

Having looked at words hidebound in their traditional associations, I now want to look at two words which are being used more and more often, and are being loaded with complex religious meanings and associations. The first is 'spirit', from which comes 'spirituality', a word which has only come into common use in the last few decades. 'Spirit' has an enormous number of uses, and its dictionary definition is long; for example, high spirits, spirited, with you in spirit, the spirit of the law, methylated spirit, take in the wrong spirit, alcoholic spirits, haunted by spirits, the spirit of the place, spirited away and so on. It is defined primarily as the '*vital animating essence of a person or animal*'. Spirit conveys courage, vivacity and energy; the fact that the latter is a particular preoccupation of a modernity obsessed with speed goes some way to explaining the word's growing popularity.

Definitions of spirit also open up questions about the nature of reality; the spirit of the law is its real, if not literal, meaning. Defining 'spiritual' the dictionary says, *'concerned with the soul or spirit etc not with external reality'*. This is highly contentious, asserting both that a clear distinction can be drawn between mind and matter, and that the latter is 'real'. Twentieth century physics challenges both these assertions, having revolutionised our understanding of the relationship of mind to matter. The popularity of the word speaks to a contemporary unease about the illusory nature of external reality in an image obsessed with 'ornamental culture', as Susan Faludi describes it. The popularity of spirit as a word reveals our quest for authenticity, for an irreducible, unmalleable essence more permanent than the images manufactured by consumer materialism.

But the most intriguing point about 'spirit' is that it comes from the Latin word *spirare* meaning 'to breathe'. Yet again, we have in the origins of the word a clue to a revolutionary meaning. In the Eastern religious traditions, meditation is based on mindfulness of breathing, of developing awareness of our relationship with the world at its most basic – how dependent we are on air to keep us alive. From this awareness comes an ability to live in the moment, to be fully present and not distracted – in short, to be. In that presence, says the Vietnamese Buddhist monk Thich Nnat Hanh, you can find both peace and happiness. He sums it up in one of his books in a mantra:

> Breathing in, I calm my body.
> Breathing out, I smile.
> Dwelling in the present moment
> I know this is a wonderful moment.

The fascinating point about 'spirit' is that in its definition and use it links the vital irreducible essence which inspires our lives with something we do every second of every day without thinking about it, something on which our physical life depends: the most mundane with the most vital and the most real.

The last word to look at is 'life'(and I am indebted to Don Cupitt and his book *The New Religion of Life in Everyday Speech* for the insight that an immense level of significance is currently being loaded onto this word. Cupitt points out the popularity of the word: get a life; that's life; she loved life; there's more to life; I want to get my life back together again; my life has fallen apart; life goes on; I've got a life to live; live dangerously; quality of life; right to life; that's what life is all about; I've only got one life; live life to the full.' He comments: 'It seems that the object of religious concern and attention is no longer something hoped-for after death or at the end of history, but something that gives itself to us, and in which we are immersed in the here and now: life.'

Once the use of 'life' has been pointed out, one notices it everywhere. It pops up in the lyrics to music: for example Elton John's hit composed for a friend who died, 'Song for Guy', includes death as a part of life. The only lyrics of the largely instrumental song, are 'life, isn't everything, isn't everything, life.' The lyric tapped into a common stoicism – 'it's all part of life's rich pattern' expresses the same sentiment. I think it is even significant that Elton John's lyric is part question; he's not entirely sure about what he is asserting, hinting at the uncertainty that we all share about the meaning of suffering, pain and death. In another example I noticed recently, the actress Isabelle Adjani was talking about her devotion to her children as a priority over her film-making: 'The glamorous facade of appearances and auras are mere phantoms. The fall of an actress begins when she considers herself a star. We should love life much more than cinema.' What is so interesting about her comment is that 'life' is not the celebrity world of film-making; she is making a judgement about what is not real, but the reality she asserts is vague. What she means by 'life' is anyone's guess. We are all using the word 'life', but it can have hugely different meanings for people; in the evolution of its use, we can see that fumbling towards a new formulation of faith.

Cupitt identifies some characteristics of the uses of the word 'life'. Life has an imperative: one must keep up and play one's full part in it, one has a responsibility to enjoy and explore it – 'live life to the full'. The best tribute to be paid at a funeral is that the deceased 'loved life'. Loving life means accepting its vicissitudes: 'we are learning to love life disinterestedly' is how Cupitt puts it. Loving life is living in the present, and finding in the moment an intensity and authenticity of experience: 'there's more to life than this'. I would argue that the fascination for drugs and sex amongst late adolescents and young adults is part of a quest for an intensity of experience amidst the banal, empty images of consumer materialism. But this search for the spontaneity and richness of life is not simply a contemporary preoccupation. The Hebrew word for sin means to just miss the target. That relates to the Gospel theme of Christ's love for sinners; the prostitutes and the drinkers were at least trying to find life – as opposed to the law-abiding Pharisees. Life is what Christ promised his followers.

Cupitt concludes by claiming that, 'We have supposed that what has been happening has been the secularisation of religion, and we have failed to see the much greater event of the sacralisation of life, even though it has already deeply affected all of us.'

We now have the bones of a new vocabulary:

Religion: a way of thinking to which we are devoted, which expresses our sense of obligation, bonds, and reverence.
Devotion: giving of ourselves to this way of thinking.
Sacred: that which is whole and revered. The sacred is safeguarded and protected by our religion.
Holy: whole, complete of itself.
Spirit: the essence at the core of every second of every minute.
Life: living in the present; accepting the ups and downs; and recognising our responsibility to experience in every second the whole – ourselves and our obligations, bonds, reverence.

The most dramatic difference in this new formulation of faith is that it has abandoned the Western preoccupation in the intellectual and rational. People are not interested in what you believe but how you live your life; it is the practice not the theory which now preoccupies us. Theology – the bringing to bear of intellect upon faith – seems a particularly arcane activity. Creed-based religion – one preoccupied with theory rather than practice – has been violently rejected and is scorned; it has produced huge violence in Europe in the last five hundred years as thousands have died in religious conflict over fine points of theological dispute. Furthermore, Creed-based religions have lost intellectual credibility: firstly because so many of their former truths have been proved wrong by the likes of Copernicus and Darwin; and secondly because of their misguided hostility to intellectual endeavour.

A NEW FAITH?

The new formulation of faith has lost its cosmological ambition; it cannot explain how the universe happened or how and why we emerged from the mud in evolution. The purpose of faith has been re-cast as something to help us find happiness, reduce our suffering and achieve peace of mind and meaning in this life. It is no longer preoccupied with life after death, but life before death. The emphasis has moved to intuition, emotion and empiricism. Some would argue that the pendulum has possibly swung too far, and that intellect does have a role; without it there is a danger of a credulity in which cults and quackery flourish.

The core principle of this faith is individual autonomy. 'No one can tell you how to run your life'. All previous religions have developed hierarchies and figures of authority. Now, everyone is on their own journey. What is lost is judgement, bigotry and condemnation, and what is gained is tolerance. At its best, this radical democratisation of religion places huge responsibility on each individual. At its worst, it suggests that everyone is reinventing the wheel because there is no respect for tradition or for the role of teacher. The new tolerance opens us up to the globalisation of religion. A hundred years ago, Western Christians' understanding of Hinduism and Buddhism was negligible; the great 'religious revolution' of the twentieth century has seen a huge growth and understanding of other religious traditions. Arnold Toynbee declared that one of the great events of the twentieth century would come to be seen as the arrival of Buddhism in the West. The dialogue between faiths and the discovery of a commonality of many principles and beliefs is happening all over the world, although it attracts much less publicity than the conflicts between faiths. The exclusive claims of the monotheistic faiths become harder and harder for many people to subscribe to.

The spiritual has moved into daily life and is no longer something separate and apart which properly belongs in the church; the Western understanding is of the sacred and secular as being totally distinguishable. Now we are much closer to the Hindu or Confucian practice where the gods are worshipped in the home; potentially, we can now place the sacred in everything, implicit in and underpinning all of daily life. But alongside that gain must be put the loss of the institution, and the ways in which that fostered the tradition: the study of religious texts and the appreciation of the importance of spiritual disciplines of prayer, meditation, fasting and penance in overcoming the strength of the ego. All the major religions have at their heart a concept of personal liberation. In past centuries, in the Christian West the liberation was from the temptations of the devil; in Eastern traditions, *moksha*, or release, is from the tyranny of the ego which has to be tamed and subdued to achieve true happiness and autonomy rather than being driven by the compulsions of the ego.

In the new faith, the emphasis on personal autonomy has been at the impoverishment of the collective. We no longer have collective rituals to celebrate our faith together. But religion is deeply social because it is about responsibilities and bonds; it cannot but draw people together if they become aware of those as essential to their happiness and fulfilment. So spiritual fellowship is found everywhere though it is rarely understood as such. It is the principle behind AA, Al-anon and the huge self-help therapy movement that has grown up. It can be found in charity fundraising, in voluntary work, in the companionship of the office, the prison cell and the hospital ward. Spiritual fellowship is about solidarity, compassion, generosity, warmth and laughter.

The social aspect of religion is stressed in all religious traditions; it encourages and supports the individual in a spiritual quest – for God, nirvana – which requires great determination and struggle. The central ritual of Christianity is communion, where the congregation finds union with each other and God; Christianity also talks of fellowship, known as *agape*. In Islam, you become one of the *ummah*, the world-wide community of believers. When Muslim men pray on Fridays, they are supposed to bunch so close together that they can feel physically the support of their brothers. In Buddhism, the prayer of 'taking refuge' or conversion is: 'I take refuge in the Buddha, I take refuge in the Dharma (teaching), I take refuge in the sangha or community of other Buddhists'. The community is as vital to your spiritual development as the inspiration of the Buddha and his teaching.

So, where can this new faith be found? What is the Sacred Life? The first three areas that came to my mind – the list is not definitive – indicate an unexpected continuity: the Sacred Life can be found where it has always been – in our relationships with the natural world, with other people and with ourselves.

THE NATURAL WORLD

The natural world has frequently been a source of spiritual inspiration and connection; the revival of Celtic spirituality shows how contemporary society is searching to articulate this. The Romantics powerfully articulated a sense of the immanence of a spiritual presence (many would not describe it as God) in the natural world which was in danger of being marginalised by the Enlightenment's emphasis on analytical reason. Wordsworth's words in Tintern Abbey are frequently quoted:

And I have felt
A presence that disturbs me with the joy
Of elevated thoughts: a sense sublime
Of something far more deeply interfused,
Whose dwelling is the light of setting suns,
And the round ocean and the living air,
And the blue sky, and in the mind of man:
A motion and a spirit that impels
All thinking things, all objects of all thought,
And rolls through all things.

Environmentalists rightly point out that our relationship to nature has been corrupted and become exploitative and destructive. But alongside that, for millions of people there is another relationship to nature which is deeply personal and vitally important to their sense of well-being and happiness. In the UK, the two most popular hobbies are gardening and angling. Birdwatching and walking follow closely behind. The biggest charity in Western Europe is the Royal Society for the Protection of Birds and the National Trust is not far behind. We may be a largely urban society, but the impulse towards a relationship with nature is still powerful. Why? I would suggest that part of the sense of satisfaction brought by occupations such as gardening and fishing is a recognition of the processes of the natural world which are independent of human intervention. To watch the toil of an ant, the work of a worm, the journey of a toad, the daily growth of a potato patch or a flowerbed, is to be an observer of a cycle of life of astonishing complexity and sophistication. Birdwatching is all about observation, and observation is a form of what Buddhists would call mindfulness or awareness, when you are absorbed in the present moment and in the information of the senses, the eye, ear and nose. Observation requires patience; for an angler or birdwatcher, it requires stillness and an alertness. How good a gardener, angler or birdwatcher you are depends on your mindfulness. Absorption in the present, patience, stillness, alertness: these are all qualities regarded as essential to the practice of meditation in Eastern religious traditions.

The process of observation of the natural world also inspires awe, perhaps in the gardener who has painstakingly cultivated a beautiful flower or in the birdwatcher as she watches the flight of a rare eagle. Richard Dawkins writes of the awe of the scientist for the natural world; he argues convincingly that science can replace religion in inculcating awe and reverence. The enormous popularity of natural science television programmes and books on science in the last decade are evidence of this. Dawkins quotes the physicist Karl Sagan, who claimed that the gods of religious men are small, but the gods of scientists are vast. But this sweeping generalisation omits a point which Dawkins has missed in his well-known aversion to religious faith: the 'gods of religious men' have been, in the world's major faiths, part of an understanding of self-transformation. Awe, and the worship which expresses it, is not a one-way process; there is a 'kickback' in which the awe gives the worshipper a sense of place and identity. Awe is a deeply satisfying emotion because it comes as a relief in our ego-centric, anthropocentric culture that there are complex, sophisticated, powerful processes outside our control and manipulation. It answers a human need to be part of a greater whole, to let go and to give up attempting to control everything – a pervasive drive in contemporary culture but one which is always ultimately futile.

That may seem to make no sense in relation to gardening and angling, given that both involve human intervention in nature. Not so. No gardener or fisherman would claim they can control everything; their skill depends on recognition of their dependence on nature. The ripened apple still warm from the sun which I pick off my apple tree is not my creation; I may (or may not) have sprayed it, planted it, pruned it, but the apples are created by the sun, water and earth. I may have caught a trout because of my knowledge of the river, my skill with the rod and fly, but I had to wait for the beautiful fish to choose to swim near me and to go for my fly. Both the gardener and the fisherman are acutely aware of the inter-dependence of human activity and the natural world – the interconnectedness of everything (a key Buddhist concept). Any good gardener knows how much he/she owes to worms, let alone sun soil and water. All religious traditions have celebrated this interdependence, and our partnership in creation with the awe-inspiring natural world – for example harvest festivals and Thanksgiving in the Christian West. Where the environment was harsh, religious beliefs incorporated a concept of stewardship to maintain the fragile eco-system on which human life depended, underscoring that each generation's use and enjoyment is temporary. Now that the whole planet is threatened, it is that concept of stewardship which is desperately needed to combat an environmental catastrophe.

SACRED RELATIONSHIPS

Whereas people will happily and frequently relate the sacred to the natural world, relationships are vastly more complex. Yet this is a vital area in which to regain a sense of the sacred; a sense of awe and reverence, and presence, without expectation or demand, with an Other person. This is the biggest and most testing experience of our lives, to come to love – understand, respect and appreciate – another human being. To break out of our narcissistic, egotistical preoccupation to encounter and love another person. But just as our relationship to nature has been corrupted into one of exploitation, so have our relationships to other human beings. Many of our relationships with people have been reduced to a money transaction; we buy or sell services or products from others. Even when money is not involved, it has corrupted our perception, and many relationships are cast in terms of a contract; they are conditional. Nowhere is the corruption more obvious and pervasive in consumer culture than in sex. The most powerful and most intimate drive in human beings, it is commercialised, trivialised, demystified and portrayed as a vehicle for domination and aggression rather than self-exposure, trust and intimacy.

The one relationship which is explicitly excluded in contemporary culture from this corruption, and which is the focus of high ideals and huge emotional investment, is that between parents and children. For many people, being a parent is the most sacred part of their life; it brings them a sense of fulfilment, purpose , contentment and fun quite unlike anything else. Why? It's a huge subject, and I have only limited personal experience, so my suggestions at an answer are not intended to be definitive. They are just working notes. What comes to mind immediately is awe, the emotion which is so powerful in our relationship to nature. Pregnancy and giving birth to a baby are both mundane and awe-inspiring. The awareness of having participated in the creation of a new human being is astonishing. Not just the parents, but others, regard a tiny new-born with reverence. In time, after sleepless nights and dirty nappies, the reverence gives way to a more down-to-earth but no less sacred appreciation of this growing baby. But the awe never completely disappears; every now and then a sudden stab of awareness reminds you of how you have participated in the creation and nurturing of this increasingly independent person with his or her unique personality; you are stunned by what you have succeeded in creating, but, at the same time, by the evidence of so much in them which is nothing to do with you. The Chief Rabbi, Dr Jonathan Sacks, captured something of this when he said that when you watch your children play, you glimpse the mind of God.

Within Romanticism, one strain of thought was that children were born whole and pure and were corrupted by life. One only has to watch toddlers fighting over a toy to question this theory, but in many respects the Romantics had a point. There are some childlike qualities which tend to diminish as we grow older, such as spontaneity, enthusiasm, innocence, trust, faith, appetite for happiness and absorption in the moment. As we spend time with children, these qualities inspire (often, not always) generosity and love in us. We learn the wisdom of the paradox in the Gospels: it is in giving that you receive. Furthermore, spending time with children has the capacity to re-awaken in us those childlike characteristics – spontaneity, fun, perhaps even the most precious of them, trust and innocence – which are regarded as spiritual gifts in many religious traditions. This should not be taken as a romanticisation of a difficult task in which everyone at some time or another discovers their limits – the exhausted parent who snaps, etc. Yet even those difficulties are part of what makes parenting sacred; we learn, often the hard way, about patience, and are deeply challenged ourselves to tolerate and accept the Otherness of the children we have created.

OUR SELVES

Finally, I want to look at the search for self. Arguably this is the most prevalent and powerful form of the sacred life. The search for an authentic knowledge of self has replaced the Judaic-Christian search for God. Under pressure from an increasingly demanding, competitive and insecure world of work and relationships, people have retreated psychologically into themselves. What becomes important is the personal narrative we develop, with the help of therapists, pop psychology and self-help books, to explain and give meaning and dignity to the often brutal insecurities of our lives.

The personal narrative is replacing the grand theological narratives of religious tradition – of the Fall and Redemption in Christianity, or the suffering of the Jewish people in the Old Testament, for example. The personal narrative serves the same purpose as the theological narrative, in giving us a sense of identity, a perception of our past, of where we belong and where we might be going. Our personal narrative defines our obligations, bonds and what we hold holy. A huge part of media culture is occupied now by people's personal narratives. Celebrities are called to tell us the narrative of their lives, and an extraordinarily large number of people are prepared to tell their innermost secrets on television, in print or on radio. Some argue that this is our obsession with fame, and in part that may be true, it may be evidence of our need to feel self-worth by projecting self; but there is another impulse in this obsession, which is about trying to connect one's own, often painful, experiences with others. The response to recent columnists writing about their struggles with cancer has been enormous, and they themselves have used that response as justification for their writing. We may have personal narratives, but we still want to connect those to the personal narrative of others; the impulse towards shared experience is as powerful as ever. It was this very public search for self which made Princess Diana such a compelling public figure. Her flaws, her evident suffering in her loveless marriage and affairs, spoke powerfully to millions who struggle to reconcile themselves to lives full of pain and suffering, in a culture which puts no value on pain and elevates an often impossible ideal of happiness. The fascination with other people's lives, the impulse in many people to expose the most intimate and painful parts of their lives in the media, all speak to a huge curiosity to understand and be understood, to share and learn from others in the negotiation of our increasingly difficult lives.

The virtues of this sacred inner life at its best are a search for honesty, freedom, personal authenticity, emotional courage, humility and generous tolerance of others. What is also gained is a sense of obligation to ourselves, a responsibility to be happy in the precious, short miracle of our own life (though we may be less than skilful in knowing how to fulfil our obligation to ourselves, or how to find our happiness). And this does not fit comfortably with the Western Christian tradition of self-sacrifice. What is often rejected in these personal narratives are traditional religious concepts such as responsibility, duty and self-sacrifice; and this preoccupation with self is often criticised as indulgent and selfish. In an interview in *New Musical Express*, Madonna spoke of her decision to have a baby on her own: 'It's sad, it's not a perfect, ideal situation. It's much better for a family to be whole, but y'know, you have to be true to yourself and you have to be happy, and if a situation is better one way than the other then that's the way to go.'

At the start of this essay, I identified consumer culture as the biggest obstacle to the expression and celebration of the sacred life, because it hijacks it, commercialises and corrupts it. Thus, for example, gardening becomes a billion pound consumer industry in which customers are seduced into a myriad of needs, aspirations and dissatisfaction – your patio is not as good as the one on television or in the magazine. A garden becomes the means to project your identity as a consumer rather than to develop a relationship with the natural world. Children become a reason and an excuse for extending one's consumerism into children's clothes, toys and decor.

This corruption often prompts a cynicism in which one's perception of the sacred is obscured by the paraphernalia of consumerism. Take for example the current taste in natural materials in interior decor: wooden floors, coir matting, beach pebbles and linen. Candles, with their soft, intimate light, are on sale in unprecedented volume. The colours are natural: browns, whites and all shades of cream, oatmeal and beige. Similar trends can be seen in fashion. This is a consumer trend which indicates an impulse away from our techni-coloured, high technology culture towards something softer, more harmonious, and gentler on the eye and the soul. The cynic dismisses this impulse along with the desire for organic food, gardening, fish tanks and Feng-shui as nothing more than a consumer fad – which in many cases it may be. But for some it is a stumbling after the sacred, a way of living which is harmonious and wholesome for us and the rest of the planet.

Cynicism is a defining characteristic of our culture, along with its close relation, apathy. This is understandable given how many false promises consumerism makes. For cynicism is connected to a history of betrayed high ideals, resulting in emotional withdrawal in which nothing matters much. What we have failed to see, through a misplaced idealism, is that the sacred life has always been intertwined with the commercialised. There has never been a time when the sacred has been 'uncontaminated'. Look back at the beautiful cathedrals of the middle ages, and then remember that those cloisters which speak so power-fully of prayer and peace were built by vainglorious kings and prelates, from the taxes of peasants. The splendours of pilgrimage centres were crudely assessed commercial propositions in the middle ages. Or look to Weber's linking of Protestantism and capitalism, to see the same fusing of sacred and commercial.

What is new about the spiritual crisis of our times is the lack of a common language, and this inhibits the shared celebration of our continuing, powerful sense of the sacred, and the ways in which that animates and shapes our lives. Millions of people have that sense of the sacred, but rarely the words to articulate it, or share it. That is what cripples our capacity to change ourselves and our societies, because a shared experience of the sacred has the capacity to unleash huge energy and commitment. In the absence of a common language, the dominant discourse of cynicism and apathy, and the emotional retreat it produces, both from personal relationships and society, goes unchallenged. Cynicism is the result of disillusionment; only those who once had great ideals and hopes can become cynical . We need a language in which we can once again assert the possibility of hope – for personal happiness as well as for a just society – and of faith that we will be able to realise these hopes. Faith and hope, along with charity (for when you or others fall short) were, according to St Paul, the greatest spiritual gifts. Or, to put it another way, as any business analyst will tell you, belief is self-fulfilling.

ZOMBIE CATEGORIES

Ulrich Beck

Ulrich Beck has in recent years has become one of Europe's best known sociologists, particularly for his work on the Risk Society. Perhaps less well-known is his writing (together with Elisabeth Beck Gernsheim) on relationships, love and family life. Beck argues that in today's modern Western societies individuals have been removed from traditional commitments and support relationships. These new individualised cultures foster a belief in individual control and the desire for a 'life of one's own'. There is however a paradox. Changes are occurring faster in people's consciousness than in their behaviour and social conditions. This mixture of new consciousness and old conditions has created what he describes as Zombie categories – social forms such as class, family or neighbourhood, which are dead, yet still alive. He is interviewed here by Jonathan Rutherford.

Your concept of individualisation provides a convincing explanation for what is happening in society - the transformation of work; the decline of public authority and increasing personal isolation; a greater emphasis on individuality and self-reliance; the changing balance of power between men and women; a redefinition of the relationship between private life and the public sphere; the emergence of a culture of intimacy, informality and self-expression. You describe it as the 'disembedding of the ways of life of industrial society (class, family, gender), and the re-embedding of new ones'. Can you explain what you mean by individualisation?

There is a lot of misunderstanding about this concept of individualisation. It does not mean individualism. It does not mean individuation – a term used by depth psychologists to describe the process of becoming an autonomous individual. And it has nothing to do with the market egoism of Thatcherism. That is always a potential misunderstanding in Britain. Nor, lastly, does it mean emancipation as Jurgen Habermas describes it.

Individualisation is a concept which describes a structural, sociological transformation of social institutions, and the relationship of the individual to society. It is not simply a phenomenon of the second half of the twentieth century. Earlier historical phases of individualisation occurred in the Renaissance, in the courtly culture of the Middle Ages, in the inward asceticism of Protestantism, in the emancipation of the peasants from feudal bondage and in the loosening of intergenerational family ties in the nineteenth and early twentieth century. European modernity has freed people from historically inscribed roles. It has undermined traditional securities such as religious faith, and simultaneously it has created new forms of social commitment. I use the concept of individualisation to explore not just how people deal with these transformations in terms of their identity and consciousness, but also how their life situations and biographical patterns are changed.

Individualisation liberates people from traditional roles and constraints in a number of ways. First, individuals are removed from status based classes. Social classes have been detraditionalised. We can see this in changes that have taken place in family structures, housing conditions, leisure activities, geographical distribution of populations, trade union and club membership, voting patterns, etc. Secondly, women have been cut loose from their 'status fate' of compulsory housework and support by a husband. Industrial society has been dependent upon the unequal positions of men and women, but modernity does not hesitate at the front door of family life. The entire structure of family ties has come under pressure from individualisation and a new negotiated provisional family composed of multiple relationships – a 'post-family' – is emerging. Thirdly, the old forms of work routine and discipline are in decline with the emergence of flexible work hours, pluralised underemployment and the decentralisation of work sites.

At the same time as this liberation or 'disembedding' occurs, new forms of reintegration and control are created ('re-embedding'). With the decline of class and status groups the individual must become the agent of his or her own identity-making and livelihood. The individual, not his or her class, becomes the unit for the reproduction of the social in his or her own life world. Individuals have to develop their own biography and organise it in relation to others. If you take for an example family life under conditions of individualisation, there is no given set of obligations and opportunities, no way of organising everyday work, the relationship between men and women, and between parents and children, which can just be copied.

Alongside the freeing of individuals from traditional constraints, a new standardisation occurs through the individual's dependency upon the employment market. This simultaneous individualisation and standardisation of our lives is not simply a private experience. It is institutional and structural. The liberated individual becomes dependent upon the labour market and because of that, dependent on, for example, education, consumption, welfare state regulation and support, possibilities and fashions in medical, psychological and pedagogical care. Dependency upon the market extends into every area of life. As Simmel noted, money both individualises and standardises.

The individual is removed from traditional commitments and support relationships, but exchanges them for the constraints of existence in the labour market. In spite of these new forms of constraint, individualised cultures foster a belief in individual control – a desire for a 'life of one's own'. There is a paradox here. On the one hand epochal changes are occurring – especially in the area of sexuality, the law and education. On the other – except for sexuality – these changes exist more in people's consciousness, and on paper, than in behaviour and social conditions. This historically created mixture of new consciousness and old conditions sharpens in people's minds the continuing and intensifying inequalities between men and women, rich and poor.

What's changing here, people or institutions?

I'm talking about Zombie categories.

Zombie categories? Sociology and horror?

Because of individualisation we are living with a lot of zombie categories which are dead and still alive.

Can you name some?

Yes. Family, Class, Neighbourhood.

Zombies are the living dead. Do you mean that these institutions are simply husks that people have abandoned?

I think people are more aware of the new realities than the institutions are. But at the same time, if you look at the findings of empirical research, family is still extremely valued in a very classical sense. Sure there are huge problems in family life, but each person thinks that he or she will solve all those problems that their parents didn't get right.

You write a lot about the family and relationships.

Yes. The family is a good example of a zombie category. Ask yourself what actually is a family nowadays? What does it mean? Of course there are your children, my children, our children. But even parenthood, the core of family life, is beginning to disintegrate under conditions of divorce. Families can be constellations of very different relationships. Take for an example the way grandmothers and grandfathers are being multiplied by divorce and remarriage. They get included and excluded without any means of participating themselves in the decisions of their sons and daughters. From the point of view of the grandchildren the meaning of grandparents has to be determined by individual decisions and choices. Individuals must choose who is my main father, my main mother and who is my grandma and grandpa. We are getting into optional relationships inside families which are very difficult to identify in an objective, empirical way because they are a matter of subjective perspectives and decisions. And these can change between life phases.

If you ask what is a household, the answer seemed quite straightforward ten or twenty years ago. Today there is no simple answer. It can be defined as a geographical unit of one place, an economic unit in which individuals are economically supported and dependent upon one another, or a social unit of individuals who want to live together. And of course these definitions can contradict one another. There is also the dramatic increase in single households in the last twenty years. In cities like London and Munich, more than 50 per cent of all households are single households, and it is a tendency which is increasing. But this category itself is not homogeneous. There are old widows, or men after divorce, maybe before remarrying; and there are single households where people are living in quite close relations with others, and some where they are not.

We are living with a rhetoric about the crisis in family life; but the family is not the cause of the historical conflict between men and women – it is the surface upon which this conflict becomes visible.

Everything which strikes the family from outside – for example the contradiction between the demands of the labour market and the needs of relationships, the employment system, the law – is distorted in the personal sphere. The tension in family life today is the fact that equalisation of men and women cannot be created in an institutional family structure which presupposed their inequality. In personal relationships conflicts are initiated by the opening up of possibilities to choose: in conflicting needs over careers, in the division of housework and child care. In making decisions people become aware of the contrasts in the conditions of men and women. With the lack of institutional solutions people are having to learn how to negotiate relationships on the basis of equality. This is transforming what we mean by the family.

I want to ask you what you think has determined these changes. I ask because you've tipped the conventional Marxist view that material conditions determine people's consciousness onto its head. You talk about how people's consciousness has changed but the institutions they live within, even their actual practices, haven't done so to the same extent.

Yes, that's true.

I accept that. I find it a paradox which is very interesting.

Let me pick up the question of this paradox . Marxist sociologists argue that capitalist societies, despite the changes I mention, are relatively stable structures of social inequality. They point out that the difference between the groups occupying the bottom, middle and top of society haven't really changed. They argue that this proves we are still living in a class society, and that class remains the dynamic of modern capitalism. I argue that the dynamism of the labour market, backed up by the welfare state, has dissolved the social classes within capitalism.

You've called this transformation of society, capitalism without class.

It is true that in Germany, patterns of social inequality have remained relatively stable. Yet at the same time the living conditions of the population since 1960 have changed dramatically, and this has set in motion a diversification and individualisation of lifestyles and ways of life. This development is related to the expansion of education, the increase of

THE ART OF LIFE

social security and wealth, even the patterns of inequality. I want to think about these changes in terms of democratisation. I would make a distinction between political democratisation, social democratisation related to the welfare state, and what I would call cultural democratisation. Individualisation relates to this third description. If you look closely at the changes we are living through you find that principles of democracy are being picked up, and believed in, as principles for the organisation of everyday life and relationships. We are living under the preconditions of internalised democracy: the belief in equality in relationships, and in dialogue – rather than violence or the imposition of authority – as the main element for reaching agreement. The capitalist market of instrumental relations under the conditions of the post-welfare state has produced something no one really imagined it would – an individualisation which is infused with ideas of cultural democratisation .

The situation is different now, in the late 1990s, but let us stick with the 1970s and 1980s. I don't think you can make sense of what has happened in all Western European countries in terms of social movements, changes in family life, sexuality and love, a growing interest in the politics of everyday life and more direct forms of democracy, if you do not accept at least a part of this interpretation of cultural democratisation.

I agree with you broadly speaking. What seems to be crucial to your analysis is this notion of culture - something which is not, as the more conventional Marxism has argued, a determined activity but is rather a relatively autonomous and transformative experience and activity, in which human beings act upon and create their material world. Conventional Marxism would argue that against the power of capital cultural practices are relatively incidental and incapable of producing the kind of ideological political blocs which could resist exploitation, the globalisation of capital, or the commodification of society.

I would agree to some extent. First of all it is right that these changes in the family are only one part of the picture of what is happening in modern society. It is not the whole picture. But I wouldn't agree with the old mechanical Marxist picture of capitalism which provides too singular a description of the way society is constructed, and one which has to be understood as a natural law. There is something more significant going on, which this old type of Marxist analysis cannot recognise. Over the last few hundred years in Europe we have been living in modernity, an experience of industrialisation, democratisation and modernisation. We are now in a situation where this first modernity is being transformed into a second modernity. The first modernity was based upon a nation state society, on given collective identities such as classes, families, ethnicities. Central to it was the principle, if not the practice, of full employment, and a mode of production based on the exploitation of nature. This modernity is being challenged by several developments. First of all individualisation. Second, by globalisation as an economic, sociological and cultural phenomenon. Third, by under-employment or unemployment, not simply as the consequence of government policy or a downturn in the economy, but as a structural development which cannot easily be overcome. And, fourthly, it is being challenged by ecological crisis. In this second modernity, we are heading not only for minor changes – in personal relationships, for example – but for a different form of capitalism, a new global order, a different type of everyday life. We have to begin to ask very basic questions about how we are living, how we can respond to these changes, and how we can analyse them in sociological terms.

In your books you talk about the global conflict between societies like ours which are entering a second modernity and those that are either in, or entering, their first modernity. Do you think there is a similar uneven development within societies?

Of course. We shouldn't simplify this process. There are very different speeds of development and individualisation in different societies or subcultures, and these are happening simultaneously. In most countries where these processes are well advanced, you can still find areas in which they have scarcely begun.

And these different formations in society must each give rise to different politics and values? I just wonder whether individualisation is not describing the culture of a metropolitan educated elite, perhaps the emergence of a new knowledge-based class?

No. I do think class is a zombie category. The discussion about indi-vidualisation got started in Germany in the early 1980s, after I published an article, 'Beyond Class and Status'. Why did I do this? Because in the late 1970s and 1980s I had more and more trouble explaining class categories to my students. The conventional Marxist analysis of class bore no relation to their own experience, and they could not make sense of it. I had to translate class to a more individualised culture, concerned with quite different basic questions. The students did not think of themselves in an unconscious way as members of a class. Their cultural self perception was somehow different to the picture presented by a class analysis of culture and society.

In Britain you still have a sociology which believes in the centrality of class as an explanatory category. You find this even in the writings of Anthony Giddens. Relativised yes, but still believing that we cannot say goodbye to the class category. Maybe this is related to experiences in Britain which I am not aware of. But if you look at how a class-based sociology defines class categories, you find that it depends upon what is going on in families and households. Empirical definitions of class identity are founded on categories of household defined by either a male head of household, or at least the leading person of the household. This is a completely fictitious way of defining class. No-one can really say what a household or a family is nowadays, not in economic or social terms.

Let me give you an example of how the individualisation debate has been picked up in Germany. First of all there has been very important research on the individualisation of the poor. This challenges the misunderstanding that individualisation is a matter for the rich. Research has shown that there is now a much greater degree of mobility in and out of poverty amongst a wide range of people and at different periods of people's lives. There is still, of course, an increasing number of people who are poor in the long term. But in the middle there is a coming and going. Because of individualisation, there is a lack of political organisation of the poor. Capitalism without classes does not mean less inequality in the future, it will mean more. The current idea of exclusion can only be properly understood against the background of individualisation, or to be more precise atomisation. It creates institutional circumstances under which individuals are cut off from traditional securities, while at the same time losing access to the basic rights and resources of modernity.

Are you using the term poverty in the sense of material deprivation, to describe something which is new? Perhaps it has to be redefined for this second modernity?

Yes I agree. Even poverty to some extent is a zombie category because we don't know what hides behind this term. This does not mean that these people are not poor but it does mean that we cannot predict by one indicator what kind of life they lead and what kind of consciousness is going to develop out of this condition.

It is very difficult to work in a rich empirical way with class categories. You can only develop them on an objective income basis, or on structures of work and employment. You can't relate them to how people live and think, eat, how they dress, love, organise their lives and so on. If you are interested in what is going on in people's minds, and the kinds of life they are leading, you have to get away from the old categories. And if you want to know what this all means politically, again you have to get away from objective class categories. Then you can draw a picture of a differentiated society with different cultures of individualisation and different reactions to it. It is possible to identify a variety of what I will call collective life situations – not classes – and all of these have a different political meaning.

Such an analysis differs from the old class analysis by concentrating on changes in everyday life. In the 1980s and the beginning of the 1990s, this analysis identified that between 30 and 40 per cent of the population in Germany were interested in some form of experimental way of life, and were at the same time highly political in a new sense. No one could understand this for quite a while because they were not involved in any political party, not the liberals, the SPD, the conservatives or the greens, nor were they part of union membership. Nevertheless they were still active politically in a very direct way both around their personal relationships and around wider issues. It is these individualised sub-political cultures which helped to alter the political landscape of Germany. Nobody expected it. These people want an experimental politics to happen. They want politics to adjust to the new realities they perceive.

You don't think that this 30 or 40 per cent is the formation of a new class category and consciousness?

No. If it is, you have to think of class in a different way.

I'm quite happy to. Your work reminds me of the humanist, cultural Marxism of E.P. Thompson which describes how working people organised around the shared experience of exploitation and created their own class cultures and a class consciousness. It seems absolutely right that class cultures and consciousness, under different conditions, will change or disappear. What takes their place?

I think the approach I have been describing relates to this tradition of cultural Marxism quite well. At least in terms of the importance it attaches to what people think and believe, and how they organise their lives. But there is one big difference, which we probably need to have a debate about – and that is the need to acknowledge the individual as the basic unit of democracy, the republic, and political organisation. All old class conceptions and politics presupposed that the individual and individualisation was a basic illusion, which had to be overcome in order to rebuild collective identities, and to organise political life and represent the individual in political democracy. I think this is a basic mistake. Just the opposite is necessary. Political parties nowadays have to recognise and acknowledge individualisation, not as something to overcome, but as a new form of cultural democratisation and self consciousness of society. A new form of society in which politics is related to individual freedom, and the political freedoms and rights of groups in their everyday life. If political parties fail to understand this situation and always try to go back to a given collectivity or class they will completely misunderstand the political forces and ideas of this society. The basic mistake of communitarianism is to react to individualisation. It is 'reactionary' in its attempt to recuperate the old values of family, neighbourhood, religion and social identity which are just not pictures of reality any more.

There are residues of class identity and discrimination in British society which remain immensely powerful. I wonder whether this emergence of a second modernity could ever break away entirely from the institutions and categories of the first modernity. The psychological residues of class identity provide people with a personal history, a way of making sense of their own life experience or at least the experience of their parents. I'd extend this to the level of a society's perception of itself. Even if we now aspire to leave our class, it still remains as something which defines where we came from. It still appears to hold water in terms of defining the unequal distribution of educational opportunities, and social and cultural capital.

Of course there are different situations in different countries. I am aware of Britain being a more everyday class-bound society than, for example, Germany. Again it is different in France. In the second modernity there are powerful transnational actors changing the social and political landscapes. There will be winners and losers, so maybe we will need redefined class categories to understand the relationships and dynamics of a cosmopolitan society. But a society and politics which only reacts to globalisation and individualisation, and which tries to reactivate old values, is failing to understand the process of 'reflexive modernisation', and grasp the historical changes we are living through.

Do you think it's simply about political parties not understanding? Surely they can't do anything. They are first modernity institutions trying to grapple with a landscape beyond their language.

Yes. Take the example of full employment, which is a zombie category. We are living with two models of employment. One is the postwar, welfare-state model of full employment, characterised by very low unemployment; a male family wage earner; normal, usually secure, work contracts; the idea of a career for the middle classes; and a job for life. The other model is what we could call fragile or flexible employment, which means flexitime, part-time work, short term contracts, people juggling different types of work at the same time. This second category of fragile employment is increasing rapidly in industrialised countries worldwide. We don't have the categories to describe it. Politics, and governments in Britain, Germany and France, are reacting to this pluralisation and flexibilisation of work – even in relation to the most advanced areas of the information economy – by trying to enforce the full employment principle. It is one example of an outmoded politics trying to engage with the new conditions of individualisation.

You describe an emerging society in which family and personal life has become individualised, employment has become less secure and more fragmented, and the political system appears to be incapable of engaging with these processes. Is representative liberal democracy one of your zombie categories?

This is a very difficult question to answer. I think we need to democratise democracy. For Germany our admission ticket to the democratic age lies with Immanuel Kant, who took it upon himself to label parliamentary democracy 'despotic'. Representative democracy contradicts the self determination of the individual. It is founded upon the rule of the common will against the individual which, as Kant says, is a contradiction of the general will with itself. The alternative to national majority democracy is what I call a cosmopolitan republicanism. By this I mean the revaluation of the local, and the self-responsibility of civil society – an active society where political processes are not simply organised in Parliament and in the government but at a local and every-day level of the citizen. Civil society is in poor repute amongst politicians because it does not meet their standards of efficiency. The technocratic plastic speech of so many politicians is a cancer on democratic culture. Politics cannot be simply rational. Efficient solutions to problems are important, but so is passion. Politics has to be about emotional life. It is about the ability to listen, justice, interests, trust, identities, and conflict when necessary; these involve more than a belief in some optimal path. We need a society which is not simply centred on work but is willing to finance, by for example a citizen's income, those forms of self-organisation and experimental life forms which are already going on. Such a democraticisation of democracy also needs to happen on a transnational level. We need a European civil rights movement which, in respect to foreigners, brings Europe's political identity into focus and helps develop it further. The more successful the Euro becomes the more urgent is the question of Europe's soul, and the need to democratise the Union.

Who are the enemies of this process of democraticisation?

Individualisation doesn't automatically mean that people want to live as individuals and relate to one another as individuals. It could mean a new form of reflexive fundamentalism as well, which attempts to redefine collective identities – nationalism for example – and use them to resist or attack this process of individualisation.

Do you see where this might be happening?

If you look back at history, Hannah Arendt explained German fascism as a reaction to an earlier phase of individualisation (or, again, more accurately, the atomisation of society). That was a picture-book example of creating a collective identity by politics. I am not saying this is being repeated today, but there is a fundamentalist reaction to individualisation in all parties and social groups which may become a more open conflict in the future. There will be resistance in the second modernity to individualisation, and to the way globalisation deterritorialises national cultures. It will come in particular from religious movements, the revival of ethnicity, and counter-modern movements, paradoxically using the information technology of the second modernity to organise themselves globally.

You say in your writing that we are living in a crisis of freedom and choice.

Yes.

The second modernity seems to be founded upon freedom, choice, the individual, and an existential uncertainty, and it is this last one that people draw back from, seeking those old collective identities and certainties.

Yes, of course you have to see this in the institutional context of the welfare state, the nation state and a work-oriented society. There is not a simple choice between the new or the old. For example in Germany the politicisation of the ecological crisis is part of individualisation and the second modernity. And yet out of this there is the possibility of a reflexive ecological fundamentalism as a reaction to this new culture of freedom.

What comes to mind in the relationship of the first modernity to the emerging second modernity is an antagonism between a large majority of the world's poor, who might adopt a fundamentalist view of the world, and a liberal minority of the rich societies. An antagonism which would also exist within the rich societies. I'm thinking about Islam both in Europe and in Britain where there are certain strands which mobilise fundamentalist interpretations of Islam to articulate an anti-imperialist politics, and the grievances of Muslims against racism and injustice. The Islamic tradition of religion as central to everyday life and as a source of political expression poses a challenge to the secular pluralism of the second modernity.

Yes, indeed, this is one of the plausible future scenarios.

Second modernity against the first modernity. Privileged against the poor?

No, I wouldn't agree to just opposing first modernity to second modernity. It isn't that easy. The experimental cultures I speak about are not universal, they are a part of European culture. There are what I will call 'divergent modernities' and 'contextual universalisms' in Asia, Africa and South America to be recognised as well. This means we cannot think about societies as we did before, as existing within the container of the nation state with clear boundaries and relationships to others. We have to think globally. People are no longer living even simply local cultures any more. The poor population, even in a world wide perspective, is changing. The meaning of being poor is changing. In the first modernity, poverty, as Marx said, was determined by a class's or group's access to the labour market. The situation today is dramatically different because nobody needs the poor any more. Capitalism is creating joblessness and excluding swathes of populations. The second modernity is not simply a positive development. We in Western Europe are highly individualised but at the same time we are confronted – in a world which doesn't have the same borders any more – with people who are excluded and yet still living inside our lives. They are excluded but a part of our life. We have to relate to them. There are really dramatic challenges coming up. We have to rethink society in a cosmopolitan order, redefining the essential notions of justice and solidarity. At the moment, most of the philosophical debate is based on the assumption of a national container model of society, with its self-definitions of community, justice and democracy.

Going back to the 17th and 18th century, when society was radically changing with the emergence of capitalism and the first modernity, there existed a similar preoccupation with the self and with individual values and ethics. What do you think will be the values and ethics which emerge in this second modernity and which will lay the foundations for a different kind of politics?

They will not be the ethics from those periods of early individualisation. The late eighteenth and early nineteenth century witnessed the emergence of subjectivity and romanticism in everyday life. There was a dramatisation of romantic love which created not only the notion of an individual biography, but also a moral and emotional complex which helped to create the couple, and their history, against society. If you look at the cultural artefacts of the time – love letters and diaries – you are persuaded that people invented themselves and their relationships through love. The secular religion of love was invented at this time. You will also discover in these same love letters the invention of divorce as well. Today both romantic love and divorce have become ordinary and democratised.

The first impression one might have of individualised subcultures today is that they are similarly centred on the dramatisation of their own egos. But research by Robert Wuthnow, a US sociologist of religion, has challenged the idea that we are living in a 'selfish society'. His study showed that for 75 per cent of the American population, solidarity, helpfulness and concern for the general welfare are as important as self-actualisation, professional success and expansion of personal freedom. Individualised cultures do develop their own altruistic ethics. Being an individual does not exclude caring about others. In fact living in a highly individualised culture means you have to be socially sensible, and be able to relate to others, and to obligate yourself, in order to manage and organise your everyday life. In the old value system the ego always had to be subordinated to patterns of the collective. A new ethics will establish a sense of 'we' which is like a co-operative or altruistic individualism. Thinking of oneself and living for others at the same time, once considered a contradiction in terms, is revealed as an internal, substantive connection.

And are you willing to give up for others ?

Yes, willing to give up and having a lot of dilemmas and paradoxes about it. Let's think about it on the level of personal relationships. On the one hand you want someone who will always support you in your own development. On the other, you have to support their own development if they are to support yours. More than this, you have to acknowledge the other's freedom and also his or her need to be loved. This is the dilemma: you must allow your beloved to be free, but in wanting them to love you, you restrict their freedom. Each partner wants his or her freedom, and at the same time to be chained in the hands of the beloved. Out of the struggle with this dilemma between love and freedom a new ethics will emerge about the importance of individuation and obligation to others. No-one has the answer as to how this will work.

This is the business of growing up as children, learning the give and take of life, learning to be with others, reconciling our desire for autonomy with our need of dependency on others. Always that

*negotiation. Is this the ethical experience out of which a new poli-
tics will emerge?*

Yes. We have to understand that individualisation presupposes a
conscience and a reflexive process of socialisation and inter-subjectivity. You have to construct and invent your inter-subjectivity in order to
be an individual. But it is not a Robinson Crusoe society, where everyone is for himself. It's the opposite. It is in the everyday experiments in
living that we will find out about a new ethics which combines personal
freedom with engagement with others, and even engagement on a
transnational basis. I think we are living in a highly moral world
despite what the cultural pessimists try to tell us. But it's not a world
of fixed obligations and values. Rather it is one which is trying to find
out how to combine individualisation with obligations to others, even
on a global scale.

Does this ethical impulse have a political expression?

It does.

Where?

First of all on a sub-political level, where changes in attitudes do not
amount to an inflation of material demands for more income, more
consumption, more career. At the centre of the new ethics is the idea of
the quality of life. What does this imply? For one thing, control over a
person's 'own time' is valued more highly than more income or more
career success. So, for example, providing there are basic securities, a
lack of waged work means time affluence. Time is the key which opens
the door to the treasures promised by the age of self-determined life:
dialogue, friendship, being on one's own, compassion, fun, sub-political commitment. In some ways this marks a shift away from the struggle for the distribution of material goods which still dominates public
politics, towards a demand for the distribution of scarce immaterial
resources which cannot be expressed in the exchange of money. I'm
thinking of rest, leisure, self-determined commitments and forms of
working, relationships, family life. Of course these are the values of a
self-oriented culture which is sensitive to ecological concerns.
    It is an ethics of everyday life which is developing its own sub-poli-
tics, which is often very local and concrete and which politicians don't

recognise, because they don't know about the cultural nerve systems of these individualised cultures. It is an 'anti politics'. We are witnessing today an actively unpolitical younger generation which has taken the life out of the political institutions and is turning them into zombie categories. This Western variant of anti-politics opens up the opportunity to enjoy one's own life, and supplements this with a self-organised concern for others which has broken free from large institutions. It is organised around food, the body, sexuality, identity, and in defence of the political freedom of these cultures against intervention from outside. If you look at these cultures closely what seems to be unpolitical becomes politicised.

Your vision of a positive outcome to an individualised society relies upon there being a moral impulse. I can see an alternative to this optimism here in Britain as we have moved away from the European model of social democracy, towards the American model of a flexible deregulated market economy. A more libertarian culture certainly, but one in which the poor and excluded and those needing support and help (and that means all of us at some time in our lives) are left to flounder alone. If the market is left to distribute freedoms in the way it distributes wealth then we're in deep trouble. There will be nothing left of the social democratic institutions which were created in the first modernity to defend people.

This is very true. Arguing for the centrality of risk in understanding the dynamics of our time, I am aware of the dark sides of individualisation and globalisation as well. But I can't help feeling bored by the habit of concentrating on the catastrophes ahead. It doesn't challenge us to think. How do we know that everything is getting worse? Neither the pessimist nor the optimist can foresee the future. It is very difficult and therefore intellectually challenging to open up a thinking and acting for realistic utopian opportunities. Maybe I underestimate those threats of second modernity because I am still very much connected to the continental political movements of the 1970s and 1980s.

I like that. It gives your work an optimism, and hope for the future.

Re-thinking Work

Suzanne Franks

Work more than ever before is the defining characteristic of social worth. If Descartes was around and still philosophising today, he might well have added that 'I *do* therefore I am'. So it follows that anyone who does *nothing* is in danger of social invisibility. According to contemporary social description it is the newly invented category of the 'workless household' that has become the dreaded badge of social exclusion.

The same is true at the other end of the social scale. Never until the present generation has the son of the monarch bothered his head about finding work. Indeed a whole class of men was once quite comfortable to write 'gentleman' under the occupational category on their passports. But now even Prince Edward has to find employment and to *become* a television producer. Sure enough he has never worried about earning any income, but he has to have a job because just like anyone else he would have been socially excluded had he failed to find work. Once upon a time the Marx brothers used to snigger that 'If work was so great then how come the rich don't do it?' Alas now they do, and judging by the hours of the city types or the corporate lawyers, they are often working harder than anyone else. In many cases there is even a direct relationship, so that the longer the working hours then the higher the job status and the more important is the person.

Of course it was not always the case that work was inextricably part of social status. For the ancient Greeks it was completely the other way around. Work was itself the badge of social exclusion – something to be done by the underclass and the excluded; notably women and slaves. No self-respecting Athenian citizen would demean himself by working. It was certainly not the route to social acceptance but something to be avoided in favour of leisure and all kinds of other social and civic activities.

So how is it that work has become so central to our definition of self?

Work has always been with us. By comparison the social construct of 'the job' is a comparatively modern invention. Many pre-modern societies did not even have a word that meant 'work'. It was just something that went on according to seasons and needs with everyone participating as necessary, mostly in and around the home. Working wasn't readily distinguishable from other activities: and 'in so far as it was recognised as a distinctive type of activity, it was not something which was associated with a male role'.[1] This is the pattern that had existed for thousands of years, and it still persists in many non-industrial societies, where families depend upon agriculture or small scale home-based craft activity, and everyone – adults and children – plays a role, alongside general domestic life.

In the west the industrial revolution changed all that. Men went off to work in jobs. In fact the practice of seeing the family as a single employment unit continued for a while after industrialisation, so that women and children were sometimes jointly employed in an enterprise. But this habit soon disappeared and women were left to preside over the domestic sphere, even though many poorer women still had to earn an income. A woman was not meant to work and have a job; her place was in the home and – provided her husband brought home a 'family wage' – that is what she was expected to aspire to. At home she did not have a job and so was no longer officially working. The 1881 census officially designated housework as unproductive and so the category housewife became a non-occupation. Whatever a woman was doing in the house – it was not work.

Real work was inextricably associated with having a job – which was something that men did all day, in the years after full time education and before retirement. And gradually the concept of having a job became fused with moral meaning and personal identity. Its converse, which was unemployment, left a man devoid of social value. At the same time the biggest social revolution of the twentieth century has been the entry of women into the public domain and one of the consequences has been, perhaps unsurprisingly, that their status has, like that of men, become more and more closely associated with what they do. 'Just a homemaker' is no longer socially sufficient; whereas at the beginning of the century any other role (certainly for a married woman with children) was greeted with suspicion. Today the label housewife and 'staying at home to look after...' invariably means second class, low status and something to be excused.

In most modern industrial societies work has become a necessary component of social status for everyone. This is not just a feature of capitalism, which only values what is done in exchange for money. It was equally true of the planned economies of Eastern Europe. Every able-bodied individual had to participate in the labour market, in order to have a socially meaningful existence. And the same philosophy underlies much of New Labour's welfare reform. There are plentiful tax credits and childcare assistance for the poor who want to enter paid work, especially the lone mother. She is encouraged to take a job – even if it is a lowly paid position in a call centre or perhaps as a childcare worker looking after other people's children. Paid work is the route to salvation; no matter how menial it may be, it is socially sanctioned, whereas unpaid caring remains socially unrewarded – despite the convenient political slogan about the so-called 'Giving Age'.

The paradox is that paid work has become *more* significant in a period when it is also increasingly precarious. The scenario of the stable job market, reliably low unemployment and a pattern of full-time, lifetime work feels like ancient history. How unfortunate it is that regular and secure work is more difficult to find and to hold on to just at the moment when it is also more critical to our concept of self and status. Perhaps there is a direct causal link whereby we revere work because it is harder to achieve?

In the new-model labour market individuals are typically juggling portfolio tasks or switching in and out of short-term contracts, and experiencing the insecurity that was previously absorbed within institutions. Redundancy and retraining are part of the familiar economic furniture; but the experience of losing a job, particularly in middle age, can be catastrophic. Stress in the workplace is a growing theme and it has even become the subject of litigation as individuals find themselves under greater pressures. The real meaning of the famous 'flexible labour markets' is that individuals now have to be able to absorb uncertainty that was previously contained within institutions. Once it was jobs that were described as flexible because the hours were convenient or adjustable. Now the term represents something quite different; which is that individuals have to fit in and be flexible whether this means zero hours contracts, anti-social shifts, Sunday opening hours or constant availability to clients. In a recent gloomy but very accessible account, Richard Sennett has described in detail the effect of this ever-mounting insecurity and risk in the workplace. His book is aptly titled *The Corrosion of Character: The Personal Consequences of Work in the New Capitalism*. It looks at the negative effect upon both individuals and communities of the continual and frantic change in the workplace.[2]

The pace of economic transformation means that it is conceptually difficult to understand the new employment landscape. So many organisations and individuals feel more comfortable with the familiar and traditional world of employment as it used to be. School 'careers' lessons, trade unions, benefit agencies, financial institutions and other areas of officialdom often still operate on the principle that we live in the old world of the normal, full-time, 9-5 employee. Even the idea of education as a lifetime process and the need for new and transferable skills is a difficult one for a bank to grasp hold of when considering a loan application. When the management guru Charles Handy's children left university he admonished them with the words: 'I hope you are not going to go out and look for a job now'. His vision was of course that they should develop a series of skills, which they could then 'sell' into the market in a sequential, portfolio existence. For the majority of parents it can be an alarming prospect to have to change their perceptions of what work really means and to envisage how school leavers today will find themselves 'living without a map'.

It is not just our immediate pre-conceptions about work which are being turned inside-out. J.K. Galbraith pointed out recently that the word work itself is in any case 'our most misleading social term' ... 'It designates the occupation of those who would be very unhappy without it. And yet we also use the same word for hard, repetitive, even physically painful toil. No word in the English language stretches over such different conditions.'[3] In the view of right-wing orthodox economists, work operates according to the same supply and demand as any other commodity. It is a 'disutility ' which we perform simply because we have to. Leisure is a 'utility', which we give up solely because work enables us to earn a wage, and we will only forego leisure at the point where the price for our labour is sufficiently attractive. Other economists have described how this is far too crude an analysis; and indeed work is for many people a 'utility' which itself provides all kinds of social advantages.[4] Moreover many people derive enormous enjoyment from work. Indeed those who enjoy their work most often receive the highest pay. A further paradox is that those whose product is most socially useful may well receive the lowest wages. In the scramble for work this rather obvious distinction is often lost. For many other workers there are only limited utilities beyond their pay packet. In a casualised labour market, trade unions are weaker and less able to protect people, so invariably working conditions have become degraded. It is only for the lucky ones, who inhabit quite a different universe, that work is a life-enhancing, exciting and rewarding prospect.

The confusion about work goes even wider than this. If work is defined as having a job, then the counterpart to work is seen as leisure. Everything else is invisible. So a time chart which reads: rise at 6 to feed a baby, spend a day full of cleaning the house, cooking, attending to the needs of elderly relatives, shopping, washing, childcare, finishing with a night-time feed, would not officially count as work. It is the same in a labour ward; the midwife, anaesthetist, tea-lady, doctor, nurse and cleaner are all working, because they are paid. The woman who is 'in labour', producing a future member of the human race, is not considered to be doing any productive work, because her effort is not recorded in the Gross National Product.

Work is only work when money changes hands. And every first year economics student knows that 'when a man marries his housekeeper, the GNP will drop'. She may be performing identical tasks as an unpaid wife but they will no longer count as work. Indeed such are the paradoxes that according to orthodox economic definitions an unemployed man is defined as 'economically active' even if he lies in bed all day, whilst a homemaker/mother for statistical purposes, no matter how busy she is with caring and voluntary effort, is defined as 'economically inactive'. Now that women, especially married women and mothers, have increasingly come to participate in the visible world of paid work, it has thrown up awkward questions about priorities. If time is supposed to divide into work and leisure then how does all this other activity fit in?

The assumption behind the traditional sexual division of labour is that men's paid work relies upon a shadow economy of unpaid women's work. If women are now also in the formal paid workforce then what is the status of what had always been a 'labour of love'? One solution is to argue that the concept and values of the market must extend to incorporate what has always previously been considered non-work. According to some interpretations, the traditional 'free' labour of women should be seen as a form of taxation whereby society benefits from their input, just as if they were paying directly to the state.[5]

This idea that the invisible 'love labour' should have a monetary value is a new concept; it has only become seriously recognised since mothers started going to work and employing someone else to under-take domestic activity, which then suddenly became real paid work. (To some extent women may have colluded in the continuing invisibility of domestic labour. It was never a good idea to mention family concerns in the workplace, as this detracted from being seen as a committed employee.) Of course, anyone who has undertaken unpaid care in the home knows all too well that it is not invisible but very real. It is only in the terms of the official paid labour market, and the formal economic measuring tools, that it is invisible.

These contradictions were particularly clear in the former planned economies of Eastern Europe, where the demands made of women demonstrated the 'double burden' with particular clarity. A woman of working age was expected to participate fully in the labour market (in 1989 the former East Germany had a participation rate of 98 per cent of women of working age – compared to only 54 per cent in the West). So a woman would typically pass her day in a factory, driving buses or mending the roads. Yet after that she would rush off to spend hours on all the time-consuming duties associated with the home; the rules of gender segregation, even in the so-called socialist states, dictated that these were strictly 'women's activities', not to be shared.

Under these systems the nature of the 'invisible work' was exces-sively demanding because of the peculiarities of the economic system; yet despite the official credo of an equal society, this burden still fell exclusively on women – and it was still officially invisible.

Until recently the idea of paying for domestic labour, and campaigns like 'Wages for Housework', were treated as a joke. But gradually the discovery of 'unpaid work' has emerged from feminist theory and entered the mainstream. The insurance company Legal and General recently produced a survey entitled 'The Value of a Mum', which stated authoritatively that Mum's work an average of 62 hours a week, and that the value of this work was £313 in March 1997. From an insurance point of view if Mum is not around this is what it would cost to replace her efforts.

Another indication that women are doing something of value came when the UK government, after a long battle, agreed to change the system of paying benefits to widowers. Historically widows have been treated very generously by the benefit system, in order to compensate for the loss of their 'breadwinner', whilst a man who was left with dependent children after his wife died has received almost nothing from the state. After an interminable legal wrangle in 1999 the government agreed that losing a wife and mother might also have financial implications for a family, even if she had been at home working without pay!

Housekeeping and the care of young children are not the only roles that have had no official recognition as 'real work.' At the other end of the life cycle, the growing number of carers who undertake responsibilities for the elderly also throws into relief the substitution value of such effort. An estimated six million people have some form of caring responsibility for the old and the sick, and a third of them have a full-time job as well. Even amongst women in their twenties, it appears that 16 per cent now put in between twenty and thirty-five hours a week as 'carers' – a proportion which has doubled in the last few years. The potential savings in residential care and nursing are enormous, because it is all done for 'free' – or if any caring allowance is paid it covers only a tiny fraction of the equivalent institutional cost. The numbers in need of care are steadily increasing so there is a growing awareness of the paradox of this officially invisible effort. In fact elder care might become pivotal in the association of women with unpaid domestic labour. All the arguments about 'maternal instinct' and the task of breast feeding, which link women with caring for young children, disappear when it is the case of the elderly that is under consideration. After all there is unlikely to be an innate biological reason why a woman is better than her spouse at emptying her mother- or father- in-law's bedpan.

Outside the home, voluntary and communal effort – all those myriad tasks that provide the invaluable social capital held so dear by sociologists – are equally part of the shadow economy. It has hitherto been predominantly women's work; but if women are entering the paid labour market in a serious way then what happens to this 'invisible' effort – the parental involvement in schools, the support for meals on wheels, the staffing of the scout troop, or citizen's advice bureau, or the thousands of other institutions that depend upon voluntary work?

Many industrial countries have decided that the time has come to acknowledge the 'informal economy' alongside the official calculation of the Gross National Product, which measures only the financial transactions in the economy. In Britain the Office for National Statistics, formerly an offshoot of the Treasury, decided that from October 1997, for the first time since housework became a non-occupation in 1881, they were going to start putting a value on it.

According to economists who specialise in this area, if we were to put unpaid work in the United Kingdom, measured in the 'Household Satellite Accounts', alongside the official GNP, it would amount to between 56 per cent and 122 per cent of the entire economy, depending upon the rates of pay.[6] No mainstream voice is yet suggesting that housework should be paid for – after all where would the money come from? The objective is simply to demonstrate how much effort and value resides in this sector. Even this is historically significant because it officially exposes for the first time all the hidden activity which has hitherto been carried out very largely by one gender and not the other. In 1973 there was a groundbreaking sociological study by Young and Willmott called *The Symmetrical Family*, which looked ahead to a world where women were entering the labour force en masse.[7] It predicted that instead of a couple having two jobs – his in paid work and hers in the home – they would henceforth have four jobs between them. The woman would now take on a job outside the home and thereby have the burden of two jobs. Eventually though, the authors predicted, her partner would take on his share of tasks in the home so that they would both have two jobs – one inside and one outside the home. Unfortunately the symmetry is still missing in the majority of households; in general there are still three jobs (two for her and one for him) rather than the anticipated four. There is an interesting calculation which follows from this – to add up paid and unpaid effort and see how much time is left – for this is the real definition of genuinely 'available leisure'; unsurprisingly, men have a great deal more of this (at least eight hours a week) than women.

Unpaid work continues to be unfairly distributed between the genders. At the same time, paid work is more unevenly distributed than ever across the social spectrum, which has lead to the clichéd contrast between the work/rich and time/poor versus the time/rich and work/poor. At one time the prediction was that we would all be working a thirty-hour week by the start of the new millennium. But in fact the picture is more one of a world where half the population work sixty hours a week and the rest do not work at all. Despite all the glorious prophecies of the leisured society, it turns out that extensive leisure is largely restricted to those who have no money to use it.

No matter how it is disguised, worklessness is a problem in both industrial and non-industrial economies, and the major economic challenge of the twenty-first century is to overcome this. If work is so crucial to social well being and status then we must be able to spread it around more evenly. Some economists, for example Mauricio Rojas, are remarkably sanguine, and anticipate that we will be able to adjust.[8] A larger number of them paint a frightening picture of a substantial economically disenfranchised underclass who lack the skills to belong to the workforce. Professor Ian Angell of the LSE is typical of this voice: 'The lights are going out for whole categories of employment. We are entering an age of hopelessness, an age of resentment, an age of rage. Whole sectors of society who previously felt their future secure can see it slipping away.'[9] Their only hope of an occupation is in the poorly paid service sector, where they will service the needs of the hard-working and high-earning highly skilled, whose time is too precious to spend on any menial task.

We need to find not only a fairer way of allocating paid work, but also a better balance between paid and unpaid effort. It is vital that we lift the status of caring and other non-remunerative but vital activity. Maybe the route is through some form of citizen income in recognition of these efforts. We need to develop a political economy of time, which takes into account paid and unpaid effort and acknowledges the need to limit and redistribute paid work. In France, for example, there has been a conscious effort to limit working hours – well beyond the tentative steps of the European Union. In Germany there is evidence that status and long hours should not be regarded as inextricably linked – the last car in the car park at the end of the shift is often a sign of its driver's inefficiency rather than dedication. However, although there are benefits to be gained in resisting the 24-hour service society, there is a risk that they will be largely achieved at the expense of restricting women's opportunities, and preserving a traditional attitude to gender identity.

So far no society has managed to achieve a harmonisation of work and parenthood, as well as other forms of caring – without giving women a hard time. There have been many attempts but they frequently result in the unintended consequence of reinforcing gender stereotyping. For example, well-intentioned policies of parental leave are invariably taken up by one gender only. In Germany only two per cent of those who have taken the 'child upbringing break', and its associated benefit payment, are fathers. The official Department of Trade prediction in Britain is that only two per cent of fathers will be asking for the unpaid parental leave which has recently been agreed. The only solution is to make such benefits non-transferable and financially worthwhile. Interestingly this proposal of non-transferability was suggested by the European Union in the 1980s but was never introduced.[10] When Sweden switched some of its paid parental benefits so that they were non-transferable it had the effect of increasing paternal involvement.

There is another sense in which paid work and home need to be harmonised. If the workplace is increasingly stressful and insecure then the private domain has to absorb these fluctuations. In his recent book Richard Sennett has given a grim account of the consequences of job market insecurity for individuals.[11] He describes the inability to plan or to develop ties of obligation and responsibility which arises as a result of the ever-shifting contemporary workplace. In a rather less gloomy account William Bridges talks about the brave new freelance world which will replace the old vision of jobs.[12] He predicts that everyone will redesign themselves as You & Co to sell their skills into the market; but he still worries that people who are for hire – as are today's independent workers – 'lack a centre to their lives': 'in a new world of non-stop change ... they are living with ambiguities produced by the disappearance of any meaningful economic slots to settle into ... experiencing tension between doing different things for different clients at the same time in ALL fields.' He refers to a workplace where, since organisations operate in such a turbulent environment, no arrangement serves for very long, so that individuals 'need the ability to bend and not break, bounce back quickly from disappointment, to live with high levels of uncertainty'. His conclusion is to find your security from within rather than from outside. Yet the rising rates of divorce and family breakdown mean that the trend is likely to be towards less rather than more security being found in the private domain. Indeed it is likely that domestic upheaval can be a direct result of the changing workplace. Britain has the longest working hours and the most deregulated labour market in Europe, as well as the highest divorce rate. So just at a point when the home is more vital than ever, as a 'haven in a heartless world', it is likely to be an area of unrest.

It may well be that after all the emphasis on downshifting, contracting out and the need to improve the bottom line, we are discovering that other costs and side effects can be incurred through deregulation and flexible markets. The impact of employment insecurity upon communities and upon the social fabric sometimes presents itself in a direct way, such as in the high public costs of family disintegration. At other times it is much harder to measure. It is also evident that the stress of flexible labour markets will fall heaviest upon those who are doing the 'invisible' work.

The challenge is to civilise work and spread it out more evenly. At the same time we need to balance the three-way equation of paid work, unpaid work and meaningful leisure to be enjoyed. And if we could emphasise the significance of, and encourage a higher status for, unpaid caring and community effort, we could achieve a more equitable redistribution between men and women of both paid and unpaid responsibility. The consequences of this for the upbringing of future generations, especially for young boys – who are the focus of much current concern – would be immeasurable.

NOTES

1. Anthony Giddens, *Sociology: Third Edition*, Polity Press, Cambridge 1997.
2. Richard Sennett, *The Corrosion of Character: The Personal Consequences of Work in the New Capitalism*, W.W. Norton & Co, New York 1998.
3. J. K. Galbraith, LSE lecture, 28 June 1999.
4. Will Hutton, *The State We're In*, Jonathan Cape, London 1995.
5. Howard Glennerster, 'Paying for Welfare: Issues for the Nineties', Welfare State Programme Paper WSP/82, London School of Economics 1992.
6. Interview with Henry Neuberger, formerly Economist with Office for National Statistics and Household Satellite Accounts, HMSO, 1997.
7. Michael Young and Peter Willmott, *The Symmetrical Family*, Routledge, London 1973.
8. Mauricio Rojas, *Millennium Doom: Fallacies About the End of Work*, Social Market Foundation/Profile Books 1999.
9. *Independent*, 25.9.96. See also Jeremy Rifkin, *The End of Work*, G. P. Putnam, 1995; or Viviane Forrester, *The Economic Horror*, Polity Press 1999.
10. Jane Lewis (ed), *Women and Social Policies in Europe: Work, Family and the State*, Edward Elgar 1993.
11. Richard Sennett, *op. cit.*
12. William Bridges, *Jobshift: How to Prosper in a World Without Jobs*, Nicholas Brealey, 1995.

THE ART OF LIFE

Jonathan Rutherford

'What will we get out of these questions?' asked the second disciple.
'The promise of a new question', replied Reb Mendel.
Edmond Jabès *The Book of Questions*

At the university where I work, I organise a course on autobiography.
When the students first begin this course many think there must be a
catch: 'You mean we can write about anything?' They can write about
anything and they do, and most of them do it well. It never is about
'anything'. Anything very quickly proves to be something. Even those
students who have spent three years trawling bottom grades excel in
their insightful depictions of childhood, and the nuances of family relationships. They put their personal hopes and aspirations into this writing. They document parents who loved them and parents who have let
them down; sisters, brothers, grandparents who have died; families
split by violence, and families in which the children have been secure
and happy. It's an opportunity for them to make sense of the confine-
ments imposed on them by social inequality, the difference of race, and
the ambivalences of sexuality, love and need. In this final term of their
university careers, in the moment before embarking on their lives, they
write down their story however shocking or ordinary.

The popularity of the course amongst students reflects broader
changes in culture. Despite historically unparalleled degrees of social
stability and affluence, we are living through a period of profound
change in our personal and emotional lives. Capitalism is reconstruct-
ing the economic and geographical conditions which produced the old,
work-centred class categories. Globalisation, the emergence of new
knowledge-based, post-industrial sectors, and the expansion of the
service economy have radically altered the time and rhythm of work.
The end of empire, post war new Commonwealth immigration, and

radical changes to family life and sexual values are transforming the social character of English ethnicity. Individuals are being freed from the constraints of the old order, but the new opportunities have brought new risks which mirror the injustices of the old class society. Greater degrees of personal self-expression coincide with new forms of standardisation in which the rhetoric of the market – the supremacy of personal choice, the inviolability of individual ambition – disguises the disparate life chances of people. The dissolving of working-class ties has led to unprecedented degrees of inequality, intensifying the experience of poverty and creating new forms of social exclusion. We are, in the words of the German sociologist Ulrich Beck, entering a period of capitalism without class, in which collective relationships to the means of production have been radically disrupted by de-industrialisation and unregulated forms of 'turbo-charged' capitalism. Working-class cultures have fragmented and are unable to mobilise individuals against the new forms of risk they face; nor, in the main, can they generate a contemporary language of self affirmation and cultural empowerment. Their bonds of solidarity are now vestigial. There will be no revival of social democracy as we have known it, because the alliance of class interests which brought it into effect has disappeared.

The challenge to familiar forms of authority and collective ideals of belonging has helped to precipitate profound changes in people's personal lives. These are emotional and psychological in character and consequently it is individual consciousness and cultural attitudes rather than political and economic indices which are currently most directly affected. The periodic and cumulative undermining of patriarchal attitudes by women's struggle for emancipation has redefined the boundary between private and public life, creating new definitions of the self. What were once considered to be private personal feelings and experiences have now become publicly relevant. The diminished gap between public and private is characterised by a re-evaluation of the place of reason and emotion in society. Masculine civility, duty and emotional restraint which once dominated the public sphere are under challenge from a culture of intimacy, informality and self-expression. The turn away from collective ideologies and public discourses is both symptomatic of the individualisation created by neo-liberal capitalism and a reaction against its tendency to uproot settled patterns of life. The cultural sensibilities of the students lend themselves to a preoccupation with their own personal identities and relationships, and in this they are representative of our time.

Our increasing personal isolation in society has encouraged a greater emphasis on individuality, self-reliance, and the search for an ethics and practice of identity and emotional life. Dissatisfaction is expressed in our concern for the particular and everyday rather than in grand ideological themes. This absorption with the 'quality of life' is a response to new antagonisms and problems which necessitate people's active engagement. For those in paid work, time has become a scarce commodity. Family life has lost its common temporal rhythm and spatial focus, and requires new skills of management, co-ordinating the competing needs, interests and activities of adults and children. People's expectations of relationships are growing. Sexuality has been politicised, and the body has become the subject of ubiquitous forms of self management and modification. Personal appearance and self-presentation now embody valuable forms of social capital. The growing desire for the immaterial – rest, free time, friendship, fun, creative work – is encouraging conflict with the work ethic, and new demands for personal and social well being. The meaning of life is the subject of countless self-help books. Established religions and old fashioned notions of morality are challenged by new representations of the sacred, and by personal ethics and alternative spiritual beliefs. There is a revolt against the institutionalising of death. Banished out of sight by Victorian propriety, it is being brought back into people's lives. The things that matter to people are increasingly outside the instrumental, managerialist language of politics and the sphere of governance.

Popular culture has been absorbed by these changes. It is in music, art, literature and the new forms of media, that the images and vocabularies of these preoccupations are being invented. TV talk shows have been public lessons in a newly emerging language of intimacy and ethical decision making. They reflect a culture in which individuals are continually having to make judgements and choices effecting their life course. For all their dwelling on the spectacle of dysfunction, the shows engage with a language of care, love, friendship, responsibility, concern, permanence, continuity, longing, despair, which contradicts the short-termist, utilitarian languages of work and commerce. What were once the private domestic cultures of women have been projected into the public arena as new forms of imagined ethical communities.

There is an argument that the contemporary search for authenticity in personal life is a defeat for civic virtue and democracy; that we are hovering on the fringes of a consumerist, privatised dystopia. It is true that the modern turn to the self coincides with public apathy toward local and national elections and a general disinterest in politics. But as Adam Smith reminds us in *Wealth of Nations*, the realm of the public in modernity was originally secured by the market and the utility of money: 'every-man in some measure becomes a merchant'. Benevolence toward others was subordinated to the function of exchange value. If this instrumental and utilitarian culture of capitalism was somewhat dissipated by the social solidarities created by the Second World War and the welfare state, it returned with a vengeance in the 1980s and continues unabated. Neo-liberal capitalism has undermined representative democracy and forms of national and public authority through individualisation and its promotion of a global, standardised commodity culture, but ironically it has extended democracy into cultural, personal and family life. A new relationship between the individual, the local and the global is emerging, and it is here, not in the public realm of governance, that there is a re-evaluation of what an ethics of living might be, a search for a new vocab-ulary of virtue. The individual practice of identity making, of negotiating relationships and defending oneself against the social forces of capital, racism and sexism, is not simply an aesthetic of lifestyle, but the neces-sary emotional work of everyday life. Concern with private life and the cultivation of the self is central to the revolution in society of the late twentieth century. Contemporary preoccupations with intimacy, friend-ship, the meaning of life, death, love, family, belonging, sexuality, the body and emotions are prefigurative forms of culture and are what Raymond Williams has described as 'structures of feeling'. By this he means cultural forms which have not yet found the conditions for their collective self awareness. They exist on the edge of semantic representa-tion: 'affective relations of consciousness and relationships: not feeling against thought, but thought as felt and feeling as thought'.[1] They are a part of emergent values and identities across Western Europe.

PROTESTANTISM AND THE INDIVIDUAL

The preoccupation with the self, emotions and identity has been a central feature of the history of modernity and closely affiliated to the constitutional struggle for civic democracy. In Europe, during the seventeenth century, the emergence of finance and trade capitalism increasingly directed the private economic activity of the family house-hold toward the commodity market. This led to the establishment of a public realm of the trading and middle classes, and a separate domestic culture of family life. At the same time the Puritan revolution secured a sphere of private individual autonomy. Lacking both educational background and identification with an established denomination, Puritans could only invoke the authority of personal experience. With the Reformation, self-examination replaced oral confession and there grew up a Puritan culture of spiritual autobiographies, diary writing and personal testaments which gave rise to a self-conscious, inner life of the individual.

The Reformation had initiated an idea of human togetherness radically different from Catholicism, which had bound individuals to the church through their bodies and emotions. Protestantism promoted an imaginary community based on faith, which abstracted religion from people's everyday lives. The meaning of life was no longer fixed, but became a task of individual self-reflection and the examination and interpretation of god's word. Sensuality was identified with the despotism of the Catholic church and the absolutism of the King. The Protestant revolution was intent on ridding society of the baroque cultures and sacred communities which gloried in and upheld this divine earthly power. Emotions became ungodly and threatening to the rational order of things. The sacred gradually came to reside in the mind rather than the body and community. The Protestant revolution marked the growth of a possessive individualism integral to the rise of capitalism. Individual identity came to express a person's place in the new order of things.

Milton's epic poem *Paradise Lost*, published in 1667, was written on the cusp of this emerging culture. Its narrative of the Fall of Adam and Eve from Paradise can be read as a lament for man's essential aloneness, the failure of his revolutionary consciousness in the aftermath of the English Revolution and the tragedy of free will. Milton, who was blind, and writing after the Restoration and the defeat of his beloved Good Old Cause, is both of god and of the devil. What captures the imagination is not the amorphous light of divinity or the righteousness of Jesus, but the heroic misfortune of Satan cast out of heaven, wracked by the human emotions of failure, jealousy and revenge; our forebear who discovers hell is within. Milton's was a new kind of allegorical politics, a turn inward, an assessment of defeat which recognised that failure lay in the psychology and consciousness of men and women.

Milton had been a part of the small marginalised radical movement – the Levellers, Ranters, Muggletonians and Behmenists – which had manifested itself in the second part of the 1640s. And it was this culture of revolutionary nonconformism which provided the seed bed for eighteenth century Enlightenment thinking in England. When John

Bunyan in *The Pilgrim's Progress* (1678) falls asleep and dreams a dream of Christian, 'a man clothed in rags', breaking out in his lamenting cry 'What shall I do?', he inaugurates a cultural revolution which symbolises the transition from traditional society. The narrative of early European modernity was this pilgrim's progress to his spiritual homeland; the transition from Providence and fate to the idea of personal destiny. But in the same instant Bunyan establishes a profound problem about the place of love, intimacy, and emotions in human life. Christian's despairing call to be saved is answered by Evangelist who tells him to follow 'yonder shining light'. Bunyan watches in his dream as Christian runs from his own door, his wife and children pleading with him to return as he stops up his ears crying, 'Life, life, eternal life'. The ambivalence of choice: human love or divine grace.

The philosopher William Godwin secularised the language of the pilgrim's progress. He evolved from a fundamentalist puritan sect to the radical individualism of his major work *An Enquiry Concerning Political Justice*, published in 1793. The narrative of modernity was no longer toward a spiritual home but toward human perfection. The application of enlightenment values of reason and persuasion would achieve the long transition to a perfect society. With the emergence of science and a metropolitan public culture, the eighteenth century witnessed the secular development of the individual's inner life. Man was governed by reason, and his mind released from the parameters of religious tradition. The religious ethic of righteousness was gradually superseded by a pragmatism and psychology of the self. The Calvinist anxiety 'how can I be good?' became the secular 'how can I be happy?' Society was constructed on the rational deliberations of its male citizens, defined by relationships which were associational and secular rather than communal and sacred. But this rise of individualism introduced new anxieties about community and what held people together. The eighteenth century abounded with theories of civil society which attempted to explain how a specifically secular and human society was possible.

The beginning of polite society, heralded by the *Spectator* in 1711, embraced every aspect of manners and morals and demanded the regulation of personal feelings. Individuals had powerful emotions which could not be suppressed, but they could be regulated, or better still refined to a 'greater Elegance'. Feelings provoked by fine literature and art were the greatest and purest of pleasures. Politeness and its codes of conduct encouraged the widespread self-reflection of diary writing and

the keeping of journals which recorded the author's efforts to understand culture and achieve good taste. But fashioning behaviour in order
to please others created anxiety about identity. 'Who am I!' wrote
Anthony Ashley Cooper, the Earl of Shaftesbury, in his private note-
books, concluding that he had 'lost My self' in 'all those supple caress-
ing and ingratiating ways'.[2] Artifice inevitably prompted a reaction – a
desire for an authentic 'language of the heart' and the spontaneous
emotion of sentiment.

The philosopher David Hume was concerned with the conflict
between reason and emotion, in particular with the sociability which
bound individuals into a society. In *Treatise of Human Nature*,
published in 1739-40, he argued that feelings permitted the expression
of social bonds upon which society was founded. Sociability and moral
values were inaugurated by the flow of emotions – sympathy – between
people. Feelings were the impetus behind human action, and a form of
communication: 'Hatred, resentment, esteem, love, courage, mirth and
melancholy; all of these passions I feel more from communication than
from my own natural temper and disposition.'[3] Hume's language of
sentiment and sensibility, shared by the novelists Laurence Sterne and
Samuel Richardson, developed into a popular cult of feelings; this was
challenged by his friend Adam Smith. Hume had written in the Treatise,
'Reason is and ought only to be the slave of the passions, and can never
pretend to any other office than to serve and obey them.'[4] Smith, in
Theory of Moral Sentiments published in 1759, argued that sympathy –
compassion, fellow-feeling – was necessary for the moral foundation of
a commercial society. However, unmediated emotions of sentiment
usurped reasonable behaviour and undermined the ties which bound
people together. To ensure the harmony of society, emotions could not
be completely private and spontaneous but had to be learnt through
social interaction. In Smith's *Theory*, the concept of sociability becomes
a calculation of self-interest which distances the subject from both
himself and from others: 'We must imagine ourselves not the actors, but
the spectators of our own character and conduct'.[5] A statement he made
more explicit in the 1761 edition: 'I divide myself, as it were, into two
persons ... the first is the spectator, the second is the agent'. [6]

In the face of this criticism Hume recanted his more extreme
pronouncements on the dominance of emotion over reason.
Nevertheless his exploration of the language of feeling had identified
the limitations of Enlightenment rationalism. In his short autobio-
graphical essay *My Own Life*, written four months before his death in

1776, he once more embraced sentiment – the unity of feeling and reason, public man of letters with the private self – in a text which expressed his desire to die as he had attempted to live, in a philosophical manner. In contrast Smith, who published *The Inquiry into the Nature and Causes of Wealth of Nations* in the same year, displaced human relatedness further still into political economy. The emergence of disinterested competitive markets and contractual relations would ensure the well being of all, without recourse to the fickle nature of human benevolence. Unsatisfied with Hume's boundless emotions and doubtful that benevolence was innate to human nature, Smith anchored morality and its regulation in the 'immense machine' of public life and government. Justice and the rule of law, not sociability, would be the ties which bound citizens to society. Society, he argued, could manage without benevolence, though it would be, as a consequence, 'less happy'. The public good would be managed by the 'invisible hand' of the market. Smith places his faith in general rules and principles which will guarantee morality, rather than any notion of sentiment.

ROMANTICISM

In 1781 Jean-Jacques Rousseau declared at the beginning of his *Confessions*, 'Myself alone! I know the feelings of my heart, and I know men. I am not made like any of those I have seen; I venture to believe that I am not made like any of those who are in existence. If I am not better, at least I am different.' It was Rousseau of all the Enlightenment philosophers who most successfully navigated a path between 'unreasonable rationalism' and 'superstitious anti-rationalism', between individualism and a recognition of democratic and egalitarian ideals. His introspection, his concern with the memory of childhood, his search for personal fulfilment and disdain for authority, established a revolutionary fashioning of the self and identity which has become a central feature of modernity. In the final decade of the eighteenth century, Rousseau's writing had a significant influence on English supporters of the French Revolution and marked the birth of Romanticism.

Romanticism in England emerged out of the political agitation for constitutional reform between 1792 and 1796 and expressed the humanitarian sympathy associated with the French and American Revolution. The *Lyrical Ballads* of Coleridge and Wordsworth, published in 1798, is its best known literary representation. In the preface, Wordsworth declared that poetry is 'the spontaneous overflow of powerful feelings'. Romanticism was a continuation of the 'Age of

Sensibility' and gave expression to an intense reaction against the rationalising tendencies of the Enlightenment and the anti-human, anti-
aesthetic influences of commerce. It emphasised the inner life of the
imagination, and sought through its depictions of nature a language of
immanence. Mary Wollstonecraft's travelogue *Letters Written During
A Short Residence in Sweden Norway and Denmark*, published in
1796, anticipates the *Ballads* and the doctrine of the sublime: 'my very
soul diffused itself in the scene ... imperceptibly recalling the reveries of
childhood, I bowed before the awful throne of the creator' (letter 8).[7]
As she writes in another letter to her lover, the American adventurer
Gordon Imlay: 'my reason obliges me to permit my feelings to be my
criterion ... though I insist that the cultivation of the mind, by warm-
ing, nay almost creating the imagination, produces taste, and an
immense variety of sensations and emotions, partaking of the exquisite
pleasure inspired by beauty and sublimity' (letter 10).

At least half of the literature published in England between 1780 and
1830 was written by women, but the growing cultural dominance of
men in the early nineteenth century has concealed the central role
women played in the Romantic movement. More than this, it obscured
how the making of the modern self and identity was a profoundly
masculine affair which reflected men's attempt to claim personal feeling as the authentic expression of the individual without succumbing to
the sentimental emotions associated with women. In *Emile*, published
in 1760, Rousseau discusses what he means by the passions. The word
comes from *patio*, I suffer, I am worked upon. To be subject to passion
is to cease to be the sole instigator of one's actions. Passion confronts
Rousseau with the loss of self, his fear of dependency and the threat to
personal well being which these imply. He describes Emile's first real
passion as his love for Sophie. 'Sophie you are the arbiter of my fate.
You know it well. You can make me die of pain. But do not hope to
make me forget the rights of humanity. They are more sacred to me
than yours. I will never give them up for you'. Sophie is Rousseau's
perfect imaginary wife, a coquette who is confined to the private realm
and subordinated to the abstract, rational ideas of public life. 'Women
have, or ought to have, but little liberty' he declared.[8]

'What nonsense!' retorted Mary Wollstonecraft in *A Vindication of
the Rights of Woman* (1792). 'Still harping on the same subject, you will
exclaim', she writes to Gordon Imlay in 1795. 'How can I avoid it,
when most of the struggles of an eventful life have been occasioned by
the oppressed state of my sex: we reason deeply, when we forcibly feel'

(letter 19). The feminism of Mary Wollstonecraft demanded women's right to reason and for a public existence alongside men. Men, cultivating their finer feelings, were unwilling to admit women into public intellectual life. Similarly they were anxious in their exploration of the emotions. If women were the unreasonable creatures of sentiment then the feelings of men had to be marked out as separate, different and superior. The aesthetic of life which became known as Romanticism evolved not so much in the absence of women writers but in their exclusion by men intent on fashioning a language of feelings denuded of feminine connotations. The degeneration of the French revolution, and political reaction in Britain, encouraged the displacement of Romanticism's original humanitarian sympathy into a cultivation of the solitary genius. A man's expression of his sentiment was less for others than for the higher things of life. He could aspire to be free from social relations, to give birth to the idea of himself. Feelings were no longer Hume's expression of sociability, but increasingly belonged to the solitary world of the exceptional individual.

By the end of the century conservatives associated sentiment with the revolutionary benevolence of the French Revolution, and condemned it as a threat to the social order. Even radicals like the young Coleridge linked it with flighty female readers of the novel. What had been a mark of sincerity had become associated with foreigners and effeminacy. British national identity forged in the war with France was defining itself in its rejection of certain forms of emotional expression – abstract idealism, public displays of sentimental emotions, introspection – in favour of a sturdy, unreflecting manliness secured by the dispassionate, the provable and the measurable.

The late eighteenth century provided the modern language of political radicalism and democracy: revolutionary ideologies; Tom Paine's writing on citizenship and equality; the constitutionalism of the 1790s; the feminism of Mary Wollstonecraft. It gave form to the social contours of modernity: the cultural differences of femininity and masculinity; the emergence of empires and the racialising of European cultures; the conflict between reason and feelings, commerce and sensibility; the divide between the public and private spheres of social life; the consolidation of the modern self and its other as a defining category of social life. Romanticism emerged as the counter culture of modernity, establishing a tradition of opposition to capitalism through its promotion of the authenticity of emotional life, its appeal to nature, and, with the rise of agnosticism, the promise of the sublime. But it too was subjected to its own counter culture, not only in the writing of women and the emergence of feminism, but in the narratives of former slaves who exposed its complicity with imperialism and the emerging discourses of racism. Ignatius Sancho, born in 1729 on a slave ship, and later becoming a friend of the sentimental novelist Laurence Sterne, wrote his best selling *The Letters of the Late Ignatius Sancho* with the intention of proving that an African possessed the same abilities as a European. Published in 1782, two years after his death, the book attracted 1200 subscribers, rivalled only by the *Spectator* 70 years before. Olaudah Equiano, the first political leader of Britain's black community, similarly wrote a best selling life story *The Interesting Narrative of Olaudah Equiano* (1789). These narratives exposed the way in which commerce reduced human lives to goods and chattels, and how the racialised character of sensibility all too frequently failed to extend its benevolence to black people.

ETHICAL LIFE

In its darker aspect, the immanence of Romanticism was subsumed into the absolutism of an authentic truth of the self, which provided the chief ideologies of the nineteenth and twentieth centuries – nationalism, fascism and Marxism – with their respective aesthetic and philosophical justifications. At the heart of these ideologies was the longing to implement the utopian desire for human completeness, a pursuit of perfection which required the total rationalisation of human conduct. Marx in the *1844 Manuscripts*, drawing on German Romanticism, attempted to address what it means to be human, to describe the ways in which commodity relations alienated the worker from himself. Capital, he argued, is the 'subjective manifestation' of man wholly lost to himself, and labour its 'objective manifestation'.[9] Behind his description of this self-estrangement lay Hegel's belief in an underlying unity of human essence and world, the notion of the inevitable progress of history toward human perfection. Marxism and its dialectic of historical materialism was the legacy of the Enlightenment's unreasonable belief in reason. As Godwin wrote in his early edition of *Political Justice*, 'Man is perfectible, or in other words susceptible of perpetual improvement'.[10] In the hands of Lenin, Marxism differed little from the punishing theology of Calvinism. One demanded the surrender of life to God, the other of life to the State and History.

The collapse of Communism in 1989 was the most recent rout of the Enlightenment project of human perfection through the application of reason and science. In contrast, traditions of English/British socialism – the Socialist League of William Morris, Edward Carpenter's brand of romantic socialism, the New Left and the social movements of the 1960s – have been sceptical of modernity's rationalising ethos and derived their languages from native Romanticism. They fostered a creative engagement with the world, antipathetic to the bureaucratic didacticism of the Fabians, the industrial ethos of Labour, and the scientism of theoretical Marxism. Their emphasis on emotions and inner experience, and the search for an authentic self, democratised personal life and redefined the boundaries of political discourse. But these traditions of collectivism also have not been saved from history. They too were a product of the culture of puritanism. Their notions of human solidarity were invented by the religious traditions of the non-Conformists, and they harboured a romantic moralism and a politics of judgementalism which became evident in their suspicion of commercial popular culture, and their prescriptive attitudes toward lifestyle and personal opinion. This moralism was a variation on the religious authority and bourgeois propriety which had previously rewarded the masses for being dutiful, emotionally restrained, self denying, or deferential. People have rejected the imposition of this class authority, and, like their religious forebears, these Left politics have also now been dispersed by secular individualism.

Today there are no more utopias, and no more dreams of brotherhood. The sign we live under is one which is ambivalent in its own meaning. It was Jacques Derrida who theorised this unending slippage of language, the impossibility of securing meaning; and Jean Francois Lyotard who described our modern predicament of identity as always arriving at our destination too soon or too late. In such a culture we are left to our own devices – adrift for the moment, but also free to take ethical decisions. There is no Left any more in the sense of an identifiable moral and political authority, only the remnants of a number of antagonistic traditions. There is no future in attempting to repair and impose one of the old ideologies, to homogenise difference, or try and stem the leaking away of identity. But equally there is little to be gained by pretending they never existed. A future politics will be fashioned in the present on the basis of the past. What then are we to do? It is a question that has haunted the texts of the European Left. It is the spectre which besets this moment of modernity, because, unlike John Bunyan, or for that matter Lenin, we no longer believe in the Celestial City where the streets are paved with gold. As Marx accurately predicted, the logic of capitalism encourages the breaking up of human ties and a more intensive commodifying of everyday life. The solution of the market is to promote the personal realisation of the few over social and moral concern for all; but there is no human respite guaranteed in the allure of profit, or the individual pursuit of wealth. Adam Smith informed his readers over two hundred years ago that commodity relations will never lead to personal fulfilment or happiness. And Marx, sixty-eight years later, perversely insisted that the 'goal of the economic system is the unhappiness of society'.[11]

In the Romantic era love became the great melodrama which would beat back the dull, patriarchal world of duty and emotional impoverishment. It was the beacon of liberation which would launch the lives of its young protagonists into the future of their dreams. The secular religion of love was invented, and it has now become ordinary and is the stuff of everybody's dreams; and yet it still holds the promise of transforming our lives, of connecting us in deep and enduring ways to other human beings. Love is an emancipation which enables us to be present in our own lives. But the Romantic tradition, in its rejection of the fractured and instrumental relations of capital, longs for an holistic, organic culture and this lends it a deep and abiding fear of cultural and racial difference. Love cannot be the basis for a politics, for it tends to reduce difference to sameness. To learn to be with oneself in the presence of other people is how an ethical practice might be simply described. The philosopher Emmanuel Levinas argues that we are not wholly alone in the world, nor are we part of a totality to which all others belong. Our encounter with others who are not reducible to ourselves, and the realisation that we must negotiate sharing the world with them, is the moment ethical life begins.[12]

It is this encounter in the contemporary democratisation of culture, family and personal life which will provide a future vocabulary of political radicalism. It will not be another singular ideology of anti-capitalism, but one which holds the potential for being a counter-culture of modernity, able to address the proliferation and dispersal of contemporary social and political antagonisms. The development of such a politics cannot begin with defining strategies, agencies or ideologies. In a post-scarcity society in which economic determinants play a less significant role in determining the fate of individuals, conventional forms of politics and sociology are no longer able to explain individual motivations and behaviour, nor do they have the language for representing people's aspirations for a better life. A beginning can be made by returning to the old question appropriated by religion. What does it mean to be alive? And with the memory of slavery and the ethnic barbarism of European Fascism, Nazism and Communism, it leads to a further, political question. What is the relationship of human life to sovereign power? Such an ethical politics requires a cultural and intellectual life which follows the spirit of Levinas's Jewish humanism – reading against the grain, interpreting rather than prescribing and legislating, placing questions at the heart of the search for identity and meaning.

It was the late Michel Foucault who recognised that such a philosophy leads us to the early Stoics and their art of living. At the beginning of the first millennium, Seneca, in his essay 'On The Shortness of Life', wrote 'But learning how to live takes a whole life, and, which may surprise you more, it takes a whole life to learn how to die.' [13] As Foucault points out in his book *Care of the Self*, the Stoic concern with the cultivation of the self – 'spend your whole life learning how to live' – was not simply a valorisation of private individualism, but indicative of a crisis of the subject: 'the difficulty in the manner in which the individual could form himself as an ethic of the subject'.[14] Norbert Elias has described the changes in the customs of the Roman upper classes and how subsequent legislation altered the balance of power between men and women in women's favour. It was this weakening of private patriarchal authority and the changing relationship between the family household and the public sphere of the state which encouraged a philosophy of care of the self. Elias argues that a central factor in fostering more egalitarian relations between men and women was the role of the state in protecting the person, property and income of women. He concludes 'the same holds true, I think, in our time.' [15]

It is the paradox of an ethical politics centred on the individual that it can only develop through new forms of social solidarity, and more specifically through the transformation of the organisation and culture of the state. Today it is necessary to live without guarantees but nevertheless with an ethical framework that acknowledges co-dependency, and that care of the self and the pursuit of self-interest is intrinsically bound to care of others and concern for society. 'If you wish to be loved: love', wrote Seneca to his 'pupil' Lucilius.[16] In an age of secular individualism in which the dread of loneliness and failure have replaced the apprehension of hunger and disease, there is a need to cultivate representations of human commonality and the pleasures of being alive. To invent a language of virtue – notions of goodness which are pragmatic and contingent and not a pious observance of the Law. In the past these were expressed in religious symbols and spaces of the sacred. They were timeless, changeless representations of a pre-modern, homogeneous culture and an undifferentiated world view. The search for a new settlement between the individual and society requires the invention of plural, non-absolutist and deinstitutionalised forms. Objects, languages and spaces in which our inner being finds an emotional connection to the world beyond, and which foster coexistence with the others who occupy it.

We can never know the truth of ourselves, we will never achieve immanence or attain transcendence. We can only ever get hold of the world indirectly though representation in language. We also are made in language. It makes us, as well as the world. The sacred is simply a metaphor for the excess of world over word. The Left died when it failed imaginatively, creatively, aesthetically and politically to help us in this act of knowing and reparation. Life is a work and it is the emotional and intellectual business of politics to invent new languages which redescribe the world and help us live in it better and with pleasure. If we live today with personal insecurity and a paucity of public languages of our commonwealth, it is within human natures to reach for something more which is beyond us, to grasp for words which will correspond to what is missing. Out of this ethical activity can emerge a renewed collective impulse for economic justice, personal emancipation and political democracy.

NOTES

1. Raymond Williams, 'Structures of Feeling', in *Marxism and Literature*, Oxford University Press, 1978.
2. See John Brewer, *The Pleasures of the Imagination: English Culture in the Eighteenth Century*, Fontana Press, 1997, p112.
3. David Hume, *Treatise of Human Nature*, ed. L.A Selby-Bigge, 2nd edition revised P.H. Nidditch, Oxford, 1978, p317.
4. *Ibid.*, p415.
5. Adam Smith, *The Theory of Moral Sentiments*, ed. D.D. Raphael and A.L Macfie, Oxford 1976, p111.
6. *Ibid.*, p113 .
7. See Mary Wollstonecraft, *A Short Residence in Sweden*, Penguin Classics, 1987.
8. See Mary Wollstonecraft, *A Vindication of the Rights of Woman*, Penguin Classics, 1992, p108.

9. Karl Marx, *Economic and Philosophic Manuscripts of 1844*, Progress Publishers Moscow, 1974, p75.

10. William Godwin, *An Enquiry Concerning Political Justice and Its Influence on General Virtue and Happiness*, London, 1985, p140.

11. *Op. cit.*, p26.

12. See Emmanuel Levinas, *Totality and Infinity*; also 'Ethics as First Philosophy' in *The Levinas Reader*, ed. Seán Hand, Blackwell, 1996; also, for an introduction, Colin Davis, *Levinas: An Introduction*, Polity Press, 1996.

13. Seneca, 'On the Shortness of Life' in *Dialogues and Letters*, Penguin Classics, 1997, p66.

14. Michel Foucault, *The Care of the Self*, trans. Robert Hurley, Penguin, 1988, p95.

15. Norbert Elias, 'The Changing Balance of Power between the Sexes – A Process-Sociological Study: The Example of the Ancient Roman State', in *Theory Culture and Society* Vol. 4, 1987, 287-316.

16. Seneca, 'Letter IX' in *Letters from a Stoic*, Penguin Classics, 1969, p49.

No place like home

Roshi Naidoo

For once, thinking about 'race', ethnicity, cultural identity and national belonging is not solely a preoccupation for Britain's black and 'ethnic' minorities. For those of us who, historically, have had constantly to negotiate and renegotiate our cultural, national, political and 'ethnic' identities, the current preoccupation with Englishness evokes a number of responses.

We fear that any assertion of an English identity will be a reactionary one, which will exclude or vilify the centuries-old presence of non-white people on these islands. As the UK divides into its four nations, the British identity that black[1] people have fought hard to assert will be lost in the supremacy of these 'ethnic' identities.[2] Will those on the left, who seem to be as preoccupied with the cultural meaning of Englishness as those on the right, come up with a more radical definition of it? But there is also an amused response to this crisis in Englishness. For so long it was assumed that it was only us, the racial 'other', who even had an ethnicity. We had to learn as children the difference between nationality, ethnicity, language and political identification when interrogated about who we were, and where we came from, while our English counterparts took it for granted that their cultural identities held no such conflicts.

The continuing problems which black people have had around national identity have not been met with uniform responses. Despite the backdrop of our persistent exclusion there is an incredible confidence amongst African, Asian and Caribbean people in Britain at the moment[3] – it is even (finally!) 'cool' to be Asian – and this can be detected in black expressive culture, and in the views and attitudes of those who assert that confident cultural hybridity leaves one in a privileged space rather than permanently culturally dislocated. At the same time there are some 'second generation immigrants' who are exploring the possibility of making a life for themselves at their parents' home, as a response to what is perceived to be the insurmountable racism and exclusion in British society. This desire for a more satisfying home is also expressed by some young people through their moves to reconnect to familial, communal and religious orthodoxies in this country.

Against these different ways of formulating belonging, the trip 'back home' – i.e. to parents'/grandparents' home – is invested with all sorts of symbolic significance. What I am particularly interested in is the notion of 'returning' as therapy: that one makes a pilgrimage there to reconnect to a 'lost' identity, and seeks that elusive sense of home through finding a unified self and a coherent cultural identity. This journey is sometimes also constructed as being therapeutic because it allows one to dismiss the 'other' place as one of alienation, and it can therefore be used to confirm Britain as home. Both these positions appear to be unsatisfactory, and are predicated on partial notions of what constitutes nation, community and cultural identity. In this piece I am primarily concerned with the idea that black people born and/or brought up in Britain can 'resolve' problems of locating home by travelling elsewhere. Can there be any closure for those who embark on this journey with that agenda?

It was with this in mind that I made a trip to South Africa, my parents' home, after a twenty-year absence. I had been aware of a heightened sense of investment in family 'over there' from those 'over here'. Many people, settlers and their descendants, were making more regular trips there, as well as planning to return for good. Obviously the nature of South Africa's political situation gave some clues as to why this would occur now. It was five years after the election of the African National Congress (ANC) and many South African Indians not directly connected to the liberation movements had adopted a 'wait and see' attitude about the country's political stability. Other factors, such as the increased availability of affordable flights, and the fact that those who came to Britain in the 1950s and 1960s were reaching retirement age and looking to go back, provided some explanations. However, my reading of this heightened investment in the 'second generation' making the trip was that it had less to do with South Africa and more to do with what was going on in Britain. It was here that I could identify this notion of the therapeutic value of going – the idea that it could provide some sort of antidote to the psychological traumas of living a marginalised existence in dominant British culture. Going home would be read as a sign of maturity, and as a journey which would add depth to cultural identity by showing us where we came from.

The narrative of return and the search for one's 'roots' is one which is deeply embedded in diaspora culture, and one which is very powerful and seductive. It implies a resistance to the history of slavery, colonialism and indentured servitude, and an unwillingness for language, culture and a sense of belonging to be lost in the mire of exile, migration and cultural dislocation. It is also one which can be deeply problematic, a narrative which can mask some of the complexities of diasporan subjectivity; it can invest the place of geographical 'origin' with a primary importance, and as a site of an 'authentic' culture, in a regressive way. I could tell from the investment others around me had that it was going to be a very loaded journey. My own confidence in my British Asian identity made me feel fairly sure that I would not want to return for good, but what exactly would my feelings be? Although I was passing it off to most as a pleasant holiday in the sun, I could feel my anxiety increasing as it got nearer. In an important sense it was my anxieties about going which proved to be the catalyst in interrogating my feelings about home rather than the actual journey.

In my mind there were always two South Africas. The first I located very strongly with the anti-apartheid struggle and the fight for human rights, social justice and the end of white supremacy which it signified. It was a place, as for so many, which symbolised the possibility of achieving something momentous against racism and the power of international capitalism. The other South Africa was the one where the small Indian community of Durban lived, where my parents were brought up. This South Africa had been mythologised to me in different ways. This was the place which seemed in my mind to be perpetually located in the 1950s – a place of family, poverty, mango trees and warmth. These two South Africas were not totally separate but joined together by all those Indians who had fought and died in the anti-apartheid struggle; but in my imagination they existed as distinct places.

I had last been there as a crabby teenager in 1979. I was fourteen years old and devastated that what was a return home to settle for good for my parents represented for me a leaving home – which had not been accounted for. On previous visits as a younger child I had loved it, but in 1979 things were very different. I went to a segregated Indian school, but was more 'other' there, in a class where a fifth of the children shared my surname, than I was in my 'multi-racial' school in North

London. After ten months (and for a variety of reasons) my parents and I had returned to Britain. This would be my first visit since then. I hoped, I suppose, for clear-cut feelings – either an embrace of the community or the 'rainbow nation', or a reawakening of the resentful home-sick child who was last there. It is always easier in narratives of returning to dismiss this latter response as the naive, silly one, and to give more credence to the mature embracing of one's 'real' homeland, but I had a feeling nothing would be that simple.

As I have said, the feelings and anxieties about going to South Africa were very illuminating, mostly because they alerted me to the fact that we of the 'second generation' have always had a limiting framework through which to conceptualise our feelings about home and belonging. It made me review the shifts that occur in how we choose to locate home, and what they are shaped by. It was particularly interesting that I found it easier to address the specifics of black identity in Britain in a theoretical context than to confront some of my personal feelings about certain issues. In my review of the various ways in which I had conceived of where I belonged I was aware that multiple subjectivity had allowed me to foreground different aspects of cultural and political belonging in different contexts and I refused the idea that this left me full of conflict. For example, one can call oneself black at a political meeting, Tamil at a social function and British at the airport and not be tormented by competing internal subjective voices. However, I was aware that, in foregrounding one aspect of who I was, the suppression of other aspects could also be troubling.

Once, at an Asian literature conference, I spoke to a woman who talked about her dislocation linguistically, in terms of feeling cut off from her tongue. I agreed with this sentiment, but later thought about whether or not I really felt like that and concluded that English as a first language served me well. I had agreed with the woman partly because I hadn't thought it through, but mostly because my status as a marginalised person put so much at stake in finding a sense of solidarity and common purpose in spaces such as this. I mention this because a desire to belong is ever present in how we present ourselves when we make the journey home; and because I think our day-to-day lives are full of these sorts of incidents and anomalies which we are constantly unpacking for meaning. We need more spaces to speak to each other about such conflicts – spaces where we can honestly address such things without fear of our conclusions being co-opted by the white supremacist culture we live in.

My trip to South Africa was a catalyst for some of the feelings about home and belonging which had been simmering below my consciousness. One of the things I had always been troubled by was the way in which communities 'back home' were spoken about. Life was always 'simpler', 'slower', more community orientated, and it was always a place where people really cared about each other. Ways of talking about the 'other' place often dovetailed into a sentimentalised primitivist rhetoric. Observations such as this skim over the plethora of social and economic hardships which people have to endure, and are often based on images formed through holidays where, by and large, visitors are protected from the day-to-day realities of people's lives. It highlighted the fact that many of the ways of thinking about our parent's homelands for us in the West are mediated through an essentialising of the 'other' place.

Discourses of primitivism can inform black, as well as white, access to 'foreign' cultures, and the 'other' can be fetishized in more complex but equally reductive ways. For example, when hippies set off to India in the 1960s and 1970s to 'find themselves', their construction of it as having certain spiritual and cosmic meanings also formed the way in which some, particularly diaspora and second generation, Indians have identified it. When white 'new age' culture speaks of the ancient wisdoms of indigenous people, particularly in relation to ecological preservation, this deeply conservative rhetoric is not one which black people are immediately immune from digesting. To locate the black 'other' as the antithesis of western rationalism is indeed a white fantasy which locates black people permanently outside of contemporary social relations and which neglects to discuss political resistance to forms of genocide perpetrated on these peoples. But we also have to acknowledge the ways in which such representations inform black people's access to Africa, Asia or wherever. Ironically, it is often those who claim an authenticity of cultural identity by dismissing all hybrid culture as 'impure' who inadvertently occupy the most white-identified discourses of the 'other' place.

Last year I taught an exceptionally stimulating group of first year cultural studies students with parental connections to all parts of the globe. Many of them, when doing an exercise on cultural artefacts, brought things from 'home', their parents' home, and talked with affection about holidays spent there. All who chose to talk of 'home' expressed the sentiment that life was better there because it was less complicated, because family was there, because it was warmer – both in terms of weather and in terms of human warmth. This can be read against the points I have just made, but I do not recall this to discredit their perceptions and feelings about their homelands; I do so to indicate that there are limitations in the cultural vocabulary we have to express such sentiments. This made me interrogate some of the ways I spoke about family in South Africa at a similar age, and it shed light on how difficult it is for descendants of settlers to voice the discrepancies between what our parents told us about 'home' and Britain and what we thought.

Some of us suppressed the desire to call Britain home as children because we knew it upset our parents. We rarely expressed this sentiment to white contemporaries (except when they told us to go 'home') for fear of this being interpreted as a negation of our cultural identities and an ethnocentric celebration of whiteness being 'best'. We said it (and continue to say it) quietly to each other – 'I wouldn't want to leave would you?'

When some of our parents became disillusioned with the vision of Britain that met them, they told us new narratives of England which both did, and sometimes didn't, match our experiences. For example, I, like many others, grew up hearing that English people were cold, as cold as the weather was. We agreed although there was much which didn't bear this out. I believed that English people didn't look after their old people – yet many of my English friends had their nans living with them. I cite this not to identify prejudice against the English but to highlight how difficult it was to separate out where our parents' sense of home differed from ours.

Much has been written about the difficulties African, Caribbean and Asian people have in participating in dominant celebrations of nationhood (such as the World Cup), and also about how we negotiate this (we hope that a black player will score the goal) – but less has been written about our relationship to narratives of other nations. I remember as a child that I and 'others' would tell English friends that we were going on holiday to Cyprus, the Caribbean, India, Kenya, etc, and present it as an exotic excursion, having the same kudos as the brochure version of those holidays, knowing full well that our trips would bear no resemblance to those. Our way of coping with exclusion here was to invest our parents' homelands with particular meanings. In stories of our glamorous trips we had much invested in the feeling that there we were wanted, which meant that we often homogenised places as having a singular community which we could unproblematically fit into. This partial view of the other place and the tendency to homogenise 'community', however, unravels very quickly under closer scrutiny.

Part of the therapeutic value was, as I understood it, to reconnect to this thing called community. While growing up, stories of nurturing communities and strong family ties were very powerful and appealing narratives. There has always been a sense in which black people here are perceived to be extensions, or diluted version of, the real thing elsewhere. I was always intrigued that, in my family of South African Indians, those who lived in Africa were perceived to be more authentically 'Indian' than those of us who lived in Britain, partly because we were smaller in number and less distinguishable at any specific locale, but mostly because geographically, historically and temporally we were a further step away from the point of 'origin'. Was it because I, like so many others, was troubled by a notion of community that I had postponed my visit for so long? Would I be, or even want to be, accepted as part of it, and would I be compromising my defiant identity as a British Asian by claiming even a partial stake in another place?

Metaphorically a community is something with an inside and outside, and deciding who does and does not belong is at the crux of defining it in either radical or reactionary ways. The sort of appeals to community which I object to are those which locate its boundaries as static and transhistoric, and describe it as a place where one can return to 'traditional' values. Would that be the sort of belonging I would be offered? That version of community was one that I lived outside of in Britain, but it did not mean that I had no sense of belonging to a community. Many people had assured me that I would feel 'at home' in South Africa. Those assurances which came from white family members were the least comforting, because white people have the ability to be 'at home' all over the world without compromising their subjectivity and cultural identity. For me to say that I was 'at home' there made me feel anxious about my British status and about my feelings of being 'at home' here.

I would like to be able to tell you now that some momentous revelation occurred when I finally went to South Africa. I would like to tell you that I loved it or loathed it, that I embraced my roots or rejected them. The truth for me was that nothing terribly momentous did happen, but it did throw light on many of the anxieties which I had before I went. I was aware that I had so much invested in the trip that I was perpetually afraid of giving offence and not being accepted. This made me realise that I was, in some ways, buying into the very homogenised notions of community which I had purported to reject. In worrying about whether my 'European ways', short hair, 'incorrect' gender behaviour, etc, would exclude me I was succumbing to the idea of a singular community. It was true that such things did matter, but it was also true that there were ways of being accepted which did not involve taking on familial or religious orthodoxies. Many of us are afraid that difference will leave us excluded from family 'back home' and so never go. South Africa made it clear that being a 'rebel' was not about taking on a white or British identity, although signs of non-conformity in women are often dismissed via this sort of analogy. Older people are perpetually located at the crux of 'traditional' notions of community, and my trip allowed me to uncover this essentialism. For example, my grandmother who insisted that her daughters be educated fully, so that they could look after themselves in case of marital disharmony, offered me a sense of belonging and continuity which I was very comfortable with. We need to be aware that community can be sold to us under a variety of guises, so that connecting to it for healing purposes is not always that helpful.

The lessons I learnt in South Africa were not the ones some hoped I would learn. I realised the way limiting boundaries of national identification can trap us. I clarified the importance of not mystifying homelands, and why we should be aware of the ways in which primitivism can inform our readings of the 'other' place. I realised that family over there felt the weight of investment that we in Britain had placed on them to perpetuate a certain picture of community life, and I admired the way they juggled their equally hectic and 'modern' lives to not disappoint us. I learnt not to be afraid to say I can't, and don't want to, 'return' – this does not make you white-identified, it does not make you disrespectful of this thing called community, and it does not make you trivial. The trip did help me to confirm that home was Britain, but it was not a case of recovering a sense of 'Britishness' against the 'other' of South Africa. It was more that I identified the affinity I had there, as I do here, with all sorts of 'others', whether located in cultural or political groupings.

When I was in Pretoria my cousins and I went to the cinema to watch *Shakespeare in Love*, which made me homesick. This was not because I enjoyed the endless signifiers of Englishness which it presented, but because the representation of an 'ethnically cleansed' sixteenth-century London made me locate myself very specifically around other black Londoners as I anticipated the conversations I would have about it when I got home. The other thing which I noted was that I was laughing at different bits than the South African audience.

This incident and the return plane trip to Britain showed me that a sense of home cannot be neatly encapsulated via national boundaries. I felt happy to see the familiar sights of old 'Blighty' out of the plane window, then angry and alienated as I anticipated my re-entry through passport control, then safe and comfortable again in my own pocket of London. Looking for the place where one can feel at 'home' can change very dramatically within miles. There are some places in Britain which I can call home and others which I patently can't and wouldn't want to. This does not easily correlate with whether or not an area is black or white although that is obviously a major factor. For example, I can be intimidated by a room full of white men in a rural country pub, or at an academic conference, or at a football match, in a way that I am not in some bars full of white men in Soho. Similarly, if one is Asian one is not necessarily 'at home' in an all-Asian area for other reasons. To claim a belonging to Britain is not to claim a belonging to all of it. It is not an all-encompassing one where I unproblematically participate in celebrations of dominant British national culture. But I must acknowledge that there are spaces where identities of cultural hybridity are expressed which do include me and which do make me feel at home. I enjoy those cultural expressions which have found ingenious and multilayered ways to formulate the complex relationship I and many others have to Britain. This is not something I can, or frankly would want to, trade for some illusory unified cultural identity and a securely placed sense of home.

So did South Africa provide some sort of antidote to the ravages inflicted on my psyche and sense of cultural belonging in Britain? Who knows? My reading of it shifts so dramatically from day to day that I feel unable to record any concrete response to this question. Home seems to come down to a number of clichés. It's where the heart is – it's a place you escape from – a place you never get to – it's sometimes hard to admit that you may be there already. If the trip home has therapeutic value it is ironic that home is also the place to need therapy to recover from. What I have learnt is that there are a range of responses to where we locate home, and that as descendants of settlers in Britain we are only just beginning to get to grips with them. However if the English are finding their home so difficult to locate and their cultural identity so difficult to define perhaps we shouldn't worry too much!

NOTES

1. I use the term 'black' in its particularly British sense of referring to those of African, Caribbean and Asian descent. I do this with an acknowledgement of the many problems associated with securing a stable meaning to this, and with a sense that it is a term which has connotations relating to a collective political identity from a specific historical moment which many perceive as outdated. However, I hope my reasons for retaining it will become clear as I suggest that many different 'black' communities have similar experiences in how they relate to the notion of 'home'.

2. See Yasmin Alibhai Brown, 'Where do blacks and Asians fit in a devolved Britain?', *Independent*, 18.3.99.

3. Stuart Hall's piece 'Minimal Selves', written in 1987, talks about young black people in London and the sense in which they appear to own the territory despite being 'marginalised, fragmented, unenfranchised, disadvantaged and dispersed'. It appears that twelve years on this observation is even more pertinent as young black Londoners have staked an even greater claim to the city despite the persistence of their marginalisation: Stuart Hall, 'Minimal Selves', in Ann Gray and Jim McGuigan (eds), *Studying Culture - An Introductory Reader*, Arnold, London and New York 1993, p134.

FRIENDSHIP

Ray Pahl

'He who has many friends has no friends'

Aristotle

'Better a true friend than a relation'

Old Turkish Proverb

'To keep friendship in proper order, the balance of good offices must be preserved, otherwise a disquieting and anxious feeling creeps in, and destroys mutual comfort'

Charlotte Brontë, 1847

Sue is a young woman of thirty-five with a personal community of 'best friends' which she has gradually accumulated, beginning at her primary school. She added others at secondary school, sixth-form college and university, and acquired a cluster after her second job. The mother of one of her female friends became her mentor and supported her as she struggled with her emotional development in her twenties. In their childhood, her sister – now more than a sister, a friend and soul mate – carried her daily letters to her friend at another primary school. Later, when Sue had a child with her current partner, she was able to see her sister and her partner as the firm social rocks of her world. Beyond this core are her circles of 'best' and 'close' friends, with whom she works very hard to maintain contact and continuity. Hour-long talks on the telephone, regular visits at weekends – often driving hundreds of miles on the round trips – and lengthy letters, all are neces-sary to keep her social support group active. With three other women, whom she met at work, she sometimes goes off for weekend holidays. They have a regular commitment to spending a night together in each other's houses in turn. Sue talks of her distinctive style of managing her friends, recognising that others manage their friends differently. She can cope with only seven or eight, but these are crucially important for her, and have provided continuity and support for her changing identity as she has moved through education, training and employment to motherhood.

As a young mother she needs the support of other young mothers living nearby to whom she can turn for advice and help in day-to-day crises. She says that she would not yet class these as part of her personal community. However, one of them is shaping up well and she accepts the possibility that, if they get to know each other better, she may make the transition to 'close' friend.

These young women are bound together through talk: they pour out their innermost feelings to each other about their jobs, relationships, partners and children. They are working out together who they are and what their emerging identities might be in a fluid world of social and geographical mobility. Sue mentions in passing that one of her friends is black, another had been a secretary at Sue's place of work but is now living with a car salesman, and another is a lesbian. Differences in class, age, ethnicity and sexual orientation can easily be accommodated in Sue's personal community. The most unusual friend, perhaps, is the woman who acted as her mentor, Lorraine, who is a psychologist and is now over sixty. At times she seems to have served as an unpaid therapist to Sue, who has perhaps made a hobby of reflexivity. Lorraine's relationship with Sue has changed for the worse, Sue hints, since her son, a scientist, has become Sue's partner. She did not meet him until long after her friendship with his mother was established. The easy basis of her friendship with Lorraine is now being suffused with quasi-kinship obligations and expectations. Lorraine is taking an understandable interest and pleasure in being a grandmother, and this introduces different dimensions, where age and status gain a new salience. Since Sue and her partner are now thinking of getting married, affinal kinship roles are likely to get stronger. Sue will then try to encourage 'friend-like' relationships to suffuse her new kin-links.

Since she works so hard in maintaining her personal community, and could not imagine existing without it, how could it ever change? The common bonds of shared experience make it a kind of 'family of choice', albeit largely of the same age range (though not homogenous in many other social respects). To know what will happen in the future we would have to follow this personal community as it grows or declines through Sue's life. We may call this group her social convoy. Some people have what I call 'fossil friends' – those who were particularly salient at one stage of life, at university for example, but who subsequently move away and are not part of an individual's current active personal community. However, if circumstances happen to change, the 'fossil friend' may be reactivated and the friendship would carry on 'just where it left off'.

Sue had no fossil friends but she had consciously dropped a friend, and was in danger of losing another. In the case of the first, it appeared that, despite being very close, this friend had racist views which for long had not been disclosed. Since friendship for Sue was about morality, integrity and the sort of person she wants to see herself as being, the friendship had to end. Another friendship was at risk because the woman in question has married 'successfully' and was moving in circles and entertaining at a level which Sue could not match. She was coming to feel socially ill at ease in her friend's new circle. Although she cared for her friend, she felt she was drawing apart from her.

The importance of communication and talk is central to these friendships. Sue does not need her friends primarily for practical support, although her less close friends locally do provide this. Her distinctions between her 'best' friends and 'close' friends are in terms of their moral qualities and emotional capacities. Friendship for her is part of a highly personal inner journey: it is part of the good life.

THEORIES OF FRIENDSHIP

Sue is just one example of the many respondents being interviewed in a research project funded by the ESRC and carried out by Liz Spencer and myself at the University of Essex. We were stimulated to rethink friendship by the rather cavalier way it is treated in most social surveys. In these, respondents are frequently asked how many friends they have, how often they see them, how far away they are, whether they are of the same social status and so on; and sometimes social networks are constructed to show the interlinkages between the various social atoms designated as friends. But classifications are typically of the crudest kind, and very rarely are respondents asked what they mean when they use the word 'friend'. In many analyses sharp distinctions are made between family and kinship and friends, in recognition that the agnatic and affinal ties are enduring, and that their rights, duties and responsibilities are commonly understood and may have the backing of family law to support them. Friends, by contrast, whilst claimed to be a significant part of social life, are seen as the accessories rather than the basic garments that surround one's social self. They are freely chosen, and the moral obligations that they may carry are less binding and important than those relating to basic kin ties such as those between parents and children – such is a commonly held view.

However, in Sue's account of the relative closeness of members of her personal community, whilst her sister was in the innermost circle, her brother was at the edge. And this wasn't simply a matter of gender: in the case of other respondents it was the other way round, with dominant or competitive sisters at the periphery of the personal community. Sue felt obliged to put her parents closer in on her map of social distance – but this was not because she was particularly close to them; it was because she recognised the social expectation that parents and children ought to be close, and that the only socially legitimate category as an acceptable intrusion between her and her parents was her partner and their children. She recognised that in reality she was much closer to some of her friends than she was to her parents – particularly her mentor Lorraine – but her model of 'kinship in the mind' was that parents 'ought' to be more significant than friends.

There is now increasing sociological evidence from the work of, for example, Janet Finch and Jennifer Mason on conventional families and Jeffrey Weekes on the gay community that the notion that kinship must, inevitably, be at the core of people's personal communities should be questioned. Some family members are more congenial and 'friend-like' than others. People are claiming more choice in deciding with which, if any, family members they want to remain in close contact. Those family and kin with whom they closely interact are becoming more 'friend-like'. Perhaps, reciprocally, those friends with which they get on most closely are becoming more 'kin-like': many friends of those dying of AIDS, for example, have found themselves in the 'next-of-kin' role. Similarly, in the case of partners, it is increasingly the case that it is not the traditional 'wifely' or 'husbandly' qualities that are most sought after but rather the qualities of a good friend: being tolerant, supportive, humorous, companionable, engaging in common interests, having strong intuitive insight and so forth.

But if the meaning and significance of friends and friendship is changing in our society, how can surveys asking precise questions about numbers and frequencies report accurately on social reality? Maybe people themselves are confused and refer to different styles and qualities of relationships. The word 'friend' covers a broad continuum of possible forms and styles of relationships.

There are two plausible, yet contrasting, theories about the nature of friendship in contemporary society. The first, going back to the German sociologist Georg Simmel, writing a century ago, claims that whole-hearted soul-mates are more difficult to establish in modern society. 'The modern way of feeling tends more heavily toward differentiated friendships, which cover only one side of the personality, without playing into other aspects of it', he wrote. Thus, according to this view, we play tennis with one friend, watch football with another and share a school run with another. The only person to whom we can come close to unburdening our deepest hopes and fears is our partner. This puts a great burden on close dyadic relationships; expectations are high and, for a variety of reasons – pressure of work, tiredness, post-parturitional depression and so forth – partners cannot always live up to them. This may explain why many divorces and partner break-ups take place. People are seeking better friends elsewhere. The great ages of friendship, according to this view, were in the past – the classical world of Aristotle and Cicero, the early Christian church or the Bohemian world of the Bloomsbury Group, for example. The present age is one of great superficiality, of networking and filo-faxing, of contrived forename mateyness at work and of gushy luvvies calling each other darling. The socialite with 'hundreds of friends' has no friends: she simply has many refractions of an ever-changing kaleidoscopic self with no centre. Such 'friends' disappear when the patronage or social advantages decline.

An alternative counter-theory is that friendship is reaching new levels of depth and complexity in the modern world. In the classical writings on friendship, the truly great 'friendships of virtue' could only exist between men of good character. Friendships between men and women were singularly rare and problematic, and friendships between women don't figure in this discourse. In the contemporary world, however, with increasing social and geographical mobility, friendship has at last come into its own. No longer the preserve of a privileged male elite, it is suffusing kin and family relationships as never before. Women rely on other women to affirm their identities, often in the face of criticism from parents unable to cope with feminist or non-mainstream heterosexual gender roles. Men have the same problem as they move to more non-traditional roles and wish to explore their feelings as fathers or as gays with other men. Parents die, children leave home, couples dissolve and re-unite; the emotional traumas of contemporary life take place in different places with different key actors. Sometimes the only continuity for increasingly reflexive people is provided by their friends. Unwilling to be perceived as social chameleons flitting from one job or partner to another, men and women may come to rely on their friends to provide support and confirmation of their enduring identities.

Furthermore, close friends may provide the necessary guidance and support for our rather muddled desire to be decent or good. How should we live in a way that in our hearts we find morally acceptable? The answer is provided by the guidance, support and example of our friends. If they knew what we are doing would they approve? Can I expect him or her to be my friend if I do not do this or that? We explore loyalty, trust and betrayal in our dealings with our friends. Our friends have the potential to shame us, but friendship cannot be based on fear. So we have to be prepared to show weakness in order to confirm that we trust our friends.

Some have argued that women now understand more about true friendship than men. According to this stereotype, women meet to talk and to explore their feelings about their partners, their children and 'what it means to be a woman'. But this rather narcissistic and inward-looking exploration of feelings could become obsessive and neurotic. Perhaps the Sue I have described was somewhat self-indulgent and manipulative; although she would say that her friends pour out their woes on her shoulder more than she does on theirs. Following the same stereotypical pattern is a dismissive scorn or patronising pity for men, who are 'unable to share their feelings', and limited to the cosy bonding based on beer in the public bar or claret in the Pall Mall club. On this view, the obsessive fanaticisms of engaging in, or supporting, sport of various kinds prevent men from really getting involved with the social micro-dynamics of their seven-year-old daughter's birthday party. However, there are signs that these stereotypical views are changing as younger women become more laddish and men more openly explore 'what it means to be a man' with their friends.

Given these two persuasive alternative theories of contemporary friendship, with their associated myths, fallacies and stereotypes, it is easy to see why people should be confused. Is friendship stronger now or weaker than it was ... when? Are there truly qualitative differences between what friendship means for men and for women? And what of different classes, ethnic groups, age cohorts and so forth? Similarly, I have not referred so far to friendship between men and women. Is it true that *eros* and *amicitia* can be kept separate, or must there always be an erotic element in heterosexual friendships? Do women truly find it easier to be friends with gay men or does this simply reflect anxiety about their own sexual identities?

If friendship is 'the one good thing', as Cicero claimed, is it available to all of us or are some inhibited by genetic endowment or social experience from engaging in deeply fulfilling friendships? Do we need particular kinds of close and secure relations with a mother or mother substitute to make later secure attachments to others? Are certain personality types or kinds of social experiences and contexts inimical to the development of close and mature friendships? Are those who are skilled at making such distinctive intimate bonds likely to make less satisfactory narrowly-focused partners, since the closeness they develop within their wider range of significant others distracts them from their prime bond? Or does such social capability reduce the danger of an over-pressured dependence on one partner? These and many similar questions have kept generations of social psychologists and sociologists busy with their experiments and surveys.

Many of those engaged in research on friends and friendship believe, with some significant scientific support, that friends make us happier and healthier. We are less likely to catch colds if we have friends; we are more likely to recover quickly from cardiac arrests, and we are less likely to suffer from various forms of mental ill-health. Those with better social support are better able to cope with stressful events and circumstances. So friendship may be a highly significant art of life enabling us to be happier and healthier with greater self-esteem. Get a friend: get a life.

I recognise that in opening up the topic of friendship I have opened many doors but gone through none of them. The sociologist who describes who does what, with whom, for how long, how often, and why, can provide some numerical data which may be manipulated with increasing sophistication. However, unless the dispute between the competing theories of more fragmented friends or more life-affirming soul-mates is resolved, we just don't know what we are talking about. Fewer friends seen less frequently may be of far more social significance than large numbers of superficial friends.

It is indeed strange that we should still be talking past each other on the subject of friendship, despite a greater concern with the topic over the centuries than almost any other form of social relationship. We may, at present, be collectively obsessed with the social relationships between parents and children. But this was not thought to be a topic of much interest or complexity until relatively recently. Friendship, however, was of the greatest interest to classical thinkers, and the issues they raised have endured and continue to exercise the minds of contemporary philosophers. It is to such matters that I now turn, hoping that by introducing the reader to some of the key debates about friendship, they may come to see how central it is to the Art of Life.

Aristotle

Anyone who is interested in exploring the nature of friendship will still find it valuable to return to Aristotle's classic discussion. About one fifth of the Nicomachean Ethics is devoted to the topic. There are, he suggests, three types of friend: those who have friends because they are useful – the friends of utility; those who have friends simply for pleasure – they are fun to do things with; and, finally, there is the friendship of good people, the friendship of virtue. This last form of friendship is enduring, combining all the qualities found in the other two types as well.

Philosophers have much debated Aristotle's third type of pure friendship. Aristotle said 'a man stands in the same relation to his friend as to himself'. Thus to approve of our friend we must first approve of ourselves. Our friend, in this context, becomes our 'second self'. This produces a paradox: seemingly, to be a good friend we have to have an interest in ourselves. Those who enjoy being by themselves are better equipped for showing the energy and imagination necessary in a good friend. Aristotle linked the love of friends to the love of self and the love of life. Somehow he managed to overcome the division between egoism and altruism. But philosophers quibble: how can we love a friend because he is necessary for our happiness but at the same time love that friend for his own sake? If, as seems plausible, friendship is an extension of self-love, why cannot we say that it is simply a form of narcissism and that in loving our friend we are loving ourself? But perhaps Aristotle is saying something different: perhaps he is claiming that it does not matter that friendship is linked to self-love, because that would merely demonstrate that self-love is inherently and by its very nature social. However, Aristotle does make clear that it is only the good and virtuous who should be encouraged to be self-lovers. Vicious people must not love themselves since they will harm others by following their base feelings.

Classical writers believed that the very closest friends should share everything and also, ideally, live together. As Aristotle put it:

Clearly you cannot live with many people and distribute yourself among them ... It is also difficult for many to share each other's enjoyments and distresses as their own, since you are quite likely to find yourself sharing one friend's pleasure and another's grief at the same time ... it is impossible to be many people's friend for their virtue and for themselves. We have reason to be satisfied if we can find even a few such friends.

This finest and closest form of friendship, in Cicero's words:

> ... sends a ray of good hope into the future, and keeps our hearts from faltering or falling by the wayside. For the man who keeps his eye on a true friend, keeps it, so to speak, on a model of himself. For this reason, friends are together when they are separated, they are rich when they are poor, strong when they are weak, and – a thing even harder to explain – they live on after they have died.

These friends of virtue or friends of hope are ultimately friends of communication. Our friends who stimulate hope and invite change are concerned with deep understanding and knowing. Each grows and flourishes because of the other in a spirit of mutual awareness. As Graham Little has said in his book *Friendship: Being Ourselves with Others*, friendship is not an optional extra but the most alive of all human relationships: it is more alive than politics, markets, churches and even families and sex. It is a social sprite and can never be the 'social juggernaut' that class or race or even gender can be. Friendship has to be marginal and, indeed, somewhat subversive of the ruling beliefs of the day. Like E. M. Forster the true friend hopes that if forced to betray either her country or her friend she would always choose the former. This deep communicating friend is psychologically and socially anarchistic. Pure friendship, the friendship of character, is an alternative to society. We do not have a separate word for this deep and communicative form of friendship, but there is a Russian word *droog* that has connotations of Aristotle's third type of friend.

Secrets and mirrors
Whilst it is helpful to go back to Aristotle and Cicero to get a sound base for a philosophical approach to friendship, it is also helpful to consider how contemporary philosophers view the nature of intimate friendship. In a recent article in *Ethics* (April 1998), Dean Cocking and Jeanette Kennet distinguish between the 'secrets' view and the mirror

view of friendship. According to the former view, self-disclosure cements the bonds of trust and intimacy that exist between close friends: the greater the friendship, the more we are prepared to disclose. The mirror view is concerned with the degree to which one's own traits are reflected in the friend. I want to explore this argument a little further before drawing some conclusions about friendship for this article.

The two types of friendship outlined point to different phenomena; the revealing of oneself on the one hand and the reflection of oneself on the other. In both approaches it is assumed that central to the trust and intimacy of close companionship is the disclosure of the self; either I disclose my self to the other or my self is disclosed in the other. Neither the mirror nor the secrets view is able to capture with complete success the essential features of the close or compassionate style of friendship.

Close friends can open up new areas of interest, activity or intellectual concern. We may respond to our friend by exploring some new area with her/him; we take up an interest in orchids or contemporary poetry because that is the passion of our friend. By coming to a new interest and enjoying it, we become more like our friend. This is not because the friend is necessarily dominant or engaged in interpersonal imperialism. We are open to change and the new interest may stay with us long after the friendship has ended. Another way in which friendship may change us is through the kindly truths and insights which friends may perceive about our characters, the expression of which we do not resent because we trust our friend. We may have a tendency to be pompous, to talk too much after a few drinks or whatever. Seeing ourselves through the eyes of one's friend should encourage us to change or modify our behaviour. The way our friends interpret us helps us to interpret ourselves. A good friend does not stick stubbornly to a position – 'That's the sort of person I am, take it or leave it. If I offend you by speaking my mind, you'll just have to put up with it'. Some may put up with such intransigence for the sake of other benefits, but a true friendship of communication and virtue is unlikely to respond well to such rigidity. Companionable people are more open to having their interests and attitudes changed. Yet this seemingly straightforward point is counter to Aristotle's position, which is that shared activities are central and that change is more likely to threaten a friendship than to help it to grow. As Docking and Kennet say, 'It is not that I must reveal myself to, or see myself in, the other, to any great extent, but that, in friendship, I am distinctively receptive both to the other's interests and to their way of seeing me'. My self is thus partly a product of the friendship.

Of course, this is not saying much more than that the self is not a static thing. We don't acquire a friend of the soul mate kind ready-made as it were. If our selves are changing and developing in a reciprocally rewarding and creative way, our friendship is likely to grow and flourish. The process of friendship growth and change involves negotiating various tensions and coming to terms with communicational dialectics. Firstly, friends need the freedom to be both independent and dependent. Clearly complete independence would imply no relationship at all, whereas total dependence would constrain us by undermining our individual integrities and autonomy. Secondly, the tensions between generosity and reciprocity or between spontaneity and obligation have to be resolved: there has to be sufficient affect in the relationship to remove the burden hinted at by Charlotte Brontë in the quotation at the head of this chapter. Thirdly, there is the dialectic of judgement and acceptance: if our friend is too censorious we get resentful; if she is too accepting we lose respect. This, and similar interpersonal dialectics, will change over the course of a friendship. Perhaps it is the coming to terms with these processes that defines the true friend. The final dialectic is between expressiveness and protectiveness. We have to put limits on our own vulnerability by what we can expect of ourselves, and we must also protect our friends' sensitivities. Whilst we encourage our friends to be honest with us, as we should be with them, we also recognise the importance of tact and discretion.

In Aristotle's view, the choosing of a friend is based on the mutual recognition of one another's virtue. This implies a fixed 'state of virtue'. So, for Aristotle, in choosing a friend we choose another self: we relate to our friend as we relate to our self. Friendship, as I have suggested, appears to be a form of self-love. This mutual acknowledgement of similarity is the Aristotelian version of the mirror view of friendship. Yet it is commonly recognised that people of strikingly different temperament and character can become close friends. Why should Aristotle insist on 'equality and likeness'?

In the case of his lesser friendship types of pleasure and utility, then similarities of interest and disposition are to be expected: we choose our drinking companions from those who enjoy a drink; the mirror view might work well enough for these types but in the case of the companionship type, more direction and interpretation of the one by the other would be expected. Simply having interests and 'virtue' in common cannot in itself generate friendship: more important is that we are responsive to having our interests changed or developed. Without such responsiveness the friendship could not develop.

In the Aristotelian mirror view, I recognise much of myself in the other and I love that as I love myself. Evidently, I cannot love my friend for any traits that I cannot love in myself. If I see a reflection of some of my less-good qualities, I am likely to be less enchanted than if I recognise some of those qualities in myself of which I am most proud.

This does indeed appear to be narcissistic, and some contemporary philosophers are prepared to accept that this may be so and that this also characterises Aristotle's position. Hence the importance of the argument that the mirror view is too static and passive. What we give back to our friend is not a reflection but an interpretation. Friendship is essentially a dynamic and creative process. We do not come as fully-formed and self-sufficient selves into relationships. Such a view is well understood in sociology, particularly in the symbolic interaction tradition following G. H. Mead and Herbert Blumer.

Aristotle believed in the importance and pleasure of knowing ourselves: when we wish to see our face we look in the mirror. Hence the importance of the friend as a second self, reflecting us back to ourselves. Thus, he argues, 'If then it is pleasant to know oneself, and it is not possible to know this without having someone else as a friend, the self-sufficing man will require friendship in order to know himself'. Friendship is necessary to attain self-sufficiency. It is one of the arts of life. Philosophically, friendship must be a dialectical process: if it were not, one gets into the dilemma that if one is dependent on one's friends to be self-sufficient, how could one ever claim to be self-sufficient in virtue, unless at some time one's virtue did not depend on others? I leave this for philosophers to resolve!

Before leaving this discussion of the mirror view, there is the question of the friend improving our character by providing us with a view of how we should be. A friend can be like an ideal mirror, reflecting back the person she would like us to be. This would be to take a highly moralised view of friendship, which is not how most people look on their closest friends.

Let us now turn to another view of friendship, one based on the bond of mutual trust – the secrets view, which sees self-disclosure as the crucial element in friendships of hope or character. We share confidances with our friend that we certainly would not share generally with others. Those who tell everyone everything are, as it were, disqualifying themselves from true friendship. By sharing secrets we make ourselves vulnerable to the other, which is a sign of trust and probably affection. We thereby give the friend a privileged access to influencing our lives.

But why should the sharing of secrets be so central to the notion of friendship? Some of our secrets are private or shameful and we would be more likely to go to a priest, analyst or a complete stranger to confess them. Secrets that cause shame or embarrassment should not be imposed on one's friend. This is illustrated well in the expressive-ness/protectiveness dialectic mentioned above. Of course friends reveal themselves to each other, but to see this as the essence of the purest type of friendship is to claim too much. Friends certainly gain great insight into each other's lives. Of greater significance is what we value, and how we choose to share what we value, and this is determined in a dialectical way through the process of friendship itself.

Neither the mirror nor the secrets view provides a satisfactory account of the appropriate governing conditions for friendship. Of greater importance is a more dynamic conception of friendship, where each soul mate is closely responsive to the direction and interpretation of the other. This would imply that those with more rigid personalities are simply unable to make such close friends. In his book *Autonomy and Rigid Character*, David Shapiro illustrates the nature of this more rigid type:

> The fixed purposiveness of the rigid person narrows his interest in the world and restricts and prejudices his experience of it. He looks only for data – or, in the paranoid case, for clues – relevant to his purposes or concerns. The compulsive man who examines each woman with a check-list in mind of certain qualifications for marriage does not see that woman objectively; he sees a selection of traits and features whose sum is not a person but a high or low score. This is a kind of ... awareness that is not open and attentive to the world but is restricted and prejudiced by the necessity to satisfy pre-established requirements and fixed purposes.

Such a person might have great difficulty in forming close friends or finding soul mates. But there is no good reason, as Cocking and Kennet point out, why such a rigid person should not share secrets or be attracted by similarity in another, particularly if the other person was able to meet some of the main criteria on a check list, as suggested above. So the secrets and mirror views of friendship cannot do much to help with the problem of the rigid person being unable to have close friends. However, the inability of the rigid person to be open to being directed and interpreted by others is likely to be of fundamental importance. Of course, those who are successful in drawing each other out are likely to do so with ease if they have common interests, mutual affection and a desire and interest to share each other's experiences. And if one or both parties in a soul mate dyad come to interpret their friends in a too rigid manner, the friendship may fade. Family and kin relationships can survive this rigidity since they are more structured and role governed, but this would not work with companion friends who need the flexibility and mutual drawing out to survive.

In a survey about friendship networks carried out in North London in the mid-1980s, Peter Willmott showed (without being too precise about the meaning of friend) that the category 'friend' was more important than relatives or neighbours for helping with shopping, house maintenance, 'keeping an eye on the house' and for personal advice. There are also indications that whilst regular visits to family and kin are declining, regular visits to friends, whilst also declining, are declining less rapidly. If friends are becoming more important than family and kin in certain respects, it is difficult to be sure why this is the case. On the one hand, the identity that friends are able to bestow on us may be more important than the ascribed identities of mother, daughter, sibling, or whatever. Whilst, as we have seen in the case of Sue, an ascribed relation can develop if an achieved friend-like relationship is imposed upon it. We then value these friends and friend-like relations more for affirming the view of ourselves that we most wish to adopt. As with Peter Willmott's survey, a number of other sociological studies have consistently emphasised the importance of friends as sources of emotional support and advice.

A theme from Aristotle and Cicero which is frequently echoed by contemporary writers on friendship is that our experience and exploration of what it is to be a good person is directly related to the way we behave to our closest friends. We expect our friends to be loyal, to keep confidences and to judge our behaviour according to certain standards. It is almost impossible to be friendly with someone who consistently betrays us. Betrayal and friendship cannot co-exist. Many contemporary soap operas on radio and television have as their main theme the responsibility and limits of friendship. These are frequently highly moral tales. How can we be loyal to a friend who is cheating on her partner who is also a close friend? Should you, as a friend, intervene in a situation of domestic violence when you are the only outsider who knows what is going on? The agony columns of newspapers and magazines provide a stream of examples. It is amongst our closest friends that we work out together what the 'right' thing to do might be. Part of the function of friendship is to provide the anvil on which we may individually beat out our own personal moralities. In this sense, friendship is a metaphor for morality. How to be a good and dutiful daughter, wife or mother is less likely to be discussed with a mother, husband or daughter than with a friend.

Yet some argue that it is now more difficult to make and nurture friends with all their medical and moral uses. Henrik Ibsen wrote: 'Friends are a costly luxury. When a man invests his capital of energy in a profession or a mission, he will lack the means to afford friends.' Are we creating a world, at least for the over-work-committed senior salariat, where people do not have the time and energy to practice one of the fundamental arts of life? Friendship requires time to flourish and develop. It is essentially about talk and communication. Some argue that with the complexities arising from serial monogamy, tiring journeys to work, more demanding and stressful work situations, more demanding and stressful parenting, caring and so much else besides, the close sharing friendship that I have been discussing in this essay is itself too demanding. Those with equal burdens are kept apart by similar time constraints. Those with unequal time burdens are unlikely to form close friendships: the one with the greater time will be perceived by the other as too demanding. If one is already suffering from emotional overload then a late-at-night call from a friend with relationship problems may be the last straw. Some people cannot be good friends. 'God protect me from my friends', they complain. 'I need space and a bit of peace for myself'. So can one say that globalisation, consumerism and family caring responsibilities are killing friendship?

Whilst many people recognise the social and economic pressures that take time away from the cultivation of friendship, they would argue that their best, and perhaps only, friend is their partner. Perhaps the phrase 'just friends' as a euphemism for not sleeping together is changing in meaning. This is an interesting area where social mores appear to be in flux. On the one hand there is the transition of beginning as friends and turning into lovers, and on the other hand there is the transition from being lovers to ending up as friends. Can the two really go together? In a survey carried out by the magazine *Psychology Today* in 1979, just under one-third of both men and women said that they had had sexual intercourse with a friend in the past month.

Respondents were heavily skewed towards the under-35s, and not too much should be made of such findings, given that we do not know how the word 'friend' should be unpacked. However, I have little doubt that there is a contemporary view that sexual love and pure friendship can fruitfully co-exist. Perhaps it is the existence of such a belief that encourages some to divorce, seeking the ever-elusive magic combination elsewhere.

In the opening scene of the 1989 film *When Harry Met Sally*, the two are driving together from Chicago to New York and Harry remarks, 'Men and women can't be friends – because the sex part gets in the way'. Many contemporary philosophers would agree, claiming that love is essentially possessive, which is inimical to the pure form of friendship of virtue. Harry elaborates his point when he meets Sally five years later, and modifies his original rule by adding, 'Unless both are involved with other people'. But he goes on to say, 'But that doesn't work. The person you are involved with can't understand why you need to be friends with the other person. She figures you must be secretly interested in the other person – which you probably are. Which brings us back to the first rule'. In philosophical terms the problems of combining *Eros* and *Philia* are not easily resolvable. In common experience there are many who would agree with Harry; but equally there are many who would strongly disagree, pointing to many historical and literary heterosexual friendships as illustrations of the highest form of Aristotelian friendship.

Since I am currently engaged in research on this and related issues, it would be unwise to come to premature conclusions on what appears to be an evolution in our most salient social relationships. There are many clear advantages attached to friends and friendship that fit the contemporary *zeitgeist*: they are freely chosen, not ascribed, they are democratic, egalitarian and horizontal. Family and kinship relations, by contrast, are, initially anyway, undemocratic, authoritarian and vertical. Certainly twins and some siblings will have more friend-like elements built into their relationships with each other, but sibling rivalry cannot be parallel with friend rivalry, although of course friends can be jealous of one another – something which Aristotle did not explore.

Because friends and friendship appear to offer more freedom and choice, they may seem to provide more space and scope for individual identity and autonomy. The flight from dependency and personal relations is surely healthy. However, the key issue remains: if friends should not be lovers, can, or should, spouses or partners be friends? Whatever the philosophers say, the answer surely must be yes. However, for this to happen men and women have to recognise their other selves: men have to become more confident with their *anima* and women with their *animus*. This will not be easy. Society does so much to emphasise gender differences. When men and women find in their partner another self, another individuality, but one whose otherness is not so overwhelming as to threaten or engulf or invade their selfhood, they are truly fortunate. In J. B. Priestley's essay on 'Talking', he handles the balance between *Eros* and *Philia* very effectively: initially, for the friendship between the two individuals to develop, sex must be relegated to the background. Each has to recognise the individuality of the other and respond to the other in the ways I have discussed above. But then, as Priestley goes on to point out, having recognised how alike they are as men and women, they 'will then go forward ... discover how unlike the sexes are ... This double play of personality, and then of sex, is what gives intelligent talk between men and women its curious piquancy'. In this sense friendship between the sexes may take us not out of ourselves but beyond ourselves, and may make us more whole, balanced and sane than we could otherwise be.

But friendship in marriage or long-term relationships cannot be presumed. Men fear engulfment; a woman fears an invasiveness that threatens the boundary she has struggled to maintain between herself and others. Each is tempted to shy away from otherness and settle for friends more like the self: women to women friends, men to their men friends. Perhaps *Eros* is necessary to overcome such fears, hesitation and timidity. *Eros* may be the trigger that helps some men and women to discover true friendship. To quote J. B. Priestley again:

> Talk demands that people should begin, as it were, at least some distance from one another, that there should be some doors still to unlock. Marriage is partly the unlocking of those doors, and it sets out on its happiest and prosperous voyages when it is launched on floods of talk.

Communicating friendship is one of the great arts of living, even though by drawing us together it may be a form of social regression as Philip Slater has argued. There is much in the modern world that prevents us from having the time and emotional security to be a true friend. Our hopes and aspirations are raised and we may be deluded into believing that there are short cuts. But the 'one good thing' of communicating friendship, is trivialised and demeaned by the superficial glad-handedness of much corporate culture. The ever-spiralling, first-name-calling networkers are the enemies of true friendship. They take up our time and lure us to the popular crowd at the symbolic bars of life. However, true friendship as an essential ingredient of the art of life needs to be respected and nourished.

Floreat amicitia.

Grass Accepts

The grass accepts the cigarette ends & brown things
thrown out of the tent.
The earth, the largest orphanage in the universe, patiently
tolerates
our childish whims & antics.
Our tears & shooting at each other ,
pouring salt into the fruit salad & placing bombs underneath
things.
A strong wind blowing, the tent clutches the earth as tightly
as a child
hangs onto its Mother's hand. I am writing in a horizontal
position, the strength
necessary to understanding this world is rising up through my
stomach.
The blades of grass straining upwards point me in the right
direction. Love,
Love gives us a chance to win through despite our own
being.

Jacek Podsiadlo

Don't Leave Me

Don't stop loving me. Not even for a second. Think of me
morning & evening, & even when praying. Even at the cost of
                                          missing a meal
even if it means you lose more weight. Feel free, watch
'Dempsey & Makepeace', look at the displays of dresses in
                                          the shop windows,
the symptoms of any disease
on your body – but just hold me in front of your eyes.

Shifting fifty kilo bags of cement I carry you in my arms.
Skipping to a reggae tune I jump after you into the fire.
Biting my nails I bite them out of longing for you.
Listening to the weather forecast I strain to hear your voice.
Sometimes I'm gasping for air
& then I know you've forgotten about me for a moment.

Jacek Podsiadlo

The Stepfather

Aftershave, the smell of aftershave
tailing him and claiming every room;
the paintwork tarted up in every room;
his pissing on the toilet seat.

We meet about the house and say 'hullo'
as though there were no walls,
no doors to keep us in.
His two shoes big enough to hold the goldfish;

three gross armchairs, each one
crowned with a mane of beige upholstery;
and flowers, flowers reach from every vase.
His hands as cold as bunches of keys.

We consider bribes, perhaps a dog. He shows me
albums filled with relatives I've never met
waiting, like babies, to be identified.
The terrible noises he makes in the dark.

Stephen Knight

A British Summer

My boredom chock-a-block
with furniture – the desk
in bits, the sofa's cushions
cluttering the bed, drawers
shoved beneath the dresser
– I stare at Wimbledon
while listening to the man
restretch then clean
the carpets in two rooms;
suds rumbling in their drum,
the smell of pine detergent
creeping up to me.

Two hours of plucky Brits,
mauve clouds, the covers on,
or grim-faced teenagers
washed up before their spots
have cleared, then I descend
like Norma Desmond, out
of touch, magnanimous;
and all the little dents
where chairs and tables stood
have disappeared, as though
the years of being here
had never happened.

Stephen Knight

Love Poem

She waltzes in as bold as you like
Unbuttons heavy coats and squats
Beside the pram sheds – pisses vats
Of pent up rage into the night.
Our laughter is loud and sweeps
So high into the wind you'd think
She'd hear us but her head is still
And blushless as she finishes.
I want to take your hand and walk
down the stairs, through the subway
Into that starless yellowing.
I want to read words sprayed on walls
But winter is too dark and grey
You're tired and I must wait for spring.

Anna Robinson

MY NAME IS ...

1

Anna

On a cold bright February night
in the year of the Rat,
start of the era of hope,
when yellow crocuses could be
seen snuggling in crunchy snow
from the hospital window –
I was born and named Anna
which means grace, favour, a small
coin worth 1/16th of a rupee, I,
and – to my mother – pale tragic
Russian women too glamorous
to live.

2

Kathryn

Granny Kate used to send me
parcels when I was four,
postmarked Southport
containing blue ribbon bars
crushed in the sorting,
melting chocolate onto white
cotton hankies, Mickey Mouse
and Donald Duck still visible
beneath brown nursing-home
stains, dancing their quick step
with no sense of remorse,
not even for the time when she
– who was not my mother's mother

after all – buttoned my excited body
into my red coat and took me
to the play park where
she forgot who we were
and where we lived.

3

Cecilia

I was confirmed in the name of Cecilia
patron saint of musicians
but wanted to be Agatha
to have my too early too large breasts
cut off – body flamed to ashes.

I'd breathe deep, drinking those church
smells, bathing in suffering left hanging
by so many virgin martyrs
till twice I fainted, once on Good Friday,
waking surrounded by nuns and water.

Two years later I met an Angel
and snogged him outside his father's
fish and chips shop to the strains
of the Love Unlimited Orchestra
and I changed my mind about breasts.

What better Martyrdom could there be
than Cecilia's? Sentenced to die
in her bathroom by steam and heat;
her music is playing now
as I reach for the scented soap.

4

Robinson

The maiden name of a scarlet woman
who'd cursed her lover so he fell
off his ladder and broke his leg,

who'd thought nothing of striding
wide stepped across railway lines
to shout 'bloody murderers'
at the back gates of the abattoir
while her son, lugging carcasses
on his bruised back, shrank, shamed,
who'd lived in a house where
all ablutions involved a mop bucket
where men came and went with raised hands
and where children and grandchildren
returned to rest from fists they
had left to escape.

Anna Robinson

ON BEING ALONE

Wendy Wheeler

'A vital imaginative life, and the deep effort to describe new experience, are found in many others besides artists, and the communication of new descriptions and new meanings is carried out in many ways – in art, thought, science, and in the ordinary social process.'

Raymond Williams, *The Long Revolution*

Perhaps I should start reading Zen again. For the last couple of years – fitfully at first, much more frequently now – whilst thinking about politics, neurobiology and utilitarian modernisation and other things which interest me, I have begun to experience an intensely pleasurable sensation, like a heat, beginning in my solar plexus and gradually radiating outwards; I find myself precipitated into a meditation-like state. No, I do not think I am going mad; I have simply committed myself wholly to the idea that, after thinking, a state of mind and body can be experienced in which ideas happen to you. And this is an intensely creative experience of mind-body. You prepare the ground by study, directed thought and so on, and then, by various means, you become still, and ideas happen. Now supposedly this state of what Keats called 'diligent indolence' doesn't count as getting 'proper' knowledge for Western societies. At least, it isn't much to be found in what Raymond Williams called the 'official' languages of Western modernity concerning knowledge.

More familiar in Eastern philosophies (though growing in the West[1]), this notion – of watching oneself having an idea – is one which will, of course, be utterly unremarkable to those whose work is avowedly creative; but it will be familiar too to many others. Einstein, apparently, 'thought' the universe spatially, like an artist 'thinks' (rather than simply copies) a face; the sums supported the picturing, not the other way around.

How did I get into this? Well, I have been thinking about what it means to be alone. I have wanted to read and think about the ways in which modernity and individualism have worked to make us feel more lonely. But also, because I have been reading and writing about the most recent developments in neuroscience, I have been aware that the neuroscientists, complex systems theorists and neo-Darwinists (who all meet in the person of Gerald Edelman, for example [2]), are disclosing a world in which subject and object, self and other, co-evolve. The world is not simply an 'out there' which the camera-eye 'films'; the world is made by our mind-brain-bodies in an 'accurate for us' way, and the eye is *not* a camera. The interaction between the senses and cognitive processes and conclusions is complex, and feedback loops operate in both directions; so, although we feel intrinsically alone in the world, it is equally true to say that we are absolutely in and a part of the world – our minds arise from a body-brain which is thoroughly enworlded; what goes on in our imaginations is not separated from the world and our bodies. Perhaps this seems a very obvious thing to say; but when you discover that it is well-known amongst, for example, athletes and musicians, that *imagining* rehearsal or training improves *actual* performance, you must come to this obviousness in a slightly different way. [3] When you are in my world, you are a part of my mind. Why are we surprised that people should suggest a link between images of violence and violence acted-out? Do companies spend vast amounts of money advertising their products because images are ineffective? In too much of our over-managed modern world the incalculable processes of human creativity appear as an affront to the managers. Education is no longer understood as an introduction to the processes of creative responses to the world, but as learning transferable skills for the great god Marketplace in which affectively isolated individuals compete. Untuned to the subtle interactions of minds with other minds and their environments, the 'official' languages of the modern world reinforce our sense of being alone.

We are not conscious of 98 per cent of our brain activity; the selves we take ourselves to be are metonyms, synecdoches, parts for whole. There is far more to us – both as whole individual organisms and as creatures ineluctably enworlded – than empirical positivistic modern science, and the instrumentalism of utilitarianism, have ever allowed. In *Order Out of Chaos: Man's New Dialogue with Nature*,[4] Ilya Prigogine and Isabelle Stengers argue that our science and our loneliness go together. In reducing nature to 'atom and void', they argue, modern science 'in turn gave rise to what Lenoble has called 'the anxiety of modern men'.[5] As Jacques Monod (one of the scientists whose work directly contributed to the deciphering of the genetic code) wrote:

> Man must at last finally awake from his millenary dream; and in doing so, awake to his total solitude, his fundamental isolation. Now does he at last realize that, like a gypsy, he lives on the boundary of an alien world. A world that is deaf to his music, just as indifferent to his hopes as it is to his suffering or his crimes. [6]

Our imagination, which is where ideas happen to us, is stunted when we constrain it to calculation and (supposedly) logical thought alone. We are self-alienated because modern ways of thinking and being have depended upon forms of social and mental and intellectual organisation which have tended to cut us off from ourselves and from the richness of our whole being in the world. In these forms of organisation, what have been valued are what have been thought of as the prizes of the head: calculation, order, conscious data, hierarchical organisation, detailed, step-by-step, forward planning of projects, accumulation, and so on. What have been devalued are what are thought of as the prizes of the heart: affects, intuitions, generosity, trust (faith). To paraphrase Lewis Hyde (who must rejoice in having occupied the wonderfully inclusive Luce Chair of Art and Politics at Kenyon College), we have ended up placing too much importance in the economy of the marketplace, and not enough in the economy of the gift. [7] That the latter is the sphere occupied by the artist is well-known (the artistic muse does not descend to the tinkling music of cash registers [8]) but what if *all* of us were able to allow ourselves to occupy this sphere also? What if the true destiny of all full human beings is fully to occupy the sacred space of the artist, and our full being to give expression to life as an art of living? What would this mean?

When Michel Foucault wrote his 1984 essay on modernity called 'What is Enlightenment?', he suggested that modernity is best characterised not as a period, but as an attitude; and, as an example of that attitude, Foucault suggested Baudelaire, in whom the mixture of *dandyism* and *flâneur* offers something close to the attempt to capture the pose appropriate to modernity. But note, this pose is not merely surface affectation; it is both a frame of mind and a ritual preparation of the appropriate, fitting and right attitude in which *something can happen* in which *one is alive to the present*. Hence, for Baudelaire, the true capturer of modernity is the artist Constantin Guys who, just when everyone else is falling asleep, captures, in a frenzy of creative activity, the essential truth of the present.[9]

What does this mean: the truth of the present? I think it means what Donald Winnicott calls 'a sense of being a live person in the world'. It does not mean *one* thing; it means being able to allow what Matthew Arnold called 'the free play of the mind' so as to allow things to make connections, perhaps in unusual or unpredictable ways; it is not precisely a question of the *thing* which circulates in this economy of the gift, but of what circulates *through* the thing. This is the creative work of Winnicott's 'transitional spaces and objects' – metaphorical spaces where 'inside' and 'outside' are not clearly separated – in which the infant (or adult) plays, making things into symbols for other things. I do not mean to say that there is no place for planning and property; but that it is a grave mistake to think that this is all a fully human life amounts to.

THE LONG REVOLUTION

> It seems to me that we are living through a long revolution, which our best descriptions only in part interpret. It is a genuine revolution, transforming men and institutions; continually extended and deepened by the actions of millions, continually and variously opposed by explicit reaction and by the pressure of habitual forms and ideas. Yet it is a difficult revolution to define, and its uneven action is taking place over so long a period that it is almost impossible not to get lost in its exceptionally complicated process ...
>
> In naming the great process of change the long revolution, I am trying to learn assent to it, an adequate assent of mind and spirit. I find increasingly that the values and meanings I need are all in this process of change. If it is pointed out, in traditional terms, that democracy, industry, and extended communication are all means rather than ends, I reply that this, precisely, is their revolutionary character, and that to realize and accept this requires new ways of thinking and feeling, new conceptions of relationships, which we must try to explore.
>
> Raymond Williams

There's nothing new, of course; just things seen in a new light. In *The Long Revolution*, Raymond Williams was close to where this present essay is nearly forty years ago. At one level we can oppose art to science, or emotion to reason; yet the activities described by these names are in fact deeply related parts of the whole human process. We cannot refer science to the object, and art to the subject, for the view of human activity we are seeking to grasp rejects this duality of subject and object: the consciousness is part of the reality, and the reality is part of the consciousness, in the whole process of our living organisation. Coleridge spoke of 'substantial knowledge' as that intuition of things which arises when we possess ourselves as one with the whole. This realisation, the capacity for 'substantial knowledge', is the highest form of human organisation, though the process it succeeds in grasping is the common form of our ordinary living. At a less organised level, we fall back on what Coleridge called 'abstract knowledge', when we think of ourselves as separated beings, and place nature in antithesis to the mind, as object to subject, thing to thought, death to life.

The antithesis of nature to the mind, 'as object to subject', we now know to be false; yet so much of our thinking is based on it that to grasp the substantial unity, the sense of a whole process, is to begin a long and difficult revolution in the mind. [10]

How is this revolution to be achieved? How, from the bases of languages that we know, can we introduce new 'revolutionary' languages? How can an holistic 'feel-thinking' count as a source of knowledge, 'officially' as it were, as much for the scientist and the politician as it does for the artist and the mother?

Perhaps an example from the best of modernist art might help. At the 1999 Royal Academy *Monet in the Twentieth Century* exhibition, the visitor was confronted with fifty-one paintings of waterlilies in the pond of the artist's garden at Giverny. To make any sense of this act of communication, the viewers must open themselves to the artist's obsession. Slowly at first, colour, light, pleasure, contrast; then, realising that the artist is pushing you around a bit – where can I make sense of this from? Am I to attend to the fragmenting form, the brushwork? Where do I have to stand? O here, not fragmented at all! Perfect, exquisite realism! But why make me see these fragmentations? Why, standing me at the distance at which a classical work would appear realistic, show me blobs, meaningless daubs? And then, much further away, let me see an equally attentive capturing of reality. What is he saying about reality, about distance and perspective? And so on, utterly absorbed in the effort to understand the language of lilies, gallery after gallery, people look close up, run away, crane their necks to see over crowds from the other side of the room. He has us running around as we learn. Then, finally, the last big gallery. Heroic paintings – two on the left; two on the right – and, there, right in front of you opposite the entrance: the death painting, painted near the end of the life. It's 3 am, but the gallery is full. People stand twenty or thirty deep, some at the front kneel or sit on the floor. Dart quickly across the (empty sacred) space people have left in front of only *this* painting to look at the brushwork close up: it's like discoloured artex. From the door, far away, it's just more lilies in the mist, and you have learned the language and the modernist poem which the obsession writes.

> Representation
> all gone from us now?
> Say it with lilies.
>
> Speak with the body
> which remains real as the earth
> and pond in blossom
>
> I can make you see
> and read in a new language
> lilies, given time.
>
> A philosophy
> encapsulated in this
> painting of lilies.

For Williams, this is what the successful work of art does; it 'struggles to remake experience'. But this 'struggle to remake ourselves' – to change our personal organisation so that we may live in a proper relation to our environment – is in fact often painful. Many neurologists would say that the stage before description is achieved, the state of our actual organisation before new sensory experience is comprehended, the effort to respond adequately while the new experience is still disorganised and disturbing, is biologically identical with what we call physical pain'. [11]

With God or gods the individual was, of course, never alone. He or she lived in a world teeming with relatedness – however hierarchical and oppressive. The modern self's pain is in our experience of an alienation which feels fundamental (which is to say, we feel it in our guts). For Williams, our long revolution lies in finding our way back to the world, and that entails finding a new way of talking about and describing it. It also means a different regard for feelings, and an attending to our gut feelings which are also our imaginative lives.

THE SEA OF FAITH

Dover Beach

The sea is calm tonight.
The tide is full, the moon lies fair
Upon the straits: – on the French coast the light
Gleams and is gone; the cliffs of England stand,
Glimmering and vast, out in the tranquil bay.
Come to the window, sweet is the night air!
Only, from the long line of spray
Where the sea meets the moon-blanch'd land,
Listen! you hear the grating roar
Of pebbles which the waves draw back, and fling,
At their return, up the high strand,
Begin, and cease, and then again begin,
With tremulous cadence slow, and bring
The eternal note of sadness in.

Sophocles long ago
Heard it on the Aegaean, and it brought
Into his mind the turbid ebb and flow
Of human misery; we
Find also in the sound a thought,
Hearing it by this distant northern sea.

The Sea of Faith
Was once, too, at the full, and round earth's shore
Lay like the folds of a bright girdle furl'd.
But now I only hear
Its melancholy, long, withdrawing roar,
Retreating, to the breath
Of the night wind, down the vast edges drear
And naked shingles of the world.

Ah, love, let us be true
To one another! for the world, which seems
To lie before us like a land of dreams,
So various, so beautiful, so new,
Hath really neither love, nor joy, nor light,
Nor certitude, nor peace, nor help for pain;
And we are here as on a darkling plain
Swept with confused alarms of struggle and flight
Where ignorant armies clash by night.

Matthew Arnold

Romantic love: the eroticisation of loneliness. But, for many of us, this no longer works. Individualism, the individual's right to pursue happiness, means that, once the brief moments of romance have gone, romantic love is no more, and we are returned, willy-nilly, to our alienation.

But, asks Williams, how have we come to this habitual way of thinking and, thus, being and doing? In his customary way of making us alert to the ways in which semantic change offers us the chance of seeing social and psychological changes at work, Williams discusses the origin of the contemporary meaning of individual. In its medieval use, it was used to describe individual members of a class of same things: to invoke an individual was, thus, actually to invoke the group of which the individual constituent was a member. The growing emphasis on the individual as individual rather than as a member of a group seems to stem, in England, from the late sixteenth and early seventeenth centuries. A similar shift occurs in the movement from humanity – understood as having a common destiny in God – to individual destinies and the individual's unmediated relationship to God brought in with Protestant theology. Equally, the stress on individual destiny, and its lying in the hands of the individual and his own self-effort, is lodged – as has been noted before – at the heart of capitalism as a successful form of economy; and democracy is one of the most logical outcomes of this. It seems as though Western, especially Anglo-American, cultures have been steadily moving in the direction of an increased emphasis on the individual, and his or her 'rights' and freedoms, finally arriving on the threshold of the triumph of global capitalism, with the inalienable 'right' of capitalists to do more or less whatever they want to whomsoever they please at more or less any cost to our earth home. And are we happy?

Viewed with the necessary effort at a little distance, and knowing as we do that the individual is always the product of networks of relations, we might consider that our widespread, and too often unhappy, loneliness suggests that things have gone a little too far on the individualism side of things. But, certainly, no contemporary individual – being as highly individuated as we now are – is likely to wish to put on again what seems, to contemporary sensibilities in industrialised countries, to be the yoke of more traditional and convention-ridden societies.

Perhaps, as Williams thought, it remains a question of languages; what is required is a language of and about society and the individual which has neither the negative associations of state socialism, nor the moralising of liberalism – a language which affirms the *fact* of our actual mutual dependence and connectedness, as well as our fundamental singularity. But, surely, such a political language can only grow out of a wider commitment. Many have written of modernity as the disenchantment of the world. When Williams speaks of a new language, I think he can only mean a better and more generous understanding of what constitutes a fully human life. The rationalising temper says we should do away with these untestable things of faith, which are observed in the power of liturgy and other social rituals; they are merely rituals. But, in saying this, the supposed rationalist fails to recognise that rituals are part of a wider, richer language than the rationalist allows himself to hear.

Writing that the significance of what he calls 'threshold gifts' lies in the way they manage death, Lewis Hyde says that the tokens we receive at points of change in our life 'are meant to make visible life's reciprocation': 'They are not mere compensation for what is lost, but the promise of what lies ahead. They guide us toward new life, assuring our passage away from what is dying'.[12] Reporting a joke from Woody Allen's stage act in which the comedian would pull out a pocket watch and say 'This is a family heirloom. My grandfather sold it to me on his deathbed', Hyde says, 'The joke works because market exchange will always seem inappropriate on the threshold ... A man who would buy and sell at a moment of change is one who cannot or will not give up, and if the passage is inevitable, he will be torn apart. He will become one of the done-for dead. Threshold gifts protect us from such death.[13] The 'new' languages may, in fact, spring from a new kind of cultural studies: an anthropology of modern society, in which we are able to relocate the realm of the gift banished by rationalisation.

In modern societies, we have ceaseless change but a reduced capacity to recognise the ways that *good* change requires a different economy. Hyde writes, 'we should really differentiate two sorts of death ... one that opens forward into a greater life and another – a dead-end death – that leaves a restless soul unable to reach its home. This is the death we rightly fear. And just as gifts are linked to the death that moves toward new life, so, for those who believe in transformation (either in this life or in another), ideologies of market exchange have become associated with the death that goes nowhere'.[14]

It is, perhaps, a commonplace to note that modern societies are becoming places which only recognise value (exchange value); the dominance of market relations means that worth (use value) is too often poorly recognised. Hyde makes a similar distinction between work and labour: work is what you do by act of will; labour, on the other hand, 'can be intended but only to the extent of doing the groundwork, or of *not* doing things that would clearly prevent the labor. Beyond that labor has its own schedule. Things get done, but we often have the odd sense that we didn't do them'.[15] 'Labour' in Hyde's sense belongs to the realm of the gift. In a society that only recognises work, and doesn't understand the importance of the essentially human creative business of labour, very many lives will be only half-lived, the empty spaces where labouring might have been done now stacked full of commodified leisure.

I am talking about a question of degree, about the extent to which our modern societies are moving too far towards 'value', 'work' and commodification, and increasingly (and 'rationally') failing to under-stand the importance of a symbolic economy in which the symbols are lived, not bought. The point is that the symbolic life which the gift economy enacts establishes bonds between people. Hyde rightly points out that the 'free society' is the society where everyone feels free to choose, to be perfect strangers without the ties and bonds of more traditional societies; but that is why we feel lonely; we are free and yet we long for 'real', authentic relatedness.

It sometimes seems to me that modernity has produced such an impoverished world that we are in danger of gradually losing our humanity altogether. The opposite of the labour of gratitude estab-lished by the gift economy is narcissism, which resists openness to change in the self and is frightened witless by death.[16] The increase in cases of narcissistic borderline personalities, noted in, for example, Christopher Lasch's *The Culture of Narcissism*, suggests a process of serious deterioration in the humanity of many contemporary selves. I have met people who have treated relationships – which we still think should be mainly characterised by emotional bonds and gift symbology – like market relationships. I read recently of a man who kept a detailed record of all his expenditure on his partner and, when the relationship ended, demanded repayment. This is a human being who has treated another human being as an object, a reified service-providing commodity. Of course, it may be objected that many traditional societies have treated women in similar ways, as property, and I neither wish to idealise the past nor denigrate the present. The best values of modernity lie precisely in the ways in which *all* human beings are conceived of as entitled to freedom and respect as human beings. I merely wish to make the suggestion that, in extending our ideas of freedom, we also extend our understanding of reason in the direction of an understanding of a symbolic richness perhaps once only actively available for males. If women are now entitled to work, they are also now entitled to labour.

On the other hand, I also note an increase in the number of voices raised against the fractured view of life proposed by most modern science. Fritjof Capra's *The Web of Life* (1996) and David Bohm and D. Peat's *Science, Order and Creativity* (1987) both offer, from authors who are physicists, an integrated view of life from the level of quantum mechanics upwards.[17] The imperatives of the market mean that it only understands profit in terms of work and exchange value; but what we need for our humanness is a broader understanding of profit in terms of labour and use value. A fully human life is one which values the creativity of labour: 'labour, because it sets its own pace, is usually accompanied by idleness, leisure, even sleep. In ancient days, a seventh part of a person's time (both Sunday and the sabbatical, the seventh year) were set aside for non-work. Nowadays when a worker or teacher gets a sabbatical, he or she may try to finish six years of unfinished chores. But first he should put his feet up and see what happens'.[18]

As contemporary neurobiology and various other applications of complexity theory increasingly acknowledge, there is a range of human experience which is simply mysterious. The human brain is the most complex thing in the universe. In *Bright Air, Brilliant Fire*, Gerald Edelman tells that the number of synaptic connections in the human brain is so great that, if you were to start counting them, at the rate of one a second, you would not finish counting until 32 million years had elapsed. Human creativity, upon which we all depend, is a mystery. From experience, and as an *act of faith*, some people learn how to 'prepare the ground' and then simply attend – waiting for the muse to descend; and this applies to all human ingenuity, not only to artists.

Modernity's version of knowledge and truth (based on the observational science of Descartes and Newton) is profoundly intolerant of the mysterious. Faced with the mystery of human labour, and the impulsion towards financial profit as the only *recordable* profit, the quintessentially modern response is a passion for knowing as much empirical detail about human beings and their lives as possible. Hence the constant trend towards bureaucracy, managerialism, auditing of outcomes. How terrible for the bureaucrat and manager to learn that the secret of human vitality dies at the moment at which it is recorded, calculated, and put in a ledger. Lewis Hyde tells the story of an innkeeper and a magic barrel which kept producing the most wonderful, refreshing ale without ever being refilled. An inquisitive maid determined to find out the secret of the magic barrel; she pulled out the stopper and looked inside. All she saw were cobwebs and dust; the barrel never produced any ale ever again.

An anthropology of modern life might well start with looking for the ways in which we have tried to keep the realm of the gift alive. In Britain free blood donation is one obvious example, and free health care and education are others (although under attack from market and managerialist imperatives). Most of all, we need to allow the old symbolic language of the gift to be renewed in our public discussions of value by insisting on Hyde's distinction between value and worth, work and labour. Finally, we could perhaps begin to make a distinction between loneliness and solitude: the former suggests lack of human relatedness; the latter suggests the condition into which one necessarily withdraws in order to nurture the human labour on the self which 'prepares the ground' for the gift to be received. It is surely in these mysterious, creative and incalculable processes that we learn the art of life.

Notes

1. See, for example, David Abram, *The Spell of the Sensuous: Perception and Language in a More than Human World*, Vintage Books, New York 1996.
2. G. Edelman, *Bright Air, Brilliant Fire*, Penguin, Harmondsworth 199?.
3. V.S. Ramachandran, *Phantoms in the Brain: Human Nature and the Architecture of Mind*, Fourth Estate, London 1999.

4. I. Prigogine & I. Stengers, *Order Out of Chaos: Man's New Dialogue with Nature*, Flamingo, London 1985 [Paris 1979].
5. *Ibid.*, p3.
6. J. Monod, *Chance and Necessity*, Vintage Books, New York 1972, pp172-3, quoted in Prigogene & Stengers, p3.
7. L. Hyde, *The Gift: Imagination and the Erotic Life of Property*, Vintage, New York 1999 [1979].
8. See the work of artist J. S. G. Boggs, who pays bills with notes he has drawn himself and thus, to the consternation of several governments, which have tried to prosecute him for forgery, upsets this serious distinction upon which sterile modern values are founded. See L. Weschler, *Boggs, A Comedy of Values*, University of Chicago Press, 1999.
9. C. Baudelaire, 'The painter of Modern Life' in *The Painter of Modern Life and Other Essays*, tr. & ed., J. Mayne, Phaidon, 1964.
10. R. Williams, *The Long Revolution*, Hogarth, London 1992 [1961], p23.
11. *Ibid.*, p26.
12. Hyde, *The Gift, op. cit.*, p44.
13. *Ibid.*
14. *Ibid.*, p45.
15. *Ibid.*, p50.
16. *Ibid.*, p53.
17. See also, for an overview of similar and related developments in science, chapter 5: 'Rebellious Jelly', in my own *A New Modernity? Change in Science, Literature and Politics*, Lawrence & Wishart, London 1999.
18. Hyde, *The Gift, op. cit.*, pp50-51.

When I was younger I sought answers to questions.
Silence was the answer, if I listened
I heard the wind move, a door bang.
People came and went, I rejoiced
in the unkown, forgot it quickly,
both the joy and the surprise, at home.
Now I have begun to talk to myself
as though I wanted to know this person who talks
and listens so badly, wrapped in thought.
A few words sought their way close up to me
as though they sought protection from something
that was too difficult to see. I wrote down.
This they taught me, the words that came:
farewells are parts of everything that lives
and, when I have dreamt most strongly,
a homecoming.

Bo Carpelan

I imagined that the world was outside me, great in its silence,
That that which was small, warm and bearable spoke softly,
was near. And then, this! Over the dark deeps
under the surface, deep under the water's surface those quivering deeps
    that catch stars
and, along waterways and out of the motionless choir of the reeds:
    silence.
As though a thousand screaming birds, scared flew up from the evening's
    rock
sensing that this was the world's creation, the world's destruction,
here, far in the north, in the mute, dark heart
that sees the sky's breathing like a fine mist, a wave,
heavy and great like that being space calls on with its voice's absence,
its setting sun, its darkening prayer.

Bo Carpelan

1999

I'm sitting thinking it's January
and next week I will be 49. The room is quiet.
Sunlight streams through the net curtain
suffusing lamp, sofa, desk, in a soft white haze.
I look up to appraise the walls of books.
It's a varied library – poetry, novels, lit crit, biographies,
history books, politics, cultural studies.
Who would I be without these books?
Every day I read from one, a few pages, a poem
and most days I write some lines of my own,
lay them on my desk ready to type into my computer.
A spider scurries up the wall above the lamp.
It's over by the television before I've gathered my thoughts.
Yesterday I found a small gold spider clinging to the side
Of the jar which stores curry powder.
It was dead and clung there fossilized, stiff and dull.
I've been ill and still feel groggy, but hungry now.
Yesterday I ate nothing till early evening.
Then I ate lamb and vegetable soup and some cheese
Which J had brought me home from town.
As I slept my dreams were delirious – I was frantically
sweeping and sweeping up the pine needles in our yard
as if my life depended on clearing the fallen needles.
I woke sweating with thoughts of death.
Like a friend who encourages me against fear she tells me
she is no stranger. She is always there, in the background,
sometimes moving closer, feeling the way of things.
She knows me better than anyone else,
is with me in sleep and silence, when walking alone,
while reading my books.

Frances Angela

16th June 1999

I can smell cut grass, I remember the couple who once walked here
beneath the Arch deep in conversation.

The mauve rhododendron so vibrant last month, is fading.

A woman walks through the long grass beneath a black parasol.

The smell of cut grass is difficult to describe
one can only liken it to something else

it won't do to say, cut grass

happy, buoyant you say, but soothing, calming I add.

One woman in a mustard coloured dress draws the scene,
already leaves fall and die on the path.

A baby cries. She must have brought it here
to get some peace. She gives up rocking the buggy.

Three girls in school uniform pass, one has a thick plait which rests
on her backpack.

In the field leading away from the river
a toddler learning to walk staggers across the grass.
He looks like a bee in his red cap and padded striped shorts.

I wake at 3pm my ear hurting from lying on my jacket
the sun has moved and I'm only half in shade.
There is a red patch on my leg above my sock.

I've never seen the river this low.

The Japanese woman with the shorn hair
has gone. She was sitting on the bench

some yards from my own for several hours. She
took off her trousers and loose top
and lay stretched out in the sun, resting
her head on her clothes and reading her book.

The emptiness she leaves behind is disconcerting

she was so young and beautiful.

On the phone yesterday
L sounded angry, peevish, resentful but then so might I
if I were dying and no one came willingly to see me.

The tide has changed
the banks of mud invisible now.
The water shines like thick tar.

My throat is dry. I have a persistent cough.

I am practised at being alone
I like myself more than I know.

In the silence
a boat on the river
birdsong and a water sprinkler
and the branches gently trampolining
in a sudden gust of wind.

Two barges motor upriver towards Richmond
painted in bright yellow, red and green
like Romany caravans. The distance
between them widens till one turns the bend
leaving the other alone.

Then that too is gone and the river empty.

Frances Angela

Fiction

When I first tried my hand at it,
my character moaned
not just for a day and a night, but
for three solid years.
A voice in my ear, groaning,
whinging, whining, whimpering,
sighing big heavy heaving sighs. Up and doon. Huuhh.
Puffing, oot of breath, *For crying out loud.*
She was a martyr – snivelling, Scottish.

Fed up, grief-struck, going on and on and on
and on: how she was the mug, the sucker,
taken-for-granted, how I could see *her* coming,
take her to The Cleaners. *Oh Dear.*
As for that man of hers, well he wasn't a man at all.
On she went, too close. The voice in my ear.
Heigh-ho. A widow's voice, weeping in the wee small hours,
Weary, poorly, all in the one relentless tone.
The same sorry pitiful moan.
'I've had it,' she'd say, 'Up to here.'

But she had no neck, no body, no face, bonny or raw.
She had no hands to blaw her nose
with a big white hanky.
She had no eyes to cry out,
teeth to gnash or hair to tear out.
She couldn't remember.
'Gie me peace?' she'd say.
'Does onybody think o' gieing me peace? Naw.'

One day I climbed up my steep study steps,
my heart dead, my own voice shaky and ill with it all,
paranoid, spewing self-pity,
thinking this fiction will kill me,
Up I puffed, seized by a sudden fury
to kick the life into her.

There was a blue glow in the corner.
There she was, curled on my floor, at the back,
by the attic door, covered with my father's old coat,
breathing, her face slightly flushed, shy, black,
her body plump and surprisingly fleshy.
I fell to my fat poet's knees and cried holy.

Jackie Kay

MASCULINITY: A RISKY PATH TO TAKE?

Michael Kenny and Nick Stevenson

Do we live in an era of greater 'risk'? The continuing impact of feminism, which disrupts the certainties of the gender order, the disappearance of jobs for life, the increased visibility of diverse sexualities, and the changing contours of our public and private cultures, have led many commentators to believe that modern life is becoming more anxiety-ridden than it has ever been before. Yet the implications of such trends are actually less clear-cut than is often suggested, and this is particularly so in relation to men. Masculinity has undoubtedly become an 'object' of the public gaze; and widening choice has meant that living the way our fathers did has become merely one among many paths that we might take. But are men, and specifically heterosexual men, under pressures that are qualitatively new?

If the risks of the modern world really do add up to a masculinity 'in crisis', as we are told with monotonous regularity by media pundits and the self-help industry, what exactly is at stake in this crisis? Who are its winners and losers? In this essay we try to open up a rather different perspective on the so-called 'crisis' of masculinity. We are aiming to show how different cultural forms and social locations have allowed a diversity of responses to questions that link masculinity to risk. In the realm of popular culture we will look particularly at men's life-style magazines, the 'men's movement' and the growth of a 'self-help' literature for men. We will then turn to a tradition of radical democratic argument, and suggest that this offers one way of reappraising some of the issues at stake in current concerns about masculinity.

THE NIHILIST RESPONSE

In David Lynch's recent film *The Lost Highway* – perhaps one of his most complex and unfathomable creations – one image recurs. It is the road ahead, at night, viewed from the perspective of an unseen driver. The image takes on a succession of frightening associations as a series of disturbing sequences unfold. What looks at first like a familiar genre – a story that will unfold in sequential fashion 'out there', on the road – becomes something else. The external action is revealed to form part of a complex interior world, abounding with dreams, visions and myths from which the male 'hero' is unable to escape. The open road returns, ironically, towards the end of the film, by which time it is clear that the only journey being pursued is towards a murderous destiny; what is being depicted is the road to oblivion. Lynch offers us a picture of a journey that takes the audience beyond familiar genres and traditions to chaos and meaninglessness. The road brings us back into ourselves and the possibility that we may not like what we find there.

Such nihilistic fantasies are ubiquitous in contemporary culture. And, as Lynch knows only too well, they have a unique resonance in the male psyche. Delve beneath the surface of your average guy, such pessimists tell us, and this is what you find. According to this tradition, society exists in an ambivalent relationship with men; it needs their strength and fears their destructive urges. Without men there would be no order; without men, there would be no need for order. Lynch is here tapping into an age-old anxiety about the relationship between masculinity and citizenship, and re-presenting it in a frightening contemporary guise. He does so in a way that has resonances with other aspects of popular culture.

Though Lynch is relatively unusual in seeing masculinity as a rather unyielding and unchanging bundle of primal forces, his anxiety about the nihilistic, violent and sadistic aspects of the male psyche finds strong echoes in many contemporary debates. In Britain, discussion of the comparative failure of boys in terms of educational performance is frequently linked to concerns about a male penchant for violent films, disreputable role models and the persistence of a culture of male violence in public places. One of the features of this debate is that it has brought into the cultural mainstream concerns about the groups 'at risk' from some violent men, particularly children and women. But one of the confusing features of such commentary is this: are men victims or perpetrators? Are men themselves 'at risk'? At stake in this confusion is how we are to envisage men – as patriarchal overlords, or the new losers in the risk society's game of snakes-and-ladders?

Negative representations of the male psyche occur repeatedly in current debates about the impact of changes in men's life-experiences. Such changes are often read as inexorably damaging to male self-confidence. Men, it seems, have very little to gain from contemporary social and cultural developments. The most commonly cited changes are the emergence of a new landscape of work; greater expectations of men in the private domain – in the nursery, the bedroom and kitchen; and the alleged emergence of a more emotionally expressive, feminised public culture. What these developments may mean in terms of the male psyche and the lives of individual men has been discussed at length, but in actuality such processes and their consequences are more uncertain than this commentary claims.

Much of the journalistic hand-wringing tends to ignore the rather complex responses that men, both as individuals and groups, are developing to these conditions; and it overlooks the altered emotional terrain upon which such answers are offered. Being a man now means undertaking a scarier and more uncertain 'journey' than might previously have been the case. And this uncertain situation is made even more complicated by the plethora of 'maps' and 'guides' currently on offer. How do we know which will help us? Are we so sure where we are heading?

MEN'S 'LIFE-STYLE' MAGAZINES: WHOSE LIFE, WHICH STYLE?

Many of the 'up-market' men's lifestyle magazines regularly carry items or tips that offer 'quick and easy' solutions to contemporary anxieties. *FHM* and *Maxim* carry advice (usually in list form) on how to improve your performance as a dancer, lover or father. Other magazines approach this whole terrain with hugely ironised detachment, winking at their readers whilst offering them stories of a return to a pre-feminist masculine ideal. This is what we're really like, isn't it, lads? But for all their absurdity, jokey misogyny and narcissism, these publications do illustrate one dimension of masculinity that academic analysis has missed – the pleasures still attached to being a man. In this they dovetail with other aspects of 'laddish popular' culture, from the TV series *Men Behaving Badly* to the return of 'bad boy' rock. As Sigmund Freud observed long ago, celebrating pleasure in the face of more depressing realities is hardly a model for selfhood, yet it nevertheless represents an important medium through which changes are handled.

Men's magazines can be seen simultaneously as a 'blokelash' against feminism, and as the product of more concerted forms of niche marketing. They externalise questions of risk, projecting anxieties onto men's bodies; for instance with tips on how to build and tone muscle, items on dangerous sports or hazardous holidays, and guides to the best gear to buy. The 'constructed certitude' of these features offers magical solutions to modern anxieties. No need to trouble yourself with the complex ethical and emotional questions facing heterosexual men today. Yet the anxieties are never far from the surface, erupting in perpetual concerns about the 'theatres' of male performance. Beneath these anxieties lurks the recognition that familiar forms of heterosexual masculinity can no longer be taken as a cultural given.

SELF-HELP FOR MEN

There is evidence of the emergence of a more serious-minded 'self-help' culture for men. One element of this comes in the form of that most intriguing and derided of phenomena – the 'men's movement', with its charismatic guru Robert Bly. Though the media treated this current with cynical amusement, with stories of men rushing off to the woods to find their 'inner selves', the connections with other trends in the construction of the masculine self-help industry have been missed. Bly's book *Iron John* has paved the way for the transmission of a burgeoning self-help literature and therapy culture, going beyond an established female constituency to reach male consumers. Self-help books have traditionally been written for and consumed by women. This has been the domain of the feminine. That a male equivalent has taken so long to appear says a lot about men's collective resistance to admitting feelings of weakness or vulnerability. But the emergence of this literature is indicative of a new response to men's sense of anxiety and risk, one which involves at least some capacity for self-reflection.

The philosophy and culture of the diverse American 'men's movement' is forged from a unique mix of New Age, fundamentalist Christian, cowboy and anti-feminist culture – which at the same time borrows techniques and slogans from the women's movement. This movement has not really travelled to Britain; but there have recently been men's campaigns around the rights of divorced fathers, particularly in relation to the financial demands of the Child Support Agency. And there are signs that a different kind of self-help culture, based

upon the twin goals of emotional literacy and patriarchal reconcilia-
tion, is beginning to stir here.

The first self-help guide explicitly targeted at heterosexual men to
have made a major impact in Britain is written by Australian family
therapist, Steve Biddulph. His book *Manhood* confronts the reader
with the shallow and 'inauthentic' lives men lead: men are hurting and
have reached an emotional cross-roads.[1] Biddulph argues that the
problem facing heterosexual men is that we are 'under-fathered'. A
society of one-parent families and male absenteeism has generated a
world of phoney men who do not know how to be authentic in their
masculinity. His remedies take the familiar form of 'seven steps'. The
first is to 'fix it with your father', by recognising the effect he has had
on shaping your identity, and by seeking to open new lines of communication with him. This will allow you to respect the 'father' within
yourself, and enable father and son to recognise a shared masculinity
within one another. Opening the lines of dialogue breaks the emotional
silence that traditionally exists between father and son, and takes them
towards a 'deeper' form of masculinity. Biddulph also asks men to
reflect upon their relations with women, children and close male
friends, proposing a kind of reflexive intimacy. Whilst the new men's
lifestyle magazines offer the displacement and 'externalisation' of risk
through a cheeky laddishness, Biddulph challenges men to work
through these questions internally. And the path he points to would
undoubtedly lead many men onto a relatively uncharted terrain.

But although it may be an advance on 'laddishness', Biddulph's
analysis, read against some of the literature on these topics emanating
from the therapeutic community, tends to reproduce the problem it is
meant to solve. For example, fellow Australian therapist David J.
Tracey also argues that many men are currently alienated from their
own masculine heritage; but he then makes the point that if men want
to move beyond the patriarchal rigidities of the past, it is not enough
simply to reconcile their differences with their fathers.[2] Tracey
proposes a kind of dialectic between re-connection with one's father
and detachment from the story of masculinity that we learn from our
fathers.

A common feature of much of the self-help literature – and this is a
weakness that both these books share – is the absence of women from
the story. But as Nancy Chodorow argued, the healing that is necessary
to produce strong as well as sensitive men will only come about in a
society that does not perceive femininity as weakness.[3] The shallow-

ness of much male culture is the product of men's attempts to denigrate and distance themselves from their mothers. A more reciprocal internal relationship with the feminine 'other', she suggests, would put men's psyches in touch with the more creative, caring and reciprocal sides of themselves. But this would only come about in a society that has learned to value the feminine, and where equal relations between the sexes have been allowed to mature. John Rowan argues that we might think of modern-day masculinity as a mask that hides more troubling feelings beneath the surface.[4] The decision to go into therapy, Rowan argues, may help men make connections with parts of themselves from which they have always been estranged. For Rowan, men's relationships with their parents is something to be *explored* rather than ordered around the creation of new sets of rules.

Despite the differences within the therapy/self-help literatures, there are some intriguing common features in such texts. One is the widespread concern about the development of the male self. The imagery of men that predominates in such texts is the antithesis of the well-worn stereotype of a confident, thrusting phallic masculinity. The achievement of a secure identity as a man can only be won, it seems, after a period of self-analysis and reflection. The preference within some sections of the self-help genre for offering 'rules of conduct' (though this is less a concern at the therapeutic end of the spectrum) reflects a desire to condense the variety of male experiences into a single formula for 'success'. Risk is conceived as being both external and internal, and the proposition is advanced that to re-organise one's emotional life in a given way is the best means of dealing with these kinds of risks.

What are we to make of these 'self-help' guides and the range of lifestyle advice currently aimed at the male consumer? In one sense, they are offering new 'route maps' for the male self, filled with 'dos' and don'ts' of varying sophistication, founded upon a range of social and psychoanalytic theories. In the parlance of social theory, this new self-help culture can be understood as offering an 'expert system' to cope with an increasingly contested and problematised arena of behaviour – a system founded upon new hierarchies of knowledge and golden rules. 'Expert systems' are usually analysed as being created within modern societies to handle and regulate 'external' manifestations of danger, such as environmental threat or health scares. Nowadays it seems that our very selves, our bodies as well as our psyches, need to be subjected to the security of 'regulation' by experts. To some degree this is a new experience for men (though of course women have been subjected to similar 'improving' advice from experts since at least the eighteenth century). And though the 'experts' – from pop therapists to the new men's magazines – have rushed to fill the void opening up in the lives of men, one wonders how much comfort and security they really bring. The solutions currently on offer are caught somewhere between efforts to generate more critical understanding and the avoidance of some of the more painful pathways through masculinity.

THE FALL OF PUBLIC MAN?

Underpinning the development of a culture, and markets, specialising in the male self is the profound alteration of the relationship between the 'private' and 'public' spheres that has taken place in Western modernity. And at the same time as these profound changes have taken place, men have come to recognise, sometimes grudgingly and often resentfully, that the public is a terrain that has to be shared with others, women above all. This is an important part of the background to all this current male anxiety about risk.

Nowhere are these changes in the public sphere more evident than in the world of work. The tie-up between work and masculinity has proved to be a strong one in modern industrial societies. In Europe, the emergence of modern society was accompanied by the progressive separation of the worlds of men and women in respect of public and private domains. Men's sense of who they were was largely secured through their ability to undertake paid employment outside of the home. Women, on the other hand, were restricted to the 'private' domain of motherhood and domestic labour – this was certainly the case in the upper and middle classes, and the idea of a 'family wage' being earned by the male breadwinner was also strong in working-class culture. These trends were intensified during what is often described as the 'Fordist' era: work in the Fordist ideal-type involved the refinement of highly specialised skills, mechanised production, the regimentation of time, hierarchical forms of control and relatively stable patterns of employment. It was this particular set of economic circumstances that created the conditions for the growth of unionised labour in organisations that came to sanctify the notion of the male breadwinner; and also during this period a 'mass' culture developed on the basis of highly collectivised forms of consumption.

Despite widespread disagreement about the significance and meaning of the economic changes that have taken place in the last twenty years, there is a broad consensus about the facts of change in work and cultural life. The social and cultural system of Fordism has been swept away by national and international developments in the economy, as well as by the emergence of identities and movements that disrupted the cultural collectivism underpinning it. In today's western economies, the vast majority of jobs that are created are part-time, based upon temporary contracts and team work. Most importantly of all, women have penetrated the labour market in a host of occupational areas, principally in the service and voluntary domains, but increasingly in a raft of professional locations from which they had previously been broadly excluded. The changing gender composition of the workforce has generated a set of knock-on effects for the institutions and organisations with which they were linked. The degree to which the latter have been shaped (as feminists have always argued) by residual and invisible cultures of sexism, and indifference to women's interests, is slowly becoming visible to the public eye – most shockingly in the most 'male' of professions, the armed forces and police.

The changing balance of public and private life, and the arrival of 'others' in the public sphere, necessitates a rethinking of men's relationship to the public domain, and indeed to the value and practice of citizenship. And a rethinking of this relationship has major repercussions both for the traditionally demarcated public sphere and for men's perceptions of themselves. Those engaged in ethical arguments about the character and purposes of politics have offered contrasting responses to the changes we have outlined. One of the most innovative strains of contemporary political theory, for example, stems from the recognition that our most familiar ways of thinking and speaking about politics have often assumed an artificial divide between 'affairs of state' and private matters. Feminists in particular have shown how different traditions of political thinking and action have attached value to the former over the latter. In the canon of western political thought, the public domain is often characterised in ways that presume male attributes, characteristics and even the presence of male bodies. Contemporary theorists have thus tried to assert that we require a different model and 'story' of citizenship, particularly in relation to tasks and responsibilities in what has traditionally been conceived of as private life. This opens up some interesting ethical possibilities in relation to the duties of (male) parents, for instance. A second challenge arises from some theorists' attempts to construct a more differentiated model of the body politic and the different citizens who people it. Can the ideal of universal citizenship be rendered in ways that account for some of the crucial group differences within contemporary social life?[5] Whilst existing conceptions of citizenship, both as a duty and a practice, stress attributes that have typically been construed in highly masculine terms, are there different skills and human attributes (negotiation, conciliation or empathy for instance) that might be fostered in the public domain?

Other political and social theorists have focused our attention on the apparently terminal decline of 'civil society' in liberal democracies. This is frequently connected, though often only implicitly, with a deepening anxiety about masculine identity. Whilst women have developed a range of activities, communities and networks in both the private and public worlds, it has been suggested, specifically male forms of coming-together are arguably in decline.[6] The deepening indifference towards the world of conventional politics has a particular import for men, given the degree of masculine identification with leadership and political action. In much democratic theory, the public realm is posited as the most ethical moment in the life of the citizen; in Jean-Jacques Rousseau's influential understanding it was the domain in which the male citizen learned the art of deciding on what is good for the community; and it was the domain where the ethical life of the state was settled. If, as many critics assert, there is a crippling lack of confidence about the public domain's ability to fulfil these functions, where does this leave men, given their investment in the ethical and social hierarchies underpinning such understanding of citizenship?

Though few political theorists have concentrated explicitly upon masculinity as an object of enquiry, it is easy to detect anxieties about gender beneath theoretical discussion about the collapse of patterns of authority, and the decline of community in contemporary life. Indeed, it is instructive to read some recent strands of political theory against this backdrop. One of the most influential schools of thought, communitarianism, both in its more formal philosophical guise and in its popularly expressed political forms, argues that the rights-based individualist cultures promoted by liberalism (which they associate with – and often implicitly blame for – the changing patterns of economy and society outlined above) have exposed citizens to a range of threats; communitarians argue that these developments have led to the decline of community and that this brings multiple risks. According to these thinkers, our contemporary rights-bearing individualist culture has squeezed conceptions of social responsibility, without which we are left with the unspoken assumption that we operate in a land of strangers, with no obligations beyond the constraint of not inflicting harm upon the other. The communitarians' way of countering this state of affairs – by asserting the membership nature of persons – is thus advocated as a lodestar for our thinking about individuals and their relation to society, and for engendering institutional reform and design.

Some feminist critics have perceived a call for the restoration of patriarchal authority to be underlying the perceived 'crisis' analysed in the work of Amitai Etzioni and other popular communitarian thinkers. In theoretical terms, feminists and others have revealed the ways in which many communities are in fact founded upon the suppression and denial of difference. Nostalgia for a return to old forms of community can thus be translated as a willingness to accept such suppression and denial. Some of the ambivalent comments offered by leading communitarian figures such as Etzioni about the importance of the domestic domain for women have been read as calls to restore social relations to those of an earlier era, usually the halcyon days of the 1950s.

But it is certainly arguable that not all theories that value the community, and specifically the public domain as the site of the political community, are inimical to a rethinking of the relationship between male bodies and the body politic. Some theoretical arguments in this field point to more optimistic and diverse scenarios, premised on the capacity of citizens to learn from each other, to examine themselves and their own conduct, and interact on different terms with 'others'.

One line of argument developed by those seeking to rethink the public domain along these lines focuses on the emphasis at the heart of all the multiple strands of republican theory on the public sphere as the site where citizenship is learned and practised; in particular these commentators look at the importance for some democrats of the public domain as the forum for a certain kind of talk between citizens. Critics like Jürgen Habermas have rebuked the civic republican conception of thinkers like Rousseau, William Jefferson and Hannah Arendt because they conflate the institutionalisation of a 'public use of reason jointly exercised by autonomous citizens'[7] with the idealisation of a particular form of intersubjective life (although it should be noted that republicanism, in its different manifestations, is one of the parents of the deliberative tradition of democracy that has been so powerfully revived in the work of Habermas and others). Habermas proposes a more flexible and 'decentred' understanding of 'the public' and its relations to private life and identity. A public domain established in accordance with the principle of unfettered communication is an interesting notion to consider in relation to a host of problems and issues which have been either consigned to the realm of private choice in liberal discourse (abortion and gay parenting, for instance), or have been sidelined by prevailing value-systems and mores within established communities. This account of the nature and forms of public deliberation poses some powerful questions in relation to contemporary social concerns and how these might and should be 'politicised': can a radically reconstituted set of public domains and spaces provide forums for debates on exactly the same issues which self-help books are currently trying to address? If so, risks will not necessarily disappear, but they may be handled in different, more positive ways. The deliberative tradition offers a reservoir of insight and argument about the nature, purpose and rules governing deliberation, the ends to which it might be pursued and its limitations in democratic contexts. This approach also expands the kinds of dialogue envisaged within the therapeutic community into different cultural domains, encouraging us to think too of the social dimensions of the problems currently addressed in its discourse.

Talk presumes a listener, and the listening capacity of the speaker. It provides the central motif for the tradition of discourse ethics. An ethical tradition that posits a concrete 'other' to be engaged in dialogue (real or imagined) offers a different but challenging 'procedural ideal' to be considered in the context of many current debates – about male parenting, or about ways in which men and boys in different social locations (in prisons, schools, the professions) regard women, and indeed each other. The idea here would be that learning to talk and listen to a concrete other, both within and beyond the immediate family structure, offers hope of a more 'reflexive', and less knee-jerk, form of masculinity. Despite their domination of public spaces and places, it is commonly observed that men are poor at talking about what really concerns them. Learning to 'talk', in the sense of engaging in different types of dialogue, learning to listen, and coming to terms with the essential facts of social, emotional and ethical difference, might be regarded as an ethical priority for men.

Another useful insight offered by a 'radical' communitarianism to those trying to rethink issues within this area is its recognition of the plurality of social experience that citizens encounter – a fact that disrupts simplistic notions of a 'crisis for men'. If, as radical communitarians claim, there are social, psychological and ethical benefits to community membership, we need to ask which communities individuals ought to be members of, and how freely they can join and exit them. According to leading communitarian theorists like Michael Walzer and Charles Taylor, modern societies are characterised by the emergence of multiple, interwoven communities of different kinds, and individuals belong to more than one of these. These theorists reproduce an older (Tocquevillian) vision of a pluralistic society 'laced with communities and voluntary associations'.[8] The usefulness of such an ideal in relation to the questions under consideration in this essay lies in the embrace of diverse communal membership, and the simultaneous recognition that solid communal underpinnings may be a requisite for a healthy sense of individual self-hood. This ideal can be set against the ideal-type at the heart of the male fundamentalist movement. For the latter, men have to return to a mythical, pre-modern communal ideal, to get away from the risks attendant upon a host of feminine and cosmopolitan influences. This vision fails to recognise that masculinity in the modern age can only be conceived in cosmopolitan terms; male identities develop through the playing of multiple roles, through negotiating relationships at different levels and to different depths, and through moving in and out of different social and cultural spheres. The more radical strand of communitarian thinking, as outlined above, asks us to focus attention on the different kinds of relationship in which identities get shaped and re-made. Friendship, for instance, arguably carries a large amount of social value in highly individualised social contexts, but it figures little in contemporary writing on men.

Of course there are risks in the celebration of a cosmopolitan ideal. Multiple relationships are in some ways harder to manage, adding to people's confusion and contributing to the fragmentation of experiences. In a non-traditional world, relationships between heterosexual men and women carry different cultural and social baggage. And this is not necessarily an unmitigated gain. According to Ulrich Beck and Elisabeth Beck-Gernscheim,[9] we live in more chaotic times, where love is generated for its own reflexive sake now that religion is disappearing. There is no tradition, or normative context, within the terms of which we are bound to conduct our relationships. This can make for a great deal of insecurity. And cynics (or realists?) like Ian Craib retort that such an understanding overloads relationships with social aspirations and expectations that they cannot fulfil; we live, he says, in the age of disappointment.[10] But whether or not we welcome the freedoms brought by the dissolution of old certainties, none of us will be helped by the fantasy of restitution. The regaining of a mythic, organic authenticity in the woods involves a flight from engagement with the different places and issues shaping male sensibility. The deliberative ideal, forged through the recognition of the existence of multiple notions of 'the good life' in contemporary society, offers some intellectual and ethical resources in the face of different sorts of risk.

CRISIS – WHAT CRISIS?

'Risk' has emerged as one of the most widely used concepts in social science in the last twenty years. When deployed in the context of accounts of the emergence of a so-called 'risk society', there is a danger that contemporary cultural change, for all its pace and scope, is read as irreducibly threatening. On some accounts of cultural development today, all that is solid really has melted into air, and we are left anxiously chasing shadows. The connections forged between risk and masculinity in different kinds of commentary, powerfully shaped by prevailing notions of a 'crisis of masculinity', threaten to lead us into the trap of assuming that change has to mean decline. Such a view also threatens to obscure the perspectives of history. Attention to the latter should teach us that men, just like women, have been undergoing experiences of intense change – in work conditions, in expectations, in relations with women and children, and in relations with other groups of men – over the last few centuries. Change in the configurations of masculinity and femininity is not a new phenomenon. A historical approach can also alert us to the fact that pre-modern societies could throw up risks of a physical immediacy that make contemporary society look extremely secure. Nor is the clamour of concern about men entirely novel. Debates among the political and social elites of the late nineteenth century about the 'unfitness' of the male working class are one such prior example. This is not the first time, then, that men have become the 'objects' of concern, pity, dislike and curiosity.

That there is a social trend towards anxiety about masculinity is apparent from cumulating media reports on male suicide rates, declining fertility rates, falling educational performance and the impact of long-term male unemployment. But these contemporary anxieties may be usefully regarded as one more turn of a continuing cycle of complaint and concern about male mores, attitudes and sexuality, rather than as a starting point for consideration and intervention.

Many commentators in the media industries have a great investment in presenting male behaviour as the playing out of a number of pathologies. Some 'pop' feminist and post-feminist commentators have led the way here, either castigating men for fleeing back to boyhood, or gleefully celebrating the triumph of the female at the expense of men. Neither of these 'tropes' is likely to get to the bottom of quite what is going on with men; and, oddly, such arguments let men off the hook by resorting to pathological explanations. The certainties of such positions lead to an evasion of many of the questions that could usefully be asked: for example, what choices, responses and decisions are men taking in different social and emotional locations? And with what consequences? Might they take better decisions? In what sorts of cultural environments do men become abusers and harmers? Are there exceptions? These kinds of questions rarely figure in the crisis discourse so currently pervasive.

It is possible to draw pessimistic or optimistic conclusions from contemporary developments. Much social theory has, for instance, been far more comfortable in observing that some women have benefited from the decline of the structures and mores of 'traditional society' than in focusing on the problems of contemporary masculinity. But it is not axiomatic that men have been the losers in these changing social mores. Gender is not best thought of in zero sum terms. The expansion of consumption within contemporary society has been observed to be a boon as well as a source of exploitation for women. Equally, men have embraced the practice and 'values' of consumption with a gusto that has left many on the political right and left perturbed. Have men gained from 'individualisation' as well as women? What of the increasing number of men who live single lives, in loosely formulated familial structures? Are they feckless, footloose and dangerous, or more sensitive and spontaneous beings? The response of many 'experts' – that this sort of change must involve loss, for the men involved and for the community – looks a bit too simplistic. Some evidence points to the formation of new kinds of associations, groups and collectivities, offering meaning and 'community' of different kinds; but this optimistic finding can be countered by the abundant evidence of a desire in some men to cling to some of the hackneyed aspects of male culture from days gone by. The story that needs telling is not just one of what has been lost, but of what is in flux and what is being created. We may be on the cusp of an age in which many men and women live more autonomously, and spin out a variety of 'life-projects' that are not as yet catered for by contemporary culture. We are now in a situation where even adopting a 'traditional' masculine identity involves a choice over other kinds. It is no longer simply a question of reflex. These changes are full of possibilities as well as carrying risks. (It should however be noted that, depressingly, this kind of autonomy may be beginning to appear for some, at a time when other groups of men and women, at the bottom of the economic pile, are living in ways that are highly heteronomous, socially blighted and risk-ridden.)

BEYOND THE CRISIS ...

Are there routes to male self-renewal? Can we do more than lament the 'male crisis'? From contemporary popular culture comes a confusing array of responses and diagnoses: from the Hobbesian pessimism of David Lynch on the one hand to the masculine fundamentalism of Robert Bly on the other. The former offers a path back into the untamed masculine persona of violence and chaos; the latter lays out a different road, down to the woods, to re-create the mythical male self. But are there other paths that modern men can traverse? A crude and ultimately unworkable answer came from the consumer culture of the 1980s – the 'new man', extensively re-programmed and re-modelled, a being with the 'right' answers to all the difficult questions. One of the many problems with this depressing creature was the certitude he embodied – the sense that he had to express 'the line' to keep at bay all the ambiguities and uncertainties of gender issues. Our own sense is that some men 'on the ground' are beginning to develop a variety of different, more tentative responses to contemporary dilemmas; these involve a negotiation of and reflection upon, if not an obvious escape from, our masculine heritage. These responses can be embodied in different life experiences and circumstances: men living single lives; those negotiating relationships with their children having broken up with partners, or indeed bringing kids up alone; the increasing recourse by men to self-help and therapeutic practices; and the establishment of different kinds of male networks.

To illustrate the sensibility behind all this, we end with a different aesthetic from those encased in nihilism, fundamentalism and the cult of the 'new man'. A recent album by the group Echo and the Bunnymen, *What are you going to do with your life?*, released in 1999, offers a different response to the dilemmas facing the male self. The group are no strangers to nihilistic tropes; readers are directed to the song 'Happy Death Men' on their first album, *Crocodiles* ... But in the 1990s they reinvented themselves lyrically and musically. The title track poses a question that recurs throughout the album, with tales of lost love, divorce, obsessive relationships and the uncertainty of becoming your (male) self. The album cover features McCulloch walking alone down an open road; but the feel of the maleness being explored here is neither lost nor hopeless nor striving to recreate the 'phallic certitude' of much mainstream culture. The combination of softer sound and reflective lyric is framed by a recognition of the ambivalence involved in being a man. There are even hints of a redeemed future. This possibility comes in the form of more open modes of communication with the self, and with women ('what's the use of stealing? ... she's the answer'), and the broaching of more risky intersubjective suggestions ('I need someone to help me').

No doubt, for every McCulloch there is of course a Liam Gallagher ...

It is not our aim either to resume the tedious game of standing for or against popular culture on these and other questions. But it is worth stressing the *different* cultural repertoires around risk and masculinity that are and might be available. Above all, we need to learn to distinguish those moments in the life of our culture which (as in the more formal theoretical arguments explored above) seek to promote ethical and communicative questions about men's current social standing, and to distinguish them from those that strive to close down the prospects of intimate and public dialogue. Given the ubiquitous rubbishing of our 'dumbed-down' mass culture, it is ironic that there is at the moment a greater receptivity in popular film, novels and music to the shifting terrain of male sensibility than there is in all the verbiage flowing from the self-proclaimed 'experts' on these questions.

NOTES

1. S. Biddulph, *Manhood: An Action Plan for Changing Men's Lives*, Hawthorne Press.
2. D. J. Tracey, *Remaking Men*, Routledge, London 1997.
3. N. Chodorow, *The Reproduction of Mothering*, University of California Press, California 1978.
4. J. Rowan, *Healing the Male Psyche*, Routledge, London 1997.
5. A. Phillips, *Engendering Democracy*, Pennsylvania University Press, Pennsylvania 1991.
6. H. Putnam, *Making Democracy Work: Civic Tradition in Modern Italy*, Princeton University Press, 1993.
7. S. Benhabib, 'Introduction: The Democratic Moment and the Problem of Difference', in S. Benhabib (ed), *Democracy and Difference: Contesting the*

Boundaries of the Political, Princeton University Press, 1996.

8. A. Etzioni, 'Old Chestnuts and New Spurs', in A. Etzioni (ed), *New Communitarian Thinking: Persons, Virtues, Institutions and Communities*, The University Press of Virginia, 1995.

9. U. Beck and E. Beck-Gernsheim, *The Normal Chaos of Love*, Polity Press, Cambridge 1995.

10. I. Craib, *The Importance of Disappointment*, Routledge, London 1995.

AUTHORITY

Rachel Thomson

Authority has been described as representing legitimate power – power that neither needs to be explained nor defended. In a media-saturated, diverse and discursive culture there is little that escapes such interrogation. We need only turn on the television, pick up a newspaper or magazine to find difficult questions being asked of parents, the church, royalty, state, professionals. The proliferation of confessional, consumer and self help cultural forms suggests that social institutions are having to be, or are having to be seen to be, accountable in their exercise of power. As the questions mount up, answers such as 'because we say so' or 'because it has always been that way' are increasingly unconvincing.

The relocation of authority from unquestioned tradition to the self critical individual can be understood as part of a wider process of detraditionalisation. Yet despite the historic consequences of this process in authorising the individual, it has not made us feel good about ourselves. Rather, the dominant political culture of the last twenty years has been characterised by the assumption of moral decline. While commentators argue over causes and cures, most agree that something precious has been lost. Zygmunt Bauman has articulated this in terms of 'the ethical paradox of modernity', where an expansion of the ethical arena has been accompanied by a decline of authority – while we have to make up our own minds about more and more issues, our choices no longer provide us with certainty or satisfaction.

WHO TO BLAME
Difficult questions about social change can easily slip into laments about generation. While detraditionalisation clearly impacts upon and disrupts our understandings of who we are and what we want, we have preferred to project our debate onto the adults of the future than to

deal with it in the here and now. Children and young people have become potent symbols for the loss of traditional authority – both pitied and blamed as the products of a damaged moral order. Social policies that seek to instruct young people in citizenship and moral development, or to support the parenting practices of the socially excluded, speak primarily to our need for reassurance.

Part of our trouble with young people is our confusion between the authority of 'youth' and the condition of the young. On one hand we experience youth as being very powerful. Adult men and women work hard to look young, to act young and to feel young. Toys and play are no longer the exclusive preserve of children, and, once stripped of its natural markers, 'youth' can be achieved by all who can afford it. But we should not confuse the cultural authority of youth with the material and social resources of the biologically young who as a social group are increasingly vulnerable and dependent. Unlike the baby boomers of the 1950s and 1960s, young people no longer form a formidable economic or political constituency. The disappearance of the youth labour market, free education and independent access to benefits means that dependency on parents is now extended well into the 20s. For those without family support, such as the young homeless and those living in care, independence can be premature and brutal.

So what actually lurks beneath the surface of debates about moral decline and policy initiatives to 'improve' the next generation? If we are able to disentangle our anxieties and jealousies about authority and youth we find a crisis surrounding the meaning of adulthood. The traditional markers of transition – sexual maturity, parenthood, independent housing, citizenship and economic autonomy – are fragmented in time. While it may be common to have sex before – sometimes well before – the age of 16 and, depending on where you grow up, to have a child soon after, it is increasingly rare to have independent housing or a full-time job until your 20s. Most young people are unlikely to be able to secure the identities, lifestyles and values of their parents, yet we do not trust what they will come up with in its place. It is clear that adulthood will have to look rather different in the next millennium, yet as a culture we have not yet summoned the courage to welcome experiments in its sequencing and meaning.

THE MORAL ENTREPRENEURS
While there are voices that seek to tell a more optimistic story about the young and the future – countering charges of chaos with complexity,

and selfishness with reflexivity – even the optimists fail to ask the young about what they are actually doing and thinking. Despite intense interest in their values, little attention has been given to young people as ethical agents. In a debate primarily concerned with either mourning the past or worrying about the future, there has been little room for the voices of the present. However, the recognition that young people are morally active is a crucial step in coming to terms with a future shaped by the consequences of their choices. While commentators are quick to diagnose, theorise and prescribe, few bother to ask simple questions about *how* people are living through social change and *how* they moralise and authorise their social practices and relationships. This essay does not seek to explain or theorise the moral condition of the young. Rather it attempts something more modest, and I believe more necessary – to move beyond the rhetoric and representations in order to document the ethical experiences, dilemmas, strategies and skills of specific young people today, in this case two British sixteen-year-olds.

I met and interviewed Adele and Aaron as part of a research study that sought to document the values and moral landscapes of young people growing up in contrasting areas of the UK.[1] I have chosen to tell their particular stories because they are each both ordinary and extraordinary. Ordinary in the sense that they have faced circumstances and conditions shared by many others; extraordinary because they have employed ethical strategies as a way of responding to their particular personal circumstances, inventing, from whatever resources they can muster, identities and ways of living that are different from those of many around them. I think of both of them as moral entrepreneurs, mapping out new ethical territory and forging new forms of identity and community, yet, importantly, also holding onto and defending the traditions and values of the past.

'WHEN YOU DON'T CARE YOU DON'T KNOW HOW TO BE SCARED' – ADELE

Rebellion is both complicated and necessary for Adele. It is easier to know what she will not or cannot be than it is to find a way for herself. As the daughter of a Northern Irish Orangeman, an apprentice-boy at that, she was born into a tradition of self defence. Being an apprentice-boy entails more than an awareness of history; it is 'a statement', and it ties her father to a range of traditional sources of authority and privilege that are increasingly under threat. For both her parents there is but 'one path'. While she describes her mother as sometimes looking up and around from this pathway, her father follows it straight, 'all the way down'. That means socialising with, working with, defending and marrying your own kind. It also means annually marching a path through Catholic communities.

Adele's path is to wander – literally. In a town of strict boundaries, borders and ghettos, she takes pride in her ability to cross town, to mix with the 'other side', to find others like herself who are unable to respect the boundaries of sectarianism. And she does find them. Young people like herself of both communities, who pride themselves on their difference, their individuality, their 'mellowness', who work hard to 'not care' about religion, territory and mutual fear. It is not always easy to be together and Adele finds herself getting wound up about politics, especially about marching, which she sees as a 'God given right'. She has even found herself talking of 'Fenians' and 'Taigs' in unguarded moments, only to realise with embarrassment that she is in mixed company.

Consequently, Adele and her friends tend to avoid politics; they 'don't care' about that sort of thing. While they support the peace process, they cannot afford to place faith in it: they are too aware of the power of those who are brought up to be bitter and to pass on their bitterness to others. Instead they care about fashion, about style and about music, not the pop of the undiscriminating masses, but authentic music, with a message and with meaning which speaks of other places and other people. Inevitably they see their future as being somewhere else. People at school cannot understand them (and call them 'freaks'), but her frame of reference is bigger than theirs: 'if you put us down in London we'd be normal – here we're rare'.

Economically there is little difference between Protestants and their Catholic neighbours. In fact the nice houses across from the estate boundary are now the home of middle-class Catholics rather than Protestants. Traditional boundaries are being infringed all around. Sectarian attacks are happening in the hearts of communities once considered safe havens and 'no go zones' to the other side. This physical and social proximity makes the symbolic distinction even more acute. The graffiti at the estate entrance says it all: 'don't bring Fenians into this estate, don't tout on paras or your house will be petrol bombed and you'll have 24 hours to go'. Adele knows that these are not idle threats, but she defies the bullying of those she calls 'bozzos and villains' by insisting that her Catholic boyfriend walk her to and from her door. She has heard of girls being tarred and feathered for less but laughs it off – how ridiculous, how archaic. She sees these 'hard men' as the drop-outs and failures of her own generation – the ones who did not do well at school. In her generation there has been a parting of ways. One group who really want peace, and the other group who are 'really really violent'. She is determined not to be intimidated by them – having learned the importance of fearlessness to those who need their freedom. She is prepared to break the rules and take risks but she does worry about bringing danger on her family.

Her sense of obligation to her parents and her 'area' is complicated. On the one hand she rejects their values – particularly their fear of difference, and whispered fantasies of the occult practices of priests, nuns and Catholics in general, passed from mothers to their children. She also rejects what she sees as an outmoded approach to gender roles that gives household chores and child care to daughters and the freedom of the city to sons. Yet, on the other hand she also shares some of the values of her parents and her area – in particular the right for Protestants to 'do our heritage'. Although she mixes, she also believes in returning to and defending 'her own'. In many ways Adele has reworked the loyalist ethic of 'no surrender' for her own purposes. An ethic of fearlessness and defiance in the face of the threat of violence – a threat increasingly located within her own community. When I ask Adele if she is a brave person she tells me no, not brave – 'I just don't care' – explaining that if you care it shows. Fear will stop you from doing what you want to do. 'I don't care if I get a hiding. If I get a hiding it's meant to happen. I'm not going to let it stop me' – a high risk strategy. 'If you show a wee bit of hesitation, they think they can push you about. But still I wouldn't want to put my ma in danger'.

Adele considers herself to be a feminist. Apart from loyalist marching, the only other issue that motivates her is abortion, which, again against the grain of popular opinion, she believes should be available to Northern Irish women. But she has little time for popular images of girl power: 'I don't know what girl power is, I swear to God, what is girl power. I think the Spice Girls are total prats. I bet you if you put them in a housing estate in Northern Ireland, they'd be in a mental institute by the end of the week. Their nerves would be wrecked'. It is difficult for Adele to know what she wants to be. When asked about role models she replies that she has none, just herself. While she loves her parents she has no wish to be like them; and she has little respect for her teachers whom she perceives as lazy and ineffective. Like many

Protestants of her generation, the police are no longer seen as allies, and she 'just gives them dirty looks – winds them up'. There are no big sisters or aunties who have forged the kind of path that interests her. The closest she gets to a role model is a suitably contradictory character in *Holly Oaks* who both has her own business and is a 'bad girl', getting into debt and stealing cars. While Adele has no-one to base herself on, she remarks that there are more and more girls like her coming up, thinking 'just live for yourself'.

Adele wants out. She will start by getting a training in hairdressing – either by apprenticeship in a local firm or full-time at the Tech. Then she will 'get out of this island and go to the mainland', starting in places where she has family as a way in, but not planning to live with them. She definitely does not want to take the traditional path out for a girl like her – marrying a soldier. She will leave under her own steam, and look after herself. While Adele's experience is unique to the Protestant estates of Northern Ireland, she also operates on a larger canvas, drawing on resources from a wider global culture in which she engages as a discerning consumer. Thus, she draws values of 'authenticity' and 'individuality' from a global music culture rooted in the experience of young black urbanites but consumed by young people across the world. She appropriates feminist ideas on sex and relationships from English-based young women's magazine problem pages. She takes ideas of 'mellowness' and 'chilling' from a dance-based drug culture, while largely leaving aside the drugs.

In privileging herself and rejecting traditional and external sources of authority Adele is very typical of her generation. Yet the circumstances that frame this very modern narrative of identity are quite exceptional. In particular many aspects of traditional authority in Adele's life are themselves contested and insecure. Thus while it may be comfortable for Adele to reject aspects of her parents' culture that are patriarchal, gendered and compromise the efficacy of the individual, she vociferously defends key symbols and practices of that same 'Protestant heritage'. Adele's story also draws our attention to the limits of individualism, in that she is unable to be her own moral arbiter, responsible and accountable for her own actions, since these actions have consequences for others The geography and dynamics of sectarianism mean that community has a continuing purchase in Northern Ireland. Yet who and what that community is has become a contested matter. While Adele may defend the Orange culture of her father, she is deeply hostile to the emergent version of community authority represented by the paramilitaries of her own generation. In making her own choices and imposing the consequences on herself and others she is contributing to the authorisation of new traditions and rules of conduct.

AARON: THE FISH AND THE SHARKS

Aaron knows all about ethical labour. He believes that we should 'evaluate everything we do', recognising that, although it is 'hard and time consuming … that's how we make ourselves better people'. In Aaron's world nothing is ever black or white, never simple. To see it as simple means closing your mind, taking the easy option. Instead he struggles with everything. It is important to him to hold the moral high ground and he takes risks to get there.

I met Aaron on his last day of school at an English comprehensive. He had just finished his final exam and was quietly confident about his results. Before he left to take up his place on a performing arts course at a further education college he had one duty left to perform, for himself but also for the school. Aaron had long been the subject of bullying at school and in the neighbourhood, much of it homophobic. The previous day he had heard that a teacher conducting a 'lesson on morals' had mentioned Aaron by name in a class discussion of homosexuality. This did not surprise Aaron greatly; while he liked many of the young teachers, he remarked that some of the older ones 'forget their guidelines of how they should conduct themselves'. After our interview he had an appointment with the head-teacher, at which he would make a formal complaint. In Aaron's opinion it was sometimes necessary to make teachers accountable, to make them do their jobs, to report bullying rather than fighting back, to resist collusion between teachers and pupils. He sees pointing out to teachers what they are doing wrong, and right, as part of his role in the school; as he commented, 'some of them don't like it, some of them are thankful'.

In many ways it is a good school, with a 'good building, good resources, good teaching'. But that does not satisfy Aaron: 'It's more a case of "look what we've got", rather than "look at our students, look how they're treating people outside the school, look at the way they think"'. Yet, for all its faults, at least the school has rules and policies in relation to which it can be called to account. This is not the case beyond the school gates. Although Aaron jokes that he would like to return to the school as a teacher, in practice he does not feel safe on the estate and longs to escape – to 'go anywhere, see the world, try new things, do anything'. People on the estate do not like new things. It's a place that is 'good for its traditions, the old way of life'. But people are 'narrow minded, they're not open to anything new'.

Although the estate has a reputation for tough men and women, Aaron thinks that it is a weak place. People are 'trying to live up to the tough name and bringing themselves down in the process'. Gender is a 'big thing', 'you have to sit like a man, speak like a man, play football and drink lager all day'. While women stand up for themselves on the street, this is not the case in the household situation, which is marked by strict gender roles and too much domestic violence. Aaron recognises that he disrupts this order. He also looks different. The look on the estate is conservative and expensive: Nike; Adidas; Umbro; Ralph Lauren ... Whereas Aaron is not 'a labels kind of person', more a 'piercings kind of person'. I remark to him that there is a strong sense of sameness in the school – people dress, look and speak the same. 'Yes', he agrees; 'but I'm not like that. I go the opposite way. I'm the fish swimming towards the shark'.

Although Aaron can call on teachers within school, outside he is alone, and on a number of occasions he has been the victim of violence. 'I just take it in. It's not nice immediately, but if you just look forward and think how much it's built your character then it can be okay'. This concern to learn, to develop and to take something from all experiences means that Aaron survives. He explains that 'sometimes negative experiences are better than positive ones, because if it's positive it won't last, whereas if it is negative ... you feel that then you've got to build on it, and that can make you stronger'. I ask what it is that enables him to learn from such experiences, which for others might cause or perpetuate damage. Aaron identifies the source of his ethical concern first with his family, and in particular the 'high morals' of his parents for whom language, dress and manners are of great importance. Although he does not identify with many of his parents' beliefs, describing them as having a 'one-way route', he draws strength from their respectability and pride, citing his father's daily routine of dressing in a suit despite being housebound for a number of years due to sickness. He is careful to distinguish between the values of his parents and those of the local community, explaining, 'I'm not the estate – although I'm here in the estate. I don't think you ever are where you are, you know what I mean, you're yourself'.

Aaron locates himself at the centre of his biography. He is his own invention, believing firmly that 'you choose to be something', motivated by a 'want', 'a want to be'. Rather than basing himself on particular people or role models, he describes his development as a process of cut and paste – 'we see something in someone and we like that so we'll take that bit, and in the next person we'll take that bit, so we come up with our own self – we don't just copy'. Self invention is a creative project, for which the characteristics, values and attitudes of other people and places are the raw material. Initially he found inspiration in the media, in children's television programmes such as *Blue Peter*, and *Grange Hill*, programmes that showed people 'being themselves', 'not ashamed to do things'. More recently he has developed skills and insight from a training in drama and the performing arts, which he describes in reflexive and ethical terms. For Aaron, acting does not involve pretending, but is a part of life, mimicking the process through which the self empathises with, reciprocates with and absorbs the selves of others. As in life, participation brings with it responsibilities. 'You're responsible, you've been given a script and you've got to bring the character to life ... you have to do that work for the character'. He believes that this process can give you insight into your own life, using characters as a mirror, as a way of looking back at yourself. The pay-off is that 'if there's any good in that character you can it have for yourself'; the price is that you also have to 'give to the character'.

In the light of such generosity, Aaron's views on friendship are at first surprising. He believes that in friendship one person is always trying to dominate the other, to gain power over them, to assert status and to compete. In contrast he envisages the relationship with a lover to be about equality, balance and mutual respect. I am surprised by Aaron's lack of trust in friendship and wonder if these views are shaped by his experiences of bullying and his efforts to understand his tormentors. While Aaron's position is ethically sophisticated, it also reflects his relative isolation. This begins to make more sense as he explains his views on moral authority: 'I think each of us has the authority of his own morals. It's an individual thing. It's an opportunity – we have opportunities everywhere we go and we decide what's right and wrong.' It is the experience of separateness that makes us into moral beings. People who treat others with a lack of respect do so because 'they don't know what it is like to have really made those decisions on their own'.

Aaron clearly demonstrates the reflexive, individualised and moralised self described by contemporary theorists of detraditionalisation such as Giddens, Beck and Bauman. We can also see how individualisation is the prerequisite for such reflexivity. To locate authority within the self is to have no serious alternatives, and this speaks of social exclusion as well as social differentiation. The failure of the external and collective forms of authority to include or recognise Aaron leaves him with little investment in his surroundings. Whether some experience of marginalisation is a prerequisite of such reflexive development is an interesting question. But Aaron's ability to cultivate and sharpen his reflexive skills in a way that enables him to survive the present, in the hope of a future in which these skills, values and characteristics may be valued, is itself remarkable.

Like Adele, Aaron's future lies elsewhere. He has little investment in the present; yet in engaging ethically with his circumstances he also demands reciprocity and relationship from those around him – whether that consists of forcing his teachers to deliver on their equal opportunities and bullying policies, or in providing a thorn in the side of the aesthetic and cultural landscape of the estate. Although he suffers the consequences of his difference from those around him, he also finds it rewarding because 'people can see you're different – I'm someone else to look at and people can see if they want to take that or not'. Moral relationships and reputations are by definition collective and reciprocal. [2] By insisting on engaging ethically with the people and the institutions around him, Aaron is also forcing those parties to reflect on and review their values. In this sense Aaron understands that he is a revolutionary, a person who not only changes himself, but also whatever he goes into.

ETHICS IN THE STORMY PRESENT

So what is the moral of this particular story? By documenting the everyday ethical dilemmas of these young people I hope to have challenged the representation of young people as ciphers for an uncertain future, replacing it with a sense of them as participants in a stormy present. Like the adults with whom they share their social worlds, they are much concerned with the art of life – with questions of identity and values – who to be and how to live. Yet, unlike many adults, they approach these tasks with scarce resources, often facing more than their fair share of risk and insecurity – but also bringing tenacity and creativity to the endeavour. It would be unwise to generalise about the experiences, circumstances and strategies of the young on the basis of two people's stories. Yet there are common themes in their stories that are worth noting.

First, both are marked by a partial defence of traditional values and sources of authority. In Adele's case this can be seen most clearly in her defence of the 'God given right to march'; for Aaron it can be heard in the way in which he relates to his parents' values of respectability. But the traditional and the new coexist . Each also seeks to transcend the traditional and to invoke or create new sources of identity and authority. The popular media provide both with an important resource in this process, but in unpredictable ways. While moral guardians worry about video nasties and internet porn, young people may be appropriating values of respect, equality and tolerance, from sources as diverse as *Blue Peter* and *Just 17*.

In the context of detraditionalisation authority does not disappear; rather the potential sources of authority proliferate and realign in new configurations. While it may be relatively easy to name and reject authority in traditional form, its newer manifestations can be more elusive and difficult to challenge. Thus, while the authority of the teacher may be subject to negotiation, the authority of fashion or popularity may be more difficult to articulate and resist. Both Aaron and Adele are negotiating and challenging some of the newer manifestations of authority within their local cultures. Aaron is engaged in a lonely pursuit in his challenge to the marriage of old and new community values that has produced the dominance of macho identities and reputations on the estate. In Adele's neighbourhood authority is being asserted in quite brutal ways by young paramilitaries claiming to represent and control community spaces and practices. She not only risks her own and her family's safety in challenging the legitimacy of their claims, she also asserts an alternative moral position.

While it is important to listen to these stories, we also need to look beneath their surface. In the absence of tradition, choice – the ability to choose one course of action over another – becomes the foundation of moral autonomy. Yet the rhetoric and the experience of choice cannot be equated. While the ethical rhetoric of Adele and Aaron is characterised by assertions of personal autonomy, in practice their choices are highly constrained. Heelas has characterised the uncertainties of modernity as giving rise to 'identity problems' ... 'that propel people to act, to discover "who they really are, or are capable of becoming"'.[3] This is most clearly the case for Aaron, for whom a pursuit of the moral high ground can also be understood as a very practical survival strategy, and echoes can be found in Adele's refusal to be frightened by the threats of 'hard men'.

Both young people can be understood as rebels, engaged in an active process of constructing their identity in opposition to the values of others around them, questioning the grounds of their 'authorisation of authority'.[4] Yet each could also be understood to be conventional and conservative, defending established values and traditions and accepting these claims to authority. Moreover, they are very different young people, whose values may well be at odds with one another. This apparent paradox is really no more than a symptom of the complexity and diversity of lived lives – a complexity that we tend to find whenever we move from the political, the rhetorical or the theoretical, to the particular. It is my feeling that in documenting this detail we temper our compulsion to explain and judge, and perhaps even reawaken our curiosity and ability to ask, listen and observe: important tools in the art of life.

NOTES

1. The study, *Youth values: identity diversity and social change* was funded by the Economic and Social Research Council (ref L129251020), taking place between November 1996 and April 1999. The research team included the author, Janet Holland, Sheena McGrellis, Sue Sharpe and Sheila Henderson, and involved almost 2000 young people through a range of research methods including questionnaires, focus groups and 1:1 interviews.
2. See J. Finch and J. Mason, *Negotiating family responsibilities*, Routledge, London 1993.
3. P. Heelas, *The new age movement*, Blackwell, Oxford 1996.
4. N. Rose (1996) 'Authority and the genealogy of subjectivity', in P. Heelas, S. Lash and P. Morris, *Detraditionalisation*, Blackwell, Oxford 1996.

LIVING WITH DEATH

Brian Heaphy

DEATH AND DESKILLING

Dying is one of the few certainties that we face in living, and yet in modern societies there is a poverty of cultural responses to death and a lack of resources for facing it. The fact that we die cannot easily be lived *with*, so we attempt to put it aside until we have no choice but to confront it – a task that falls to the individual and that is carried out in loneliness and isolation. That we do not know 'how to be' in the face of death exemplifies the notion that modernity has led to an emotional impoverishment with regard to core life issues. As Bauman has put it, death indicates a 'collective deskilling'.[1]

This deskilling appears in various guises, and underlies an array of theoretical narratives concerning the problem of dying.[2] These suggest that the experience of dying has become individualised in Western worlds and is now a private problem. Ever-increasing secularisation has had profound implications for our lack of shared understandings in life and death. With the loss of the sacred, and the decline of stable communities, we have been deprived of collective meanings. We have been left alone to construct values in our lives. There is a void that individuals attempt to address through the constant endeavour to maintain or create a coherent and stable sense of who we are. Lacking a more stable focal point, we increasingly centre our concern around our own bodies.

These dynamics make death and dying particularly disturbing for those who encounter it at close hand. This can help to explain the crises that individuals experience in facing the decline of their own bodies. It can also account for the reluctance of the living to come into contact with the dying, and the uneasiness they experience in doing so. In their interactions with each other, both 'the living' *and* 'the dying' have difficulty in knowing how to behave towards each other. As both have limited resources for managing the situation, the search for an appropriate way of being in this situation 'falls back on the individual'.[3] This, in part, informs the modern impulse to hide death and silence the dying.

As we have no answer to it, death threatens to overwhelm us. We hide it from view to protect our sense of self and to maintain a degree of normality and security. The hiding of death entails the allocation of appropriate places for the dying to exist (the clinic, the hospital, and therapists' consultation rooms), and the identification of authorities and experts who represent -or tell the story of – the 'realities' of the dying, and speak on their behalf. In the end, both the *inappropriate existence* and the *inappropriate voices* of the dying are experienced as highly problematic by 'the living'. The presence of these in everyday life is threatening to the sense of reality – of 'the way it is'- that the living operate with.

The crisis of death raises issues of relevance to us all. It has, however, particular implications for those who are 'chronically' or 'terminally' ill, and for the increasing number of the outwardly 'healthy' who have been identified as being at risk of death. Developments in medical technology have made it possible to identify many hidden causes of death, and offer longer dying trajectories. This implies that many individuals, like those living with HIV and AIDS, are now allocated more time to contemplate their own deaths. Faced with life threatening illness – or with the acute risk of serious illness – many individuals have little choice but to attempt to incorporate an acute awareness of their own mortality *into* everyday life.

This can, in part, explain the rise of the personal – or confessional – narrative of living in the face of death. Published autobiographies, documentaries, newspaper columns and the like increasingly introduce us to the story of 'living in the shadow of death'. In light of the limited resources available for making sense of their own demise, it appears that the authors of these are compelled to give their lives and deaths meaning through achieving celebrity. While the deskilling thesis suggests that death is silent and invisible in the operation of *everyday* life, constructing and listening to narratives of close encounters with death is emerging as a new cultural preoccupation. These narratives have much to say to us about resources for managing our living and dying. In 1993 and 1994 I conducted a study of AIDS and everyday living. The following account of one research participant, Georgina

Blake, indicates that the question of resources for living with death is a far more complex one than many versions of the deskilling thesis suggest. Personal narratives of living with death also have insights that can help in our living now *with* contingency and uncertainty.

CLOSE ENCOUNTER WITH DEATH

Georgina Blake was introduced to the acute risk of her own death at the age of twenty-six. Hers is a story of shock and crisis that began with receiving an HIV positive diagnosis as a blood donor. A key factor in shaping the impact of the diagnosis was the extent to which she had understood it to be inconsistent with 'who she was'. Georgina had assumed AIDS to be related to illicit drug use, promiscuous sexual behaviour, and particularly male homosexuality. How could 'the impossible' have happened?

> I had asked for a test in 1987, because I knew I had the herpes virus ...
> And the consultant ... said to me 'Have you ever used drugs?' 'No.'
> 'Have you ever had a bisexual partner?' 'No.' 'Or partner who's ever
> used drugs?' 'No.' 'Well there's *no way* you could be HIV positive' ... So
> I gave blood thinking that there was not a chance in the world that I
> needed to worry about HIV... As far as they and I were concerned I
> wasn't a person who was likely to test positive.

Her diagnosis required considerable reflection on the nature of her partner's (hetero)sexuality, on the extent to which 'normal' sexual lives are risky, and on popular and expert 'truths' about AIDS. It presented a challenge to her sense of who she was – particularly as it problematised the extent to which she could continue to see herself as a 'normal' woman. Popular responses to AIDS have been shaped by the ways in which it has been tied to 'deviant' sexualities and identities. The impulse to locate and blame others is indicative of the acute fear of agents of death in cultures that have been deskilled in relation to death.[4] AIDS challenged narratives of medico-scientific mastery, and the panic responses to it were ultimately about the crisis of mortality. Until very recently AIDS has conjured up the possibility of untreatable and uncontrollable illnesses associated with certain death. As such it has had the potential to bring home the contingent nature of everyday life in a particularly powerful way.

Georgina had witnessed the media panics around AIDS in the mid to late 1980s, and was only too aware of its 'terrible' implications.

Diagnosis introduced the very *real* possibility of her own death which became the background against which she has had to live her life, a situation that was initially experienced as 'a living hell'. In time, however, this gave way to an attempt to make sense of the situation, and to impose order: 'I tried everything ... I was frantically trying to keep control'. She developed survival strategies in an endeavour to prolong her life, seeking out resources to get a sense of *how* it might be possible to live.

MEDICAL KNOWLEDGE

Conventional wisdom identifies death as a medical problem, and medical knowledge is deemed the appropriate location of hope in the face of the threat it represents. However, as AIDS is one of an increasing number of conditions for which there is no final solution, Georgina was to encounter a humbled medical science. Knowledge within the clinic confirmed that what was ultimately at stake was the demise of her body: 'the only question I asked [the doctor] was the only question I cared about, which was "Am I going to die?" And then his answer to that was "Yes, most people do".'

While drug trials and medical intervention were presented as holding out some vague possibility of hope in the future, the AIDS clinic could not provide a long-term solution. It did however offer the possibility of prolonging life in the short term and the opportunity to do *something* in the form of experimental treatments. In doing so, it offered Georgina a particular way of understanding her situation and of seeing herself:

> [the doctor] told me that I should start AZT straight away. This was too much to take ... And he actually said to me 'Georgina if you don't take AZT you will get sick'. And I took AZT. It made me extremely ill almost immediately. So I went from being really well to getting this diagnosis, to being ill. And then started identifying myself as an ill person as well.

Due to the role allocated to medical knowledge for managing and controlling the problem of death, there is considerable potential for the medicalisation of people's lives at times of bodily crises. There are also, however, dynamics that can work to counter this possibility: not least the degree to which there are now a diversity of authorities that can provide resources on 'medical' issues. Georgina was to discover that her condition is the focus of a multiplicity of knowledges that claim to have access to the truth of the situation, and suggest appropriate ways of being in the face of it. These included 'complementary' and 'alternative' medicines, which offered a considerable sense of empowerment:

> I think the first thing is that you maintain some amount of control over it. You don't become a patient which is always so much work with the medical profession. And also it's usually something that's very holistic and that actually takes into account who you are and how you feel. And that's really empowering because you think 'I *can* do something about it'.

Through engaging with alternative AIDS knowledge, carrying out her own research, and in meeting others living with HIV, Georgina recognised that the illnesses she had developed were likely to be related to the prescribed course of treatment. In light of this she made her own decision to discontinue treatment: 'And, I stopped. And I just felt, within two days, I had all my energy back and I didn't feel ill any more ... And I haven't taken it for the last three years and I'm still fine.'

Georgina's experience illustrates the expanding choices that are open to the increasingly active agent.[5] It is also indicative of the degree to which death is being put back into the hands of the dying themselves - who must now weigh up the various options on offer and choose their own survival strategies. To survive they must create their own path from a wide diversity of choices available. Increased choice, however, intensifies the responsibilities that the individual carries. In light of the life and death decisions at stake, it can be a considerable burden to bear. This can be compounded by the degree to which the lack of meaning can make the task of living in the shadow of death a difficult one. As Georgina put it, 'Sometimes I wish that I was able to find some kind of spiritual meaning because it becomes hard when you don't.'

THERAPY

While a 'hybrid' strategy of medical and alternative medical resources offered Georgina the *possibility* of some control over the bodily crises that she experienced, they could not provide the solution to the emotional crisis that living with the risk of death precipitated. While they offered the possibility of more time to live, they did not provide satisfactory answers for *how* to live. Therapy provided Georgina with a particularly valuable expertise: 'I really felt that that was the best thing that I could do for my health. And I'd have to say it's the thing that has helped me, supported me probably more than anything else'. Therapy provided the opportunity for dealing with the crises attached to living with an acute awareness of the inevitability of death, and the place to encounter the problem of dying face to face. For Georgina its value is related to the extent that it enables the dilemmas attached to AIDS to be 'kept in place'. Therapy allowed her to challenge the notion that the possibility of death should be the central focus *in* everyday life. This allowed for some planning and living 'as if' she were not faced with questions of illness and death: 'It's all very well doing all the work in the room, but you need to be able to translate it to your other relationships and also translate it in a way which you can keep control of ... we've worked on strategies quite a lot over the years.'

Initially, therapy introduced the possibility of survival and 'going on'. Over time it provided the skills that could be employed in managing the emotional labour that the close encounter with death required. In doing so it provided a more dynamic sense of the possibilities of living. However, a key tension arose in relation to the role and function of therapy. While it provided a sense of the possibility of managing the dilemmas of illness and death, and of emotional control in the face of terrifying questions, it could only offer a temporary solution. Therapy could not erase the problems associated with AIDS:

> I had a real crisis in my third year ... I'd had enough. I thought 'Well, I've done that now. I've done living with HIV now and haven't I coped well?' And it's like 'I don't want to do it any more ...' [Laughs]. And at that point I went up to twice a week [in therapy] because I just ... didn't know whether I was going to be able to hold on to my life and I felt very depressed and I felt quite suicidal as well.

While the turn to therapy can be understood as the need for a 'methodology of life planning',[6] it is also symptomatic of our individualised culture. It can be depoliticising because it reaffirms that death is primarily a problem for the individual, and risks encouraging an emotional separation between 'the dying' and their networks and communities. This in turn implies that everyday interactions can remain free of the problem of death. Ultimately therapy fails the dying to the degree that it conceptualises death as an individual problem.

Therapy cannot provide the 'solution' or 'resolution' to the problem of living with death. Once its inevitability has been sharply introduced, the reality of death can not be simply put aside. For individuals like

Georgina the fragile nature of the body is always waiting to return. Hence, living with an acute sense of the risk of death can involve a sense of 'constantly waiting for something to happen'. Living as if the 'real' or 'certain' possibility of death has not been introduced into life can not be wholly effective. Irrespective of the choices that can be made, the final recourse is in the hope of the total solution:

> I wish they'd get some treatments together. Because I feel I'm doing it all on my own at the moment ... pretty much on my own. I have a badge which I found which says 'Fuck the red ribbons, find a cure'.

Doing it on my own implies constructing one's own path and being *the* expert and this is a labour intensive and lonely task. It is compounded by the burdens and intensity of the choices that are being made, and the insecurities that come with following one path and not another. The therapist can guide, but ultimately it is the individual who must decide. Georgina's narrative of her engagement with expert resources is in keeping with the notion that life and death are now purely personal dilemmas. However, this is not the whole story.

SELF-HELP

'Doing it on my own' forms part of a more complex account of how Georgina has approached her situation. She has also emphasised the importance she placed in meeting other women who shared her situation. This was a key concern immediately following diagnosis: 'I knew that's what I wanted. I wanted to meet other women with HIV'. Encountering others who shared her predicament gave her a sense that she was not 'the only person on the planet that this was happening to'. She became actively involved in self-help endeavours: 'It was the best thing I ever did ... that's where I got educated. Where I *learnt* about what it all meant ... how to cope with doctors and what complementary therapies people had tried ... and what emotional strategies people use to cope.'

Like therapy, self-help groups can be a 'lifeline' in times of crisis. They provided Georgina with sympathetic others who shared her experience – necessitated by day to day living with AIDS – of engaging in experiments. This, in turn, offered her the possibility of learning more about the shared situation, and provided insights into 'the tricks of the trade' regarding medication, possible treatments, benefits and so on. Self-help groups are the meeting place for *individual* and *collective* experience and knowledge. As such they offer the opportunity for the *generation* of collective resources, and the *production* of new critical meanings. For Georgina self-help was a route to membership of a political or critical community, and to an involvement in overtly political activities. It was also a route to more life-political activities, which were influenced by the ethic that 'the personal is political'.

The self-help endeavour has been critiqued in much the same way as therapy. It has often been characterised as a purely therapeutic encounter – as 'groups of lonely and isolated people coming together'. It has also been understood as running the same risk of individualising and depoliticising through separating the individual from their networks and communities. Like therapy, self-help groups emphasise expression and talk. Both can allow for the development of reflexive capabilities – but the latter does so within a collective and often critical context. Self-help assumes a concern for the self, but within the context of a shared concern for a collective problem.

RELATING

The notion of 'a shared concern' and the value of 'working it out together' are themes that also arise in Georgina's account of everyday relationships with her family, partner and friends. One of the losses outlined in the emotional deskilling thesis is that of no longer knowing how to manage talk about death; and this opens up the possibility of an emotional separation between the dying and the living. This issue arose most acutely for Georgina in relation to disclosure about the day-to-day dilemmas encountered in living with AIDS. The desire to limit the burden of the tragedy can make silence a preferable option, as can the considerable emotional labour that is required in managing talk about the situation:

> I think my sisters and I have got loads closer ... obviously we all thought 'Hey, we haven't got an indefinite amount of time' ... You take a little bit more time to pay attention to this other human being that you've spent the last twenty years growing up with ... So I think it's drawn us together in a big way ... [But] I still find it hard to burden them too much.

Tensions exist that can introduce uneasiness into relationships: between overestimating and underestimating the 'burdens' that are being carried; between caring for and patronising each other; between being supportive and being invasive; between reciprocity and dependence. These tensions often concern not knowing 'what to do' and 'what to say'. On the surface they suggest that Georgina and her significant others do not have an appropriate way of being in the face of the personal 'tragedy'. However, she places considerable emphasis on the degree to which it has been possible to work out new ways of being over time:

> I like to think that I have that responsibility [to support] family members. Because again, I think that didn't happen. I wasn't really expected to support anybody and it can make you an emotional tyrant. You get very used to getting what you want all the time and people not wanting to cause you stress or burden you with any of their problems. And in the end I actually started feeling isolated by that and ... also thinking 'I'm still, I should still, and I want to still, be a person that can support other people as well'.

The longer dying trajectories on offer to individuals like Georgina provide time to negotiate mutually satisfactory ways of interacting and relating in light of the crisis. There are, of course, limits to negotiation, but in Georgina's narrative the ethic of reciprocity is the central ethic at play. Where this was deemed impossible, particular relationships were discontinued: 'I think that relationship was quite *obsessed* with HIV and *obsessed* with the fact that I was, you know, "I was dying". It all got a bit too much ... I think it fed into his need to be a carer.'

Intimate relationships with partners, family and friends are key resources that inform Georgina's sense of how she can be. The challenge is to imagine and negotiate ways of living with others that can allow an incorporation of the 'realities' of AIDS and death, but that can allow for mutuality and independence. This is a labour intensive task, but for Georgina it is one that is worth it. Ultimately it is these relationships that provide a sense of having a life worth living. Death itself may remain unknowable: 'I still try and find my meaning in ... earthly terms ... I don't feel I have any idea what it means to be dead.' But living with the threat of death has given a sharper sense of value in life, and accentuated the value of particular relationships:

> I want much more continuity in my life than I ever wanted before. I want a lot more security. I want all my friends to stay friends with each other. I don't want anything to change. I can't really do anything about that. I was a person who could pack everything in a bag and leave people behind – no problem, and I'm not that person any more.

172

DEATH AND RESKILLING

What does this narrative of the close encounter with death say to us and about us? Georgina Blake's account of living with an acute aware-ness of her own mortality highlights the lack of given meanings in the face of the ultimate life challenge. It is, in many ways, consistent with the collective deskilling thesis outlined at the beginning of this chapter. Her situation is indicative of the crises that close encounters with death can facilitate for the individual. These are related to – and accentuate – a lack of resources for incorporating the inevitability of death *into* everyday life. They indicate that we do not have easy access to an appropriate way of being in the face of death.

But Georgina's account is also one of *reskilling* – where various resources are sought out in the development of survival strategies. It is, in this respect, indicative of the complexity of flows of power in contemporary societies – where various possibilities exist for impover-ishment *and* empowerment. The diversity of resources that can be accessed in reskilling implies a significant degree of individual agency. It also implies that individuals like Georgina are faced with the task of piecing together a survival strategy of choice. This can offer the promise of order in the face of crisis, but the understandings allowed for by this pick-and-mix approach can be fragile ones. While the indi-vidual is provided with a sense that they have been empowered to act, they are not provided with *the* answers: a final solution to the problem of death; or the stability in the face of death offered by given shared meanings.

Viewed from the perspective of Georgina's narrative, the deskilling thesis has considerable explanatory value. It must, however, also be understood in the broader context of contemporary concerns with the decline of old securities and the problem of living with contingency. In its various forms the deskilling thesis deploys the problem of dying as the example *par excellence* of living with loss: be it the loss of belief in the sacred, faith in meta-narratives, or the ability to maintain and construct stable (and usually narrowly defined) communities. The thesis is not, therefore, merely an account of 'how it is'. In itself it is indicative of the anxieties that come with radical social change: anxi-eties about losing control. The solutions offered are varied, but visions of mythical pasts and utopian futures are often evoked – where stabil-ity and security are the defining features of a culture, and 'order' is the name of the day.

It is against the backdrop of these concerns that we should understand the frequent recurrence of images of atomised and lonely individuals in discussions of the predicament of the dying. In this scenario individuals are caught up in circumstances over which they have no control. They face key life decisions alone and are powerless in the face of their inevitable fates. But I would suggest that emerging narratives of encounters with death can conjure up a very different image of individual *and* collective creativity in the face of the unknown. While Georgina's narrative indicates that total solutions are an attractive option at times of crisis, it also suggests the possibility of working out with others 'ways of being' in the face of radical insecurities. On the one hand it indicates that the crumbling of old securities can be productive of an intense self-concern. On the other hand it also suggests that significant opportunities can exist for the formation of new solidarities, and the consolidation of existing ones. These solidarities can provide the context for the construction of new meaning and value through the project of living *with* contingency. They can also provide the context for being transformed through it.

Encounters with death can be productive of crises for our understandings of how things are, and who we are. But they also highlight the question of how we can be and who we can be. The quest for security and stability may encourage us to put the problem of death aside, but it is one that will not disappear. As narratives like Georgina's indicate, far from 'killing death',[7] medical technologies are bringing the issue of death home to individuals in new and acute ways – and providing more time to live with the knowledge of approaching death. It is conceivable, if not likely, that the problem of living *with* this most radical of contingencies will become a more commonly shared experience. There is no cure for this contingency. The resources required, therefore, must address the question of how we can live with knowledge of this fact.

The increasing popularity of the narrative of the close encounter with death can be understood as a response to collective deskilling – as final and desperate attempts to have lives validated. There is, however, another way of making sense of this popularity. Crisis moments, Bourdieu has suggested, can facilitate the development of new knowledge and bring the 'undiscussed into discussion, the unformulated into formulation'.[8] From this perspective, the realisation that we do not know how to live *with* death is encouraging us to tell and listen to personal narratives of dying. Stories, Plummer argues, gather people around them and attract new audiences who in turn tell their stories.[9]

As such, personal stories have a key role to play in the kind of culture building that making new lives requires. In telling their stories – in private and in public – individuals and collectives are generating resources for making sense of living and dying now. In listening to these we can understand that it is possible to live *with* radical contingency – and to be transformed through it.

NOTES

1. Z. Bauman, *Mortality, Immortality and Other Life Strategies*, Polity, Cambridge 1992.
2. See D. Clark (ed), *The Sociology of Death: theory, culture, practice*, Blackwell, Oxford 1994; P. A. Mellor and C. Shilling, 'Modernity, Self-Identity and the Sequestration of Death', *Sociology* 27 (3), 1993.
3. N. Elias, *The Loneliness of Dying*, Blackwell, Oxford 1985.
4. See J. Weeks, *Invented Moralities: Sexual Values in an Age of Uncertainty*, Polity, Cambridge 1995.
5. See U. Beck, A. Giddens and S. Lash, *Reflexive Modernization: Politics, Tradition and Aesthetics in the Modern Social Order*, Polity, Cambridge 1994.
6. See A. Giddens *Modernity and Self-identity*, Polity, Cambridge 1991.
7. Bauman 1992 *op. cit.*
8. P. Bourdieu, *Outline of a Theory of Practice*, Cambridge University Press, Cambridge 1977.
9. K. Plummer, *Telling Sexual Stories: Power, Change and Social Worlds*, Routledge, London 1995.

April Morning Walk

So many of those girls I loved are gone now,
Gone to ash that skin so inexpertly kissed,
Those stomachs I was hot for, gone beyond diaries into flame.
When the years tore up our surface beauty and threw it away
Like the bright wrappings on a parcel
What was left was what links all the breathing world, an empathy,
The buried knowledge of our going.
It's so easy to forget how the years have poured away
And taken out of sequence and before their time
So many who deserved to stay longer on this lush earth.
Along the streets in which I walked with them
The horse chestnut leaves are opening like Chinese fans
The dawn's clear light varnishes houses and gardens
And freezes forever under its glittering surface
So much half remembered anguish.

Brian Patten

The Armada

Long long ago
when everything I was told was believable
and the little I knew
less limited than now,
I stretched belly down on the grass beside a pond
and to the far bank launched
a child's armada.
A broken fortress of twigs,
the paper tissue sails of galleons,
the waterlogged branches of submarines –
all came to ruin and were on flame
in that dusk-red pond.
And you, mother, stood behind me,
impatient to be going,
old at twenty-four, single,
thin overcoat flapping.
How close the past sticks to us.
In a hospital a mile or so from that pond
I kneel beside your bed and closing my eyes,
reach out across forty years to touch once more
that pond's cool surface,
and it is your cool skin I'm touching;
for as on a pond a child's paper boat
was blown out of reach
by the smallest gust of wind,
so too have you been blown out of reach
by the smallest whisper of death,
and a childhood memory is sharpened,
and the heart burns as that armada burnt,
long, long ago.

Brian Patten

I have thought that I thought of death, but in fact I don't know how one must think of death. Death is probably very hard, as hard as life, but the life is something you live piece by piece, but you die once and for all ... Once and for all you have to tear away all the lived life – seven, seventeen, seventy, and if someone is very strong, eighty years – and to let them fall into an abyss, into the void. A tiny pale bodyless soulless somebody lingers for a moment on the rim of the abyss. It is the one who has thrown away its life, it would be better to say it has let it loose. Seen from the other side, life is death, life and death are one and the same thing. Life is something you must keep and guard all the time as a rat in a cage. Because it is so hard to think of death, I prefer to think of the currants, black, red and white currants which are so ripe that they fall when you touch the bush.

Jaan Kaplinski

My poems are often not poems; they are parts of a long declaration of love to the world, a long poetic list of people and things I love. When I was young I was fond of my thoughts, my feelings, my despair, my longing and joy. I came to this world like a hot air balloon, a big and multi-coloured balloon that covered everything up. With the years the balloon has cooled down, shrunk, and I see more and more of other things, I see what simply is. This what simply is has always seemed odd to me. Sometimes I feel this oddity as elevated, sometimes it's simply funny. This feeling of oddity has not disappeared, it's probably deeper and more self-conscious than ever. The wall clock was made in Valga in the year 1902, and is still going quite well. It could even strike, if I had a chain for the other weight. But I don't believe I could get accustomed to a wall clock that strikes hours. Now it's showing 11. It's December 31st, 1992. As many times before, I am writing something in the last hour of the year. I'm not sure I would like to call it a poem. It doesn't take much time, and the emotional atmosphere of the last hour of the year suits writing well. And the ticktock of the old clock suits this atmosphere well too. I think that maybe this way the dead clockmaker from Valga sends his greetings to me and my family. I can't do the same for him.

Jaan Kaplinski

Gooseberries

Birds are chirping now rain has stopped, their songs
like the rain are silver. I hear the silence,
the music of panic, of loneliness.
Rain passes like unhappiness and birds
sing happily out of the same dull silver.
It is all the silvers of cloud and cold,
the white shine of illness. A friend lies dying
in hospital. The night I saw her there
we watched fireworks from her window, her window
filled with photos and dried flowers for real
flowers are infectious, fireworks at Christmas.
When two times meet, another friend says, stories
must end – by which he means, when day meets dusk,
the page must be marked, the book closed and children
while away their questions. I heard a story
of a child who, it was foretold, would die
when the leaves began to fall; when they did,
a sister, brother, sewed the leaves back on
but how the story ended wasn't told –
besides, the dying do not want our questions.
Today I bought a card with berries, currants,
each translucent as a heart like a small
wineglass with veins, rivers, held against light
to plot their directions. Each tiny coloured
globe marbled, jewelled. Produce of a garden.
The flurry of birdsong behind the curtain
has gone. Now and then the trill of a latecomer.
Every morning I wake alone. Today
I find the balm and bitterness. The sweetness
of pulp, pop of a taut skin, gooseberries
a friend on the phone tells me a hen used to
lay eggs under, two eggs you'd have to slide
on your belly to reach so prickly was
the bush, with hairs sun shone through on the berries

fine as the hairs on the back of a child's hand.
Twice a day two times meet. Between the two,
like a prayer between two palms, the book mark,
the memory, is placed. When day meets night,
night meets day, we must hold our breath, delay
our need for answers, live with what comes next.

Mimi Khalvati

Middle Age

There are those who are radiant addressing
death in cornflower blues and violets.
There are roofs I look on tenderly
purveying slopes to large shapes of suns
submissively as cows to the sky's gait.
I protect myself from happiness, rooting
into the search for it, mourning its youth
though it's the lesser courage that admits
to unhappiness, to gladness, the greater.
What did we vow we'd be in middle age? –
young of course. Immortal. Immune to swollen
ankles, arteries, summoning the powers
only gods command, protean, promethean.
Knowing we'd die but not knowing how tired
we'd get, even of loving, how we'd fear
emotion. No-one tells us. How we'd get
our second wind from death and even then
only those who are charmed, transformed by grace
we think a miracle – who knows what strength
it takes, who only sees those blue eyes bluer,
who only sees apparel. No one tells us
about middle age. Forget teeth, sight, hearing,
what about the heart? You'd think it a dumb
organ, stones in its well, a clobbered clock
not knowing moments from minutes, stone itself.
I tell my heart to move, it doesn't. Look
I say, what do you like out there, tail feathers?

181

It looks but it doesn't see, sees but can't name.
It's middle-aged. I think of Keats and wonder
how one so young could feel it rich to die
till I remember illness, pain. And though
here I am moaning, knowing pain will pass,
from where I am I catch the drift of it –
a wind that blows the other way. Or rather,
doesn't blow but being ever more easeful,
guides us into the shallows of its breath.

Mimi Khalvati

Youthing

It's like the process of aging.
Just a process.
Your hair starts to grow wilder,
your skin gets smoother,
your appetites increase.
Suddenly you sing in the shower and in the rain;
you discover a plant you've never seen before
and you munch it.
What's that tiny scar on your left temple?
Maybe a bird scratched it with tender claws
to prod you into flying.
And then, that dialogue with the moon
that keeps you awake,
and then, that dream of death
becomes more and more remote
– or is it the other way around?

Nina Cassian

BEING ALIVE

Interview with Adam Phillips

Adam Phillips is a practising psychoanalyst and the author of a number of best selling critically acclaimed books which include *Terrors and Experts* and *The Beast in the Nursery*. In recent years his essays on such everyday experiences as kissing, boredom, hinting, monogamy and childhood have breathed new life into debates around psychoanalysis and its relationship to literature and culture. 'In psychoanalysis', he has written, 'the opposite of ignorance is not so much knowledge (and therefore virtue) but desire (and therefore something unpredictable and morally equivocal).' His approach challenges normative explanations of human nature. We are, according to Phillips, unpredictable creatures. Life is unsettling and uncertain and the function of psychoanalysis is not to furnish us with answers to life's predicaments, but to help us live our own lives, and to find pleasure in being with ourselves. 'The psychoanalysis that I value shows how we're always fast forwarding our lives as a way of not being present in them. How it's extremely difficult not to live in the future tense, not to live aspiringly.' He is interviewed here by Jonathan Rutherford.

I'm intrigued about how you write about a sense of aliveness. I have in mind the psychoanalyst D.W Winnicott's paean to life 'Oh God may I be alive when I die'.

I think the experience of aliveness is an ordinary experience. It is, nevertheless, sometimes difficult to articulate it. One is aware that when one is doing something that one finds genuinely pleasurable or intriguing, that really engages one's curiosity or passion, or something which one becomes absorbed in – or indeed when one is with people that one loves, or desires or likes – there is a different quality to one's sense of oneself. One of the causes is that one forgets oneself, one loses a certain amount of self consciousness. In such situations or experiences questions like 'Is my life worth living?' or 'Do I love my life?' disappear because they are, in a way, answered by the experience. They don't require a justification. One might be able to tell a story afterwards about what it was about that situation or being with that person that was so pleasurable. By pleasurable I mean what enables you to be a version of yourself that you like or enjoy.

In your book The Beast in the Nursery *you describe the child as having an astonishing capacity for pleasure. A wanting, wishing, daydreaming child, able to employ curiosity and a primitive form of ruthlessness in pursuit of desire and self knowledge.*

It does look as though children's capacity for pleasure, interest and curiosity is considerable. It verges on the ecstatic. And it also seems to me to be true that experiences of pleasure are, in their own way, as much of a problem internally as experiences of pain. I think there are experiences of pleasure in childhood that are of an intensity that threatens to undo or undermine what feels like the hard-earned character structures that we evolve in growing up. Plus, there are internal prohibitions. I think that the paradox of some of these prohibitions is that they are unconsciously a relief, because they temper an instinct for ecstasy which the child begins to be troubled by. Clearly the child is asking of the adult that they contain his or her experiences and where necessary make them intelligible. But of course there is a limit to intelligibility. If we'd been having this conversation in the eighteenth century we might have been talking about the sublime. I think there is a quotidian sublime experienced in childhood, and that becomes more and more troubling, partly because it becomes so difficult to articulate and to justify, partly because it verges on the forbidden and transgressive.

You make the statement that to know what a cure is the doctor must know what a life is supposed to be like. What is it that psychoanalysis is attempting to do?

I think in psychoanalysis there has been a medicalisation of questions which from my point of view are moral or political. It is as though there is a state of nature that we can be returned to; or, paradoxically, that we are machines, and that they can go wrong and they can be fixed. In other words we already know our normal state, and therefore we can spot deviations. Clearly this is useful as a guideline, because every culture must have a category of the acceptable and the unacceptable. But our analogies for talking about these things are excessively punitive or militaristic. That is one side of the coin.

The other side of the coin is that we become preoccupied by a version of instrumental reason. Psychoanalysis becomes a means towards an end which is already known. Whereas I think that one of the things psychoanalysis does at its best is deconstruct precisely that way of constructing one's life. The psychoanalysis that I value shows how we're always fast-forwarding our lives as a way of not being present in them. How it's extremely difficult not to live in the future tense, not to live aspiringly. Now it's not that there can be pure unmediated presentness, but there can be degrees of being present at the event, which I think everyone is able to experience. One is more or less able to be there wholeheartedly – well half-wholeheartedly – feeling what one happens to be feeling in the presence of another person or a work of art or whatever it might be. Psychoanalysis, for me, is much more about showing people how they're using the ends to protect themselves from the means. And how the whole language of means and ends over-constricts experiences.

Lacan is very interesting about the notion that we are tyrannised and persecuted by our fantasies about the pleasure other people are having. One way of construing this is to say that there is projection into other people of the pleasure we fear and dread and of course long for. So I think that a lot of people in this culture live with a parallel text going on in themselves about those other people who are having a better time. This is another way of not being present to oneself. It is also a projection of a pleasurable self which is troubling. It seems to me that Klein's theory of envy is rather naive about this – naive and too knowing at the same time. Envy seems to me to be partly motivated by the notion of pleasure elsewhere – as in the primal scene fantasy. But it is also a projection of the pleasure which is ours but which for some reason we cannot bear. Which isn't to say that we can all be ecstatic all of the time; but it is to say that we are capable of these experiences of pleasure that we would rather think of other people having – pleasure which we either daydream about in a semi-musing way, or enviously or contemptuously disparage.

I think this is related to concepts of cure. The line in *Endgame* is right. We're on earth. There is no cure for that. There is nothing to cure here. The risk is that cure becomes a secular version of redemption. It seems to me it's not a question of how to cure people; it's a question of discussing the kinds of lives they might want to live, and the obstacles they create to this, but also the obstacles to those lives which do exist, which they simply have to acknowledge.

What is the fear of pleasure?

I think there are at least two things here. It isn't only pleasure that we will be present to, it is the full force of one's emotional life, the complexity of it. I think there is a sense in which everybody is what is described loosely as oversensitive. There is a degree of vulnerability or receptivity that people are frightened of. It is as though we experience more than we can process, or metabolise or represent. When we are talking about the fear of pleasure we must talk about lots of things. One is the fear of simply being overwhelmed. I think these fantasies of being overwhelmed are partly connected to pictures of water. They are linked to an idea of the self as a fortress or an object which is forever defending itself against something else. As though – and this is Freud's account – the ego is adversarial, that we are intolerable to ourselves. There is always something to ward off. What I think there is to ward off is the repertoire, the array, and therefore the disarray, of one's emotional experience. It's something to do with intensity. And with having created character types that are extremely intolerant of any emotional intensity. Emotional intensity doesn't only mean ecstasy; it must also mean experiences of hatred and of loss. Perhaps above all of emotional complexity. I think there is always an attempt to oversimplify the moral life. When we are talking about love and hate, there is a sense of relief that we have created a consensus in which the conversation is intelligible. The problem with emotional life is that it doesn't come morally prepackaged.

If pleasure is about being with oneself, it also means, as Winnicott has described it, the capacity to be with oneself in the presence of another. This is at the core of people's relationships and is what makes them so difficult

Yes. The experience of pleasure and the experience of receptivity is a very communal experience. So much work goes into warding off other people and asserting boundaries because there is an internal perception that these boundaries are fictions, defensive fictions. I don't think there is a longing for unity with others, but there is definitely a longing for an experience of community with others. We live in a political system that terrorises us with the knowledge that we are all in the same boat. We are all in the same boat. It's as though that is the trauma that is always being dealt with and expelled in this scapegoating, this creating of the state of them and us.

I think it's amazing how much pleasure people can give each other. And of course how much pain they can give.

What you're saying makes me think how central the family is to people's lives, because it is here that we learn this experience of being with others. The parents are such significant figures. The history of English Romanticism, which much of your writing alludes to, is focused on the symbolic figure of the child. But it seems to me that one of the crises in today's society is the nature of adulthood and parenthood.

One of the interesting things about Romanticism is that it's not child-hood that suddenly becomes interesting or which emerges. It is the adult's experience of the child. And what being with children does to the grown ups becomes a new object of interest. David Cooper, who is now forgotten, partly for good reasons, said in one of his books that we need fewer mothers and fathers and more mothering and fathering. I don't think we need fewer mothers and fathers, but I do think we need more mothering and fathering. The family is integral – not neces-sarily the institutional nuclear family, but the biological fact that every child has two parents, and that no child can bring itself up alone. There is a fundamental constitutive experience of being dependent and being left out. I can't imagine lives in which these are not issues.

One of the ways in which psychoanalysis has been disappointing has been in differentiating the adult from the child. What psychoanalysis needs to do is to try and work out persuasive versions of adulthood. Freud said adults are like children. But the analogy goes on. What are children like? You can construct this in all sorts of different ways. Winnicott, Bowlby, Melanie Klein and Anna Freud have all been telling us what children are like. But these are analogies. They are themselves products of desire. They're not natural facts. They're always subject to redescription. We can't go on redescribing childhood, without implicitly or explicitly redescribing adulthood. The problem of family life, and maybe this is a larger problem, is how one can go on being kind without it being at too much cost to one's vitality. Family life should be the place where kindness is learnt. I don't mean learnt as in beaten into children. I mean exemplified. For me the question is whether kindness can be learnt. Or what it means to think of kindness being learnt without it turning into another form of hypocrisy. We all know now the ironies attendant upon the whole-hearted promotion of virtue. It simply becomes a form of scapegoating. The problem of family life, which is simply the problem of living with others, is a much more interesting question than it too often seems when discussed in terms of political polarisation

In your book you quote Winnicott as saying that concern for others diminishes our own creativity and vitality. To be with oneself one must let go of concern for the other person which can leave us with fantasies of abandonment and death. I think that pleasure is tied up with this fear. To be kind we must overcome our own fear. Living in families and with others means confronting our fear.

I agree with you. I think people aren't bad, they're frightened. These two things get muddled up. We think we are frightened of our badness, whereas I think we're bad because we're frightened. The very nastiest things about us are not innate. It's more about how people internally deal with fear. And if you want to know about fear read Hobbes. You could say that all of literature is about fear. An awful lot of representations are about fear. But fear taken explicitly as a primary reaction to instinctual life, I think, is very important.

I think there are similarities between our culture today and that of the eighteenth century. Your work takes up the Enlightenment's initiation of self examination, the remembrance of the child we once were - the remembered sense of self – which has made memory central to the making of personal identity. When I think about the sublime in the eighteenth century I wonder – when people were writing about the Alps for example – if it was actually a childhood awe.

For me these eighteenth century and early nineteenth century writers are writing about experiences that seem now to be integrally related to childhood. Whether it's Wordsworth or Shelley in the Alps, or Blake in London, they're talking about experiences which threaten one's capacity for representation. They show us how identified we are with our capacities for representation. It's very difficult to separate out one's self from one's capacity to represent one's self . It's that point, at which something becomes articulable, in which there is the wish to make it known, that is very interesting.

The sublime raises the question of sociability. Is the sublime an isolating experience or a profoundly unifying experience? Not unifying me and the Alp – but unifying me and everybody else in the culture. The experience of the sublime is like a benign scapegoating; that Alp, that woman's body, that landscape, is not something I feel I can keep inside myself. What it invokes in me means I have to involve others. The problem isn't what I discover. It's that the consequences of my discovery entail connection with others.

This representing of being alive to others was also a gendered experience. The early feminism of Mary Wollstonecraft was her attempt to claim reason for women. In the way that men were looking to inner feeling, women were looking to get a hold of culture, reason and language .

I'm wary about making contemporary statements about the differences between men and women. Not because I don't think they exist but because I don't know where they are. And they seem to have a curiously prescriptive quality about them. I'm sure these are profoundly questions of gender. I don't feel able to speak up about them from that point of view.

How would you? Or would you not?

It feels to me that when I start talking about gender I start talking in clichés. I feel more than ever the ventriloquist's dummy of the culture. That in itself seems interesting. It's like a knot. It's become more and more evident as people have written and thought about the history of psychoanalysis that it was not the invention of a man or a group of men. It was a profoundly coupled experience. One could be glib about how these so called hysterics talked to Freud about psychoanalysis. It's also true. It took two of them. These are collaborative constructions.

189

There is no such thing as one sex. There is always two, and the description of those two sexes is always contentious, always subject to redescription. I prefer to use gender almost as allegory: these are the ways of dividing the emotional labour, the ways we can find of talking about things. Give one bit to the women and one bit to the men as ways of thinking about these things. That is what we should think we are doing; we should not think we are giving sensuous descriptions. They always feel like they're being too comforting or too oppressive.

When we talk about gender, the language available tends to position people, to be morally prescriptive about certain behaviours. Maybe we don't have a way of talking about it differently.

Yes – or to talk about it exposes us; it feels overexposing. It feels as if it inevitably makes us subject to certain kinds of criticism. It links us with our shames and guilts. That's why I'm surprised how easily people talk about the difference between the sexes. I'm not surprised they want to. But I'm surprised how much is written and said because the subject seems to be so recalcitrant.

This difference is being sharply played up by Neo-Darwinism, which has become a significant intellectual force in recent years. There seems to be this need to fix people in categories.

But I think what's worse, and linked to that, is the addiction to determinism. What flows from these theories is a determinism which is always waiting in the wings. Psychoanalysis has been poor in this respect. It's been very unwilling to talk about the nature of choice. That's why I think it's worth recycling existentialism. You can choose to go to bed but not to go to sleep. You can choose to make a pass at somebody, but you can't choose to fall in love with them. You can choose to vote but you can't choose to change the government. It's very important to discriminate where choice is a viable concept, rather than in some umbrella way assuming that there are no choices. That seems to be manifestly untrue. It's a counsel for political despair and political mystification. That's why I think that pragmatism is more inspiring. If one is looking for guidelines it's worth reading William James, Richard Rorty and C. S Peirce, as well as Freud or Darwin.

Your own literary interest in Romanticism has helped you rescue

Freudianism from didacticism, the pursuit of certainty and legislation and laws. It's returned us to a Jewish Freud, the tradition of interpreting the text, the strategy of reading against the grain, the use of aphorism, the answering a question with another question, the refusal ever to close a story. This unsticks the dark side of European romanticism from its desire for cloying certainties and absolutisms. However your rejection of determinism is a very frightening idea for many people. Psychoanalysis has always argued that identity can never be a certainty, or remain fixed. But you seem to take this further by saying this about life itself.

I think there is a confusion of realms. Identity is useful to do certain things with. It's useful to have an identity when you vote. I don't think it's useful to have a sense of identity when one falls in love, or when one walks down the street. Our lives are passing through us and we are passing through them. Yeats commented that civilisation is the struggle to keep control. I think the language of control is misleading. We treat ourselves as though we need a certain kind of discipline. As though discipline is the thing. That entails strange pictures of what we are like and who we are. It's sensible to say that instinctual life, or biological life, is mad. Not in a glamorised sense. By mad I mean something akin to sublime. It is in excess of our capacity to make sense of, and often to bear, our life. This doesn't mean we are suffering from original sin, or that we can't make better lives for ourselves. It does mean that we haven't invented ourselves, but we are able to describe ourselves and we are able to change ourselves by redescribing ourselves. It's like looking at the language we use about ourselves. I can remember a psychoanalytic paper by Roy Schafer in which he argued that it's not that people are out of control, but they sometimes do forbidden things. I think that's a more interesting way of putting it.

If one accepts your version of what human life is, then it is our fate to be disappointed. And disillusioned. Not just in our desire, or for the love of our parents, but the fact that we're not going to get what we want. We're going to have to give something up.

Yes. That's for sure. But the risk here is that disappointment is its own orgy. Rather than being over impressed by disappointment or disillusionment – which is a fact of life – we should be learning to find ways to bear it. So that we don't turn cynical on ourselves. So we don't start believing that the world isn't good enough for us.

Won't some people have to bear it more than others?

Of course they will. That's why we should be politically active. And that's why psychoanalysis, if it's any good, should be more politically engaged. The reality of exploitation and injustice needs to be seen, and not dissolved into personal histories, or so called insight. This is part of us all being in the same boat. It's no good going on creating more and more refuges (and, clearly, wealth is major one) from seeing what people are doing to each other, or what the consequences of people's actions are. The risk of certain kinds of political activism is, first, that they defer a future for ever; and, second, that like psychoanalysis and certain left-wing politics, they have been unremittingly grim in their ethos. It isn't that we should all cheer up and recognise how wonderful everything is. But we shouldn't have to morally cheer down, and cultivate a vale-of-tears mentality. We should learn to bear disappointment, but we should also be inspired by it to change the world, and not to merely settle in.

Your writing, and such comments as 'There is no purpose to the child's life other than the pleasure of living', remind me of a particular strand of anarchism, particularly the libertarian educators A.S. Neill and Homer Lane. It's a politics and sensibility which isn't around much at the moment. You have been able to construct yourself as a literary figure, but in terms of making political connections.

It's very dismaying. I agree. There is that tradition of, say, Winstanley, Milton, that surfaces and resurfaces. E. P. Thompson has tracked this. Curiously I have learnt more about this tradition from reading Milton scholarship than from anywhere else. I'm both inspired by these ideas and dismayed by what you've just said. It's as though this stuff disappears – the Muggletonians, Blake – as though this is not an amazing cultural resource. It amazes me that British psychoanalysis hasn't been interested enough to link itself up with these subterranean histories which I feel are utopian in the best sense of the word.

Is this because of the intellectual traditions of English empiricism and utilitarianism? British psychoanalysis – object relations theory – has never entered the realms of the abstract in the way psychoanalysis has in France. You can't use it so easily to talk about culture, language, politics. Perhaps it's also the political traditions that have dominated the left. They leave us with little sense of hope in the future. May 1997 was a wonderful experience of emancipation, but I think people are now disappointed and have retreated back into the realm of private life.

It's very troubling that the disappointment produces a retreat. Everything which reinforces our belief in the private as the true or real realm is somehow a cheat. Almost everything in my education persuaded me to believe that the best version of oneself was either alone or in a couple or in a family. This is a very misleading picture because it's as though it foregrounds something which depends upon its background. We are very interdependent. All life is group life. Our fantasies of what privacy involves come from the group. There is nowhere else they can come from. Without being too knowing, it was inevitable that there would be disappointment about New Labour. Wonderful that there was hope, and no reason retrospectively to invalidate that hope – there's a risk that there's a retrospective spoiling, a retrospective envious attack on the hope, as though hope wasn't real. I think the hope was real and the disappointment is real, and the realist thing is the next stage; that people go on trying to make New Labour be what they wanted it to be.

English culture has limited itself by its insularity. Your work draws on a much more cosmopolitan literary tradition.

Certainly for me European writers such as Thomas Bernhard and Fernando Pessoa, and lots more, are important. Psychoanalysis doesn't make sense to me in isolation or as a specialisation. American literature first of all was a liberation for me. After Romanticism it was Emerson, Thoreau, Melville, William James and Whitman, and then American philosophers and literary critics, Poirier, Bloom, Cavell, Rorty. There is more vision. A greater willingness to be imaginatively speculative, to have a more exploitative relationship to tradition. I can't say there are fewer pieties in this literature, although I'd like to believe that. But there does seem to be more of life in their writing, more living lives as experiments. And that is what I want lives to be. I can't get this from psychoanalysis in isolation. It seems obvious to me that psychoanalysis is of a piece with the period in which it emerged, a contingent invention. And it goes on being that. Freud is a great writer first and foremost.

I think the question of interpretation is linked to this in a way. What psychoanalysts don't know is what you do in psychoanalysis if you don't interpret. Ferenczi was interesting about this and so was Winnicott. At the worst, unacceptable, end of the spectrum the answer is you have sex with your patients, you kiss them, you exploit them. What we haven't got is an equally persuasive account at the benign end of the spectrum. What can happen in analysis which would produce better lives for people if interpretation wasn't the thing? It doesn't mean you would never interpret, but interpretation would be just one of the things you did. By interpretation I mean reconstruction of history, symbolic decoding, redescription.

Your comments on American literature's pursuit of life remind me of your comments about the child's ruthless pursuit of desire. The ability to be oneself in the presence of others is founded upon knowing what it is one wants. It mitigates against compliance and being robbed of one's desire.

You ditch the fantasy of losing everything. You ditch the catastrophist's view. At an aesthetic level for me these Americans are interested in sentences. Good sentences make a good life. Good sentences amuse us, interest and intrigue us, and move the story on.

It's also a question of wanting to find different ways of being genuinely welcoming of, and curious about, and getting pleasure from, the idea that things can be said and done differently. I think there has been an amazing cultural conformism in Britain. An insularity that is almost taken pride in. This then becomes a picture in its own way of what a person is. A person is somebody who successfully wards off enough difference to sustain their wished for image of themselves.

A lot of people reading this will think of analysis as happening in a room; it's paid for, an artificial experience which really has nothing to do with culture and language.

I can see their point. I think psychoanalysis needs to be woken up to the way it can become merely another narcissistic refuge amongst so many others. But there is no outside to culture. Things that go on in a room – or indeed things that go on in the health service, where I used to work – are unpredictable in their consequences. Good things can come from unexpected places. You could overhear something in a bus stop, you could hear a piece of music, you could have a conversation in analysis. All sorts of experiences and objects are potentially transformational. One really doesn't know where things are going. That needs to be included in the language of the culture. Otherwise everything becomes a form of social engineering. It becomes a form of cause and effect. I don't think there is cause and effect. I think there is array and disarray. And there are reconfigurations of things.

I do think that your writing has helped to restore the idea of emancipation. I had thought that the enlightenment belief that human beings can be emancipated from their political and material conditions had gone – Lyotard's postmodern end of the grand narrative. Yet, as you infer, in analysis one can experience emancipation, a grasping for one's life – 'we come into analysis to reconstitute our solitude'. Which is ironic, because it is about coming to know oneself, rather than being released from something.

And that's why I like existentialist writers and the American transcendentalists because they are all interested in freedom. They do want more life. And that's a good thing to want.

Culture is the place where we will come up with new meanings and language and ethics – notions of goodness. In a secular society that is such an important idea. Religions have been the producers of social solidarity and virtue in the past, and we need to find secular alternatives.

I think we need to find ways of not being so impressed by wealth and success. Until we find persuasive accounts of this, everybody is going to feel they must organise their lives around these things, whether enviously, or self-righteously, or taking a moral high ground, or getting wholeheartedly rich and successful. Money and success, stories from which none of us can exempt ourselves, are soporifics, and exhilarations and opportunities. They are narcotics. We need alternative stories about what makes a life good. Not stories which say it is better to be poor, or better to fail. But stories which get us out of this whole language.

This returns us to your language in Beast in the Nursery, *in which a central analogy of a desiring, lived life is appetite – the imaginative*

195

hunger of curiosity. What makes you want to be a successful writer? To satisfy your appetite?

Yes. And why publish books? Why not write for one's friends?

Because it's about recognition.

Yes it is, but who does one want recognition from and what for? How big is the world and how much does one want?

The child's answer to that is everything.

But that everything is not as sophisticated in its reach in actuality. A child's everything is the family, the parents, their being available. It's very interesting what Freud said – 'Why is it that money doesn't make adults happy? Because no child has ever been interested in money.' There are of course, now, children interested in money. But babies aren't, young children aren't. I think there is a lot to think about there.

The pursuit of love and happiness is replacing God. Yet the paradox is that worrying about how to be happier or how you can feel more alive means you're not experiencing these states of being.

Yes, if you're doing that, you know you're not feeling alive.

Shopping around for a place to stay

Zygmunt Bauman

> Now here, you see, it takes all the running you can do to keep in
> the same place. If you want to get somewhere else, you must run
> at least twice as fast as that!
>
> Lewis Carroll

It is hard to remember, and harder yet to understand, that no more than
fifty years ago the dispute about the substance of popular forebodings
– about what sort of horrors the future would bring – was waged
between Aldous Huxley's *Brave New World* and George Orwell's
1984.

The dispute, to be sure, was quite genuine, since the worlds so
vividly portrayed by the two prophets of dystopia were as different as
chalk and cheese. Orwell's was a world of shabbiness and destitution,
of scarcity and want; Huxley's was a land of opulence and profligacy,
of abundance and satiety. People inhabiting Orwell's world were sad
and frightened; those portrayed by Huxley were carefree and playful.
There were, of course, many other differences, equally as striking; the
two worlds opposed each other in virtually every detail.

And yet there was something that united both visions. That 'something' was the foreboding of a tightly controlled world – a world where
individual freedom would be reduced to nothingness, and indeed
would be keenly resented by people drilled to obey and to follow a set
routine; where a small elite would hold in their hands all the strings –
so that the rest would move through their lives as puppets.

That the future held in store less freedom, and more control, super-
vision and oppression, was beyond dispute. Orwell and Huxley did
not disagree on the destination, only on the road which would take us
there. At the time when they were sketching the contours of the future

they both felt that the tragedy of the world was that it was moving doggedly and uncontrollably towards a split between increasingly remote controllers and an increasingly controlled mass. The nightmarish vision which haunted both writers was that of men and women no longer in control of their lives. Just as Aristotle or Plato could not imagine a good or bad society without slaves, so Huxley and Orwell could not conceive of a society, whether happy or miserable, without managers, designers and supervisors. They could not visualise a world without a controlling tower and controlling desk. The fears of their time – and its hopes and dreams – hovered around the Supreme Office.

CAPITALISM – HEAVY AND LIGHT
One can perhaps best understand the fears outlined in the dystopias of Orwell and Huxley as being those likely to be generated by a world in which the 'Joshua discourse' is dominant – as distinct from the contemporary world which exists within the 'Genesis discourse'. According to Nigel Thrift, 'whereas in the Joshua discourse order is the rule and disorder is an exception, in the Genesis discourse disorder is the rule and order the exception'. [1] In the Joshua discourse, the world (to quote Kenneth Jowitt) is 'centrally organised, rigidly bounded, and hysterically concerned with impenetrable boundaries'.[2] 'Order' means monotony, regularity, repetitiveness and predictability; it means that some events are considerably more likely to happen than their alternatives, while some other events are highly unlikely or altogether out of the question. It means by the same token that someone, somewhere, must manipulate the probabilities, so that events do not occur at random. The orderly world of the 'Joshua discourse' is tightly controlled. Our surprise at the fears of the dystopias of a previous generation is generated because we live in a transformed world, one which is no longer orderly. And this transformation has been brought about by the transition from 'heavy' to 'light' capitalism.

Everything in the Joshua world serves a purpose, even if what that is is not clear (as yet). And this world has no room for anything which lacks purpose. What's more, for any act to be recognised as having a legitimate purpose, it must serve the maintenance and perpetuation of the orderly whole. It is the order itself, and the order alone, which does not require legitimisation; it is, so to speak, 'its own purpose'. It is there – and this all we need or can know about order. It could be there because this is where God put it, in the one-off act of Divine Creation; or it could be there because human yet God-like creatures put it there in an ongoing effort of design, build and management (and with God on a leave of absence, the task of designing and servicing order has tended to fall upon humans).

As Karl Marx suggested, the ideas of the dominant classes tend to be the dominant ideas. For at least two hundred years now it has been the managers of enterprises who have dominated the world – that have set the feasible apart from the implausible, the rational apart from the irrational, the sensible apart from the insane – and have otherwise·circumscribed the range of alternatives inside which human life trajectories are to be inscribed. It has therefore been their vision of the world – as well as the world itself shaped and reshaped in the likeness of that vision – that has fed into the dominant discourse. Until recently that was the 'Joshua discourse', which was linked to the world of 'heavy' capitalism; now, increasingly, it is the 'Genesis discourse' which prevails. The present-day meeting of business and academia inside the same discourse is no novelty; it is not something unique to our new, 'soft' and knowledge-greedy capitalism. It is simply that the dominant discourse, shared by academics and businesspeople alike, has changed for everyone.

The world sustaining the 'Joshua discourse', and making it credible, was the world of Fordism. And this world, in its heyday, was (in Alain Lipietz's description) simultaneously a model of industrialisation, of accumulation, and of *regulation*:

> The [Fordist] industrial paradigm included the Taylorian principle of rationalisation, plus constant mechanisation. That 'rationalisation' was based on separation of the intellectual and manual aspects of labour ... the social knowledge being systematised from the top and incorporated within machinery by designers. When Taylor and the Taylorian engineers first introduced those principles at the beginning of the twentieth century, their explicit aim was to enforce the control of management on the workers.[3]

But the Fordist model was more than that. The way human beings understand the world can be described as *praxeomorphic*: as always defined by the know-how of the day, by what people can do and how they normally do it. The Fordist factory, with its meticulous separation between design and execution, freedom and obedience, invention and determination, with its tight interlocking of the opposites within each pair, and its smooth transmission of command, was without doubt the highest achievement to date of order-aimed social engineering. No wonder it set the metaphorical frame of reference (even if the reference stayed unquoted) for everyone trying to comprehend how human reality works on all its levels – on the global-societal level as well as that of the individual life. Its presence is easy to discern in the Parsonian concept of a self-reproducing 'social system' ruled by a 'central cluster of values' at the top – and equally in the Sartrean 'life project', which serves as the design for the self's lifelong effort of identity building.

Indeed, at one time there seemed to be no alternative to the Fordist factory and nothing to stave off the spread of the Fordist model to every nook and cranny of society. The confrontation between socialism and capitalism, just as the debate between Orwell and Huxley, were in this respect no more than family squabbles. Communism, after all, wished only to cleanse the Fordist model of its present pollutions – that market-born chaos which stood in the way of eliminating accident and contingency and made rational planning less then all-embracing. Lenin believed that socialism would be accomplished if communists could succeed in combining Soviet power and Soviet organisation of management with capitalist progress in the scientific organisation of labour; Lenin wanted to see this 'scientific organisation' spill out from the factories, to penetrate and saturate the whole of social life.

'Fordism' was the self-consciousness of modern society in its 'heavy' 'bulky' and 'immobile', or 'rooted' phase. Capital, management and labour were all, for better or worse, doomed to stay in each other's company for a long time to come, tied down as they were to huge buildings, heavy machinery and a massive labour force. To survive, let alone to act efficiently, they had to 'dig in', to draw boundaries and surround themselves with trenches, making the fortress big enough to provide everything necessary to endure a protracted, perhaps prospectless, siege. 'Heavy' capitalism was obsessed with boundaries, with making them tight and impenetrable; the genius of Henry Ford was to discover a way of keeping all the defenders of his industrial fortress inside the walls – to ward off the temptation to defect or change sides. As Daniel Cohen argues, when Henry Ford decided to 'double' the wages of his workers, his aim was to stem the massive turnover of his labour force. He decided to give the workers a spectacular rise in order to fix them to their chains.[4]

The invisible chain firmly linking the workers to their work-place, and arresting their mobility, was in Cohen words, 'the heart of Fordism'. And the breaking of that chain brought about a decisive change in people's life experience. 'Someone beginning their career in Microsoft', observes Cohen, 'has no idea where it is going to end. In contrast, starting with Ford or Renault entailed the near certitude that their career would run its course in the same place'.

In its 'heavy' stage, capital was as much fixed to the ground as were the labourers it engaged. Nowadays, capital travels light – cabin luggage, mobile phone and laptop computer are its only accoutrements. It can stop over almost anywhere, and needs stay nowhere longer than the satisfaction lasts. Labour, however, remains as immobile as in the past; but the place to which it could previously have expected to be attached for good has lost its past solidity; searching in vain for rock, anchors meet only sands. The world itself is on the move. The 'Joshua story' sounds hollow to present-day ears.

HAVE CAR, WILL TRAVEL

The turn of events has proved to be exactly opposite to the one anticipated, and confidently predicted, by Max Weber. Weber extrapolated his vision of the future from his contemporary experience of 'heavy' capitalism (at a time when no-one was yet aware that being 'heavy' was a time-bound circumstance and that other modalities were conceivable). He foresaw the ultimate triumph of 'instrumental rationality': with the destination of human history all but preordained, and the ends of human actions determined and not open to questioning all that remained was to muster, calculate and deploy the means most adequate to the ends in question. With the question of ends off the agenda, people would tend to preoccupy themselves mostly, perhaps solely, with the issue of means – the future would be, so to speak, means obsessed. All further rationalisation would consist in sharpening, adjusting and perfecting the means. True, the contest about the ends would not stop, the rational capacity in humans being notoriously undermined by affective propensities and other equally irrational leanings; but that contest would be pushed away from the mainstream current of relentless rationalisation, and left to prophets and preachers, who operate on the margins of the paramount and decisive business of life.

Weber also delineated another type of goal-oriented action, which he called value-rational; but by that he meant pursuit of value 'for its own sake' and 'independently of any prospect of external success'. He also made clear that the values he had in mind were of the ethical, aesthetic or religious kind – the kind which modern capitalism degraded and declared irrelevant (if not downright damaging) to the process of rationalisation in which it was engaged.[5] One can only guess that the adding of value-rationality to his inventory of action-types occurred to Weber as an afterthought – under the impact of the Bolshevik revolution, which seemed to refute the conclusion that the matter of goals had been settled once for all, and to demonstrate, on the contrary, that a situation can still arise where some people will cling to their ideals whatever the chances of ever reaching them, and whatever the cost of trying; they can thus be diverted from what is their sole legitimate concern, that of calculating the means appropriate for reaching set and given ends.

But whatever one may say about the usefulness of the value-rationality concept in its Weberian rendition, it is of no use if one wants to grasp the substance of the current turn, brought about by the world of 'light' capitalism. Although, in Weberian terms, present-day 'light' capitalism is not 'instrumental-rational', neither can it be said to be value-rational. What has happened in the course of the passage from 'heavy' to 'light' capitalism is the dissipation of the invisible 'politburo', the supreme court which pronounces the non-appeal-permitted verdict about what goals are worth pursuing (the assumption indispensable and central to the 'Joshua story'). In the absence of such Supreme Office (or, rather, in the presence of many offices vying for supremacy, with none boasting more then a sporting chance of winning the contest), the question of objectives is once more thrown wide open – to become the cause of endless agony and much hesitation, thus engendering an unnerving feeling of unmitigated uncertainty and a concomitant state of perpetual anxiety. In the words of Gerhard Schulze, this is a new type of uncertainty: 'not knowing the ends instead of the traditional uncertainty of not knowing the means'.[6] The question today is no longer one of trying, with mixed success, to measure means – those we already have and those we need and seek – against a given end. It is, rather, one of considering which ends, of the many floated and dangled, are 'within reach' (can be reasonably pursued) given the available means – and taking into account the meagre chances of their lasting usefulness.

Under the new circumstances, the odds are that most of human life, and most human lives, will be spent in agonising about the choice of goals rather than in finding the means to achieve ends which call for no reflection. Contrary to its predecessor, 'light' capitalism is bound to be value-obsessed. The legendary job-seeker's small ad, 'Have car, will travel', may serve as the epitome of the new problematics of life – as can the mindset often attributed to heads of contemporary scientific and technological establishments: 'We have found the solution. Now let us find a problem'. The question 'what can I do' has come to dominate, dwarf and elbow out the question 'how can I do what I must or should do anyway'.

In the absence of a Supreme Office seeing to the regularity of the world and guarding the boundary between right and wrong, the world becomes an infinite collection of possibilities – a mind-boggling mass of opportunities yet to be caught and opportunities missed. Possibilities are many, perhaps too many; more, painfully more, than any individual life, however long, rich and active, can attempt to explore. It is the infinity of possibilities that has now filled the place left void by the disappearing act of the Supreme Office. No wonder that dystopias are no longer written: the post-fordist, postmodern world of freely choosing individuals does not worry about a sinister 'Big Brother' who punishes those who step out of line. In such a world, though, equally, there is no room for the benign and caring 'Elder Brother' to tell us which things are right, and worth doing or having, and to protect the young against bullies; and so utopias of the Good Society have stopped being written as well. It is now all down to the individual: to find out what she or he is capable of doing, to stretch that capacity to the utmost, and to pick the ends to which that capacity could be best, and with the greatest satisfaction, applied. It is up to the individual to 'tame the unexpected to become an entertainment'.[7]

Living in a world brimming with opportunities, each one ever more seductive and alluring, each 'compensating for the last, and providing grounds for shifting towards the next'[8] – is an exhilarating experience. In such a world, little is predetermined, even less irrevocable. Few defeats are final, few if any mishaps irreversible. Yet no victory is ultimate either. For the possibilities to stay infinite, none may be allowed to petrify into everlasting reality. They need to stay liquid and fluid, and have a 'use-by' date attached, lest they push other opportunities off-limits and kill the adventure in life. The awareness that the game goes on, that much is still going to happen, and that the inventory of wonders which life may bring is far from complete, is richly satisfying and pleasurable. On the other hand, the suspicion that nothing which has already been tested and appropriated is insured against decay, or guaranteed to last, is the proverbial fly in the barrel of tasty ointment. The losses balance the gains. Life is bound to navigate between the two, and no sailor can boast of having found a safe, let alone foolproof, itinerary.

A world full of possibilities is like a buffet table set with mouth-watering dishes – too numerous for the heaviest of eaters to hope to try them all. The diners are consumers, and the hardest challenge the consumers confront is the necessity of choosing. Their misery derives from the surfeit, not the dearth, of choices. 'Have I used my means to the best advantage?' is the consumer's most haunting, insomnia-causing quest.

STOP TELLING ME, SHOW ME!

'Heavy', Fordist-style capitalism was a world of legislators and supervisors. The world of goals fixed-by-others. For this reason it was also the world of authorities: of leaders who knew better and of teachers who told you how to be better. But 'light', postmodern and consumer-friendly capitalism has not put paid to authorities. It has simply given birth to too many authorities for any one of them to stay in authority: 'numerous authorities' is a contradiction in terms. When there are many authorities, they tend to cancel each other; hence the authority remaining in the field is the one who has to choose between them. It is courtesy of the chooser that a would-be authority becomes an authority. Authorities no more command; they tempt and seduce.

The 'leader' was a byproduct, and a necessary supplement, of a world which aimed at a 'good society', and tried hard to hold the bad one at a distance. The postmodern world of consumers does neither. Margaret Thatcher's infamous phrase, 'there is no such thing as society', was simultaneously a shrewd reflection on the changing nature of capitalism, a declaration of intent and a self-fulfilling prophecy: in its wake came the dismantling of normative and protective networks, which greatly helped the word on its road to becoming flesh. 'No society' means no utopia and no dystopia: as Peter Drucker, the guru of 'light' capitalism, put it, 'no more salvation by society'; and this implies, by the same logic, that it is also wrong to lay the responsibility for damnation at the door of society: both redemption and doom are all yours – the outcome of what you have been doing with your life.

There is, of course, no shortage of those who claim to be in the know, and quite a few of them have numerous followers. These are not leaders however; they are, at most, counsellors – and one crucial difference between leaders and counsellors is that the first are there to be followed while the latter need to be hired and/or fired. Leaders demand

and expect discipline; counsellors may at best count on willingness to listen and pay heed, and that willingness must first be earned by currying favour with the would-be listeners. Another crucial difference between leaders and counsellors is that leaders act as two-way translators between individual good and the 'good of us all', or (as C. Wright Mills would have put it) between private worries and public issues. Counsellors, on the contrary, are wary of stepping beyond the closed area of the private. Illness is individual, and so is therapy; worry is private, and so are the means to struggle against it. The counsels which the counsellors supply refer to life-politics, not to Politics with a capital 'P'; they refer to what the counselled persons might do by themselves and for themselves, each one for himself or herself – not to what they all together could achieve for each one of them, if they joined forces.

'We' is the personal pronoun most frequently used by leaders. Counsellors have little use for it: 'we' is no more than a collection of 'I's, and the collection, unlike Emile Durkheim's 'group', is not greater than the sum of its parts. After the counselling session the counselled person is as much alone as before, if anything reinforced in loneliness – one's suspicion of being abandoned to one's own devices has been corroborated. Whatever the advice given, it will certainly be something which the counselled person must do, and accept full responsibility for doing.

The most successful counsellor is one who is aware of the fact that what the prospective recipients of counselling wish to obtain is an object-lesson. Proceeding on the assumption that the nature of any troubles they have is such as can only be tackled by individuals on their own, what advice-seekers need (or believe they need) is an *example* of how other men or women, facing a similar trouble, go about the task. And they need examples of others for more basic reasons yet: the sentiment of 'being unhappy' is all too often diffuse; its contours are blurred, its roots are scattered, and it needs to be mapped, condensed, hammered into shape and named in order to re-forge into a specific task our equally vague longing for happiness. Other people can give us an example of such condensations. Through looking at other people's experience – getting a glimpse of other people's trials and tribulations – one hopes to discover and locate the troubles which caused one's own unhappiness, attach a name to them, and so learn where to look for ways of resisting them.

Explaining the phenomenal popularity of *Jane Fonda's Workout*

Book (1981), and of the technique of self-drill which that book put at the disposal of millions of American women, Hilary Radner points out that: 'The instructor offers herself as an example ... rather than as an authority ... the exerciser possesses her body through the identification with an image that is not her own but that of the exemplary body(ies) offered her'. Jane Fonda is quite outspoken about the substance of her offer and straightforward about what sort of example should be followed by her readers and watchers: 'I like to think a lot of my body is my own doing and my own blood and guts. It's my responsibility'.[9] Fonda's main message is for every woman to treat her body as her own possession (*my* blood, *my* guts), her own product (*my* own doing) and, above all, her own responsibility. To sustain and reinforce the post-modern *amour de soi*, she invokes the memory of a – perhaps pre-modern – instinct of workmanship: the product of my work is as good as the skills, attention and care I invest in its production. Whatever the results, I have no one else to praise (or to blame, as the case may be). The obverse side of the message is also unambiguous, even if not spelled out with similar clarity: you *owe* your body your thought and care, and for neglecting that duty you should feel guilty and ashamed. Imperfections of my body are my guilt and my shame. But the redemption of sins is in the hands of the sinner, and in her hands alone.

Let me repeat: in saying all this, Fonda does not act as an authority (lawgiver, norm-setter, preacher or teacher). Indeed, she 'offers herself as an example'. I am famous and loved, I am an object of desire and admiration. Look at my body: it is lean, flexible, shapely – and perpetually youthful. You would surely like to have – to be – a body like mine. My body is my work; if you work like I do, you can have it. If 'being like Jane Fonda' is something you dream of, remember that it was me, Jane Fonda, who made herself into the Jane Fonda of these dreams.

Being rich and famous helps, of course; it adds weight to the message. It would be foolish to deny that, Jane Fonda being who she is, her example carries 'naturally' an authority which other people would need to work hard to obtain. In general, however, one cannot be sure about the nature of the causal link between the authority of an exemplary person and the willingness of consumers to follow the example. As Daniel J. Boorstin wittily observed (in *The Image* 1961), a celebrity is a person who is known for his well-knownness, while a best-seller is a book which somehow sells well simply because it is selling well. Authority can multiply the numbers of followers, but, in a world of uncertain and chronically underdetermined ends, it is the number of the followers that makes – is – authority.

Whatever the case, in the example-authority pair it is the example bit that matters most and is most in demand. Celebrities with enough 'authority-capital' to make what they say worthy of attention before they say it are far too few to furnish the innumerable TV chat shows on our screens (and they seldom appear on the most popular among them, like Oprah's or Trisha's); but this does not stop chat shows from being compulsive daily viewing for millions of guidance-hungry men and women. The authority of the person sharing with viewers her or his life story may increase attentiveness. But lack of authority in the storyteller – her not-being-a-celebrity, his anonymity – may make the example easier to follow and so may have value-adding potential of its own. The non-celebrities, men and women who appear on the screen only for a fleeting moment, are 'people like us', as helpless and as hapless, smarting under the same kind of blows and, like us, seeking desperately an honourable exit from trouble. What they can do, I can do as well; perhaps even better. I may learn something useful from their victories and their defeats.

It would be demeaning, as well as misleading, to condemn or ridicule chat show addiction as simply an effect of the eternal human greed for gossip. In a world tightly packed with means yet unclear about ends, the lessons drawn from chat shows have pragmatic value; since I know already that it is up to me to make the best of my life, and since I also know that whatever resources this undertaking may require can be found only in my own skills, guts and stamina, it is vital to know how other people cope, faced with similar challenges. They might have come across an expedient I missed; they might have explored parts of the 'inside' which I didn't notice.

PRIVATE PROBLEMS AND PUBLIC ISSUES
Being able to learn from the example of others is not the only benefit of chat shows. As mentioned before, naming the problem is in itself a daunting task, and without attaching a name to a feeling of unease or unhappiness there is no hope for cure. Though suffering is personal and private, a 'private language' is an incongruity. Whatever is to be named, including the most private and intimate sentiments, is properly named only if the names chosen have public currency: if they belong to interpersonal, public language, and are understood by people who converse in that language. Chat shows are public lessons in as-yet-

unborn-but-about-to-be-born language. They offer words which may be used to 'name the problem' – to express, in a publicly legible way, what has thus far been ineffable, and would remain such if not for that offer.

This by itself is a gain of utmost importance – but there are more gains yet. In chat shows, words and phrases referring to experiences deemed intimate and unfit for being talked about are uttered in public, and to universal approval and amusement. Chat shows legitimise public discourse about private affairs. Thanks to chat shows, I can now speak openly about things which I previously thought were to be kept secret. I need no longer feel ashamed, wary of being frowned upon or rebuked and ostracised. These are, after all, the kinds of things people are talking about without compunction while watched by millions. Their private problems, and so also my own so similar to theirs, are fit for public discussion. Not that they thereby turn into public issues; no, they enter the discussion precisely in their capacity as private issues. They are reconfirmed as private in the discussion, and emerge from it reinforced in their privacy. After all, every speaker agrees that, in as much as these issues are experienced and lived through privately, so they must be confronted and coped with privately.

Many influential thinkers (Jurgen Habermas most prominent among them) warn about the danger of the 'private sphere' being colonised by 'the public'. Harking back, as they do, to the still fresh memory of the era that inspired Orwell or Huxley-style dystopias, such fears are understandable; however, they seem to be the wrong reading of the processes taking place. If anything, an opposite tendency is currently in operation: the colonisation of the public sphere by issues heretofore classified as private and unsuitable for public venting. What is happening is not just another re-negotiation of the notoriously mobile boundary between the private and the public. What seems to be at stake is a redefinition of the 'public sphere' as a scene on which private dramas are staged, put on public display and watched. The current definition of 'public interest' – promoted by the media yet widely accepted by most sections of society – is the duty that such dramas should be staged, and the public's right to watch the performance. While the social conditions which make such developments unsurprising and even 'natural' ought to be evident in the light of the preceding argument, its consequences may be further reaching than generally understood, and are far from having been explored in full.

Arguably the most seminal consequence is the demise of 'politics as we know it' – Politics with a capital 'P' – the activity charged with the task of translating private problems into public issues (and vice versa). It is that translation which is nowadays grinding to a halt. Private problems do not turn into public issues by dint of being vented in public; even under the public gaze they do not cease to be private, and by travelling on to the public stage they seem to be squeezing out from the public agenda problems other than private ones. What are more and more often perceived as 'public issues' are the private problems of public figures. The time-honoured question of democratic politics – what effects on the welfare and well-being of their electors have public figures brought about in the exercise of their public duties – has fallen by the board, dragging in its wake public concerns with such problems as the good society, public justice or collective responsibility for individual welfare.

Buffeted by a series of 'public scandals' (that is, public disclosures of moral laxities in the private life of public figures), Tony Blair (in *The Guardian*, 11.1.99) complained about 'politics diminished to a gossip column', and called for people to face the alternative: 'We either have the news agenda dominated by scandal and gossip and trivia or by the things that really matter'. Such words cannot but baffle, coming as they do from a man who daily consults focus groups in the hope of becoming informed about the 'things that really matter' in the opinion of his electors – a man whose handling of the things that really matter is massively contributing to a market-led, consumer-oriented and individualised way of life, which is largely responsible for the very 'diminishing of politics to a gossip column' which he bewails.

This way of life prompts men and women to seek examples, not leaders; and leads them to expect people in the limelight – all of them and any of them – to show them how the 'things that matter' (now firmly relegated to the sphere of their own four walls) are done. They are told that what is wrong with their own life comes from their own mistakes, is their own fault, and ought to be improved by their own efforts. No wonder they assume that showing them how to make such efforts is the major – perhaps the only – use of people who pretend to be 'in the know'. Why should one be puzzled if they do not expect from 'people in authority' any service other than that of setting personal examples?

In the galaxy of celebrities, politicians do not occupy a position of privilege. It does not matter much what are the reasons for that 'knownness' which, according to Boorstin, makes a celebrity. Being in the limelight has its own modality which binds everybody – film stars, top footballers and government ministers alike. One of the requirements that applies to them all, in equal measure, is that they must put their private lives on public display – and not grumble if others do it for them. Once disclosed, such private lives may prove to be unilluminating or downright unprepossessing; not every private secret contains lessons which others may find useful. This is not the crux of the problem, however; what is crucial is the fact that the way in which individual people individually define their individual problems, and cope with them by deploying individual skills and resources, is now the sole remaining 'public issue' and the sole object of 'public interest'. Having been trained to rely on their own judgement and effort, spectators and listeners seeking enlightenment and guidance will now look into the private lives of others with the same zeal and hope with which they might once have looked into the speeches and sermons of visionaries and preachers.

DAYDREAMS AND NIGHTMARES OF THE SHOPPING ADDICT

Looking for examples, enlightenment and guidance is an addiction: the more you do it, the more you need to do it and the more unhappy you feel when deprived of new supplies of the sought-after goods. All addictions are self-destructive; they destroy the possibility of ever being satisfied. Examples and recipes remain attractive as long as they stay untested: but hardly any of them deliver on their promise – virtually all of them stop short of the fulfilment they pledged they would bring. Even if any of them prove to work in exactly the promised way, the satisfaction brought does not last long, since in the postmodern world of consumers possibilities are infinite, and the volume of seductive goals on offer is never exhausted. Recipes and panaceas, and the gadgets which go with them, have a 'use by' date, but most of them will fall out of use well before that date – by having been stripped of their allurements by 'new and improved' offers. In this race the finishing line always moves faster than the fastest of runners; but most runners forced onto the track have muscles too flabby and lungs too feeble to run fast. And so one admires and praises the winners, but, as in a marathon, what truly counts is staying in the race to the end. Well, a marathon has an end as well as a beginning, but that other race – to reach the elusive and ever-receding promise of a trouble-free life – does not end once it has started.

And so it is the running itself, the staying in the race, that becomes the true addiction – not any particular prizes brought by winning. None of the prizes is satisfying enough to strip other prizes of their power of attraction, and there are always so many other prizes beckoning – alluring because (as yet, always as yet) untried. Desire becomes its own purpose, the sole uncontested and unquestionable purpose. In a world in which the volume of ends is too big for comfort and always bigger than available means, one needs to attend with great care to questions of the volume and effectiveness of available means. Staying in the race is the most important of means; indeed, it is the meta-means: the means whereby we keep the hope of other means alive.

The archetype of the particular race in which every member of a consumer society is running is the activity of shopping. We stay in the race as long as we shop around, and it is not just in the shops or supermarkets or department stores that we do our shopping. If shopping means scanning the assortment of possibilities, examining, touching, feeling, handling the goods on display, comparing their costs with the contents of our wallets or the remaining credit on our credit cards, putting some of them in the trolley and others back on the shelf – then we shop outside shops as much as inside; we shop in the street and at home, at work and leisure, awake and in dreams. Whatever we do and whatever name we attach to our activity, we also shop. The code in which our 'life policy' is scripted is derived from the pragmatics of shopping.

Shopping is not just about food, shoes, cars or furniture items. The never ending search for new and improved examples and recipes for life which we were discussing earlier is also a variety of shopping; and it is a most important one, since through it we are taught a twin lesson: that our happiness depends on personal competence, but that we are personally incompetent – or not as competent as we should and could be if only we tried harder.[10] There are so many areas in which we need to be more competent, and each calls for 'shopping around'. We 'shop' for skills needed to earn our living and the means to convince the 'job givers' that we have them; for the kind of image it would be nice to have, and ways to make others believe that we have it; for ways of making friends we want and ways of getting rid of unwanted ones; for ways of drawing attention to ourselves and ways of hiding from scrutiny; for ways to get the most satisfaction from love, and ways to stave off becoming dependent on our partner; for ways to earn the love of the beloved, and the least costly way of finishing off the union once love has faded and ceased to satisfy; for the best way of saving for a rainy day and the least costly way of spending money before we earn it; for methods of doing things faster, and for things with which to fill the time thus vacated; for the most mouth-watering food, and for an efficient diet to dispose of the consequences of eating it; for the most powerful amplifiers and the most effective pills against headache. There is no end to the shopping list. Yet however long the list, opting out from shopping is not among its items. And the competence most needed in our world of ostensibly infinite ends is that of the skilful and indefatigable shopper.

Contemporary interpretations of compulsive shopping as a manifestation of the postmodern value revolution capture at best only part of the truth; the same can be said for the tendency to represent this phenomenon as a sudden release of heretofore dormant materialistic and hedonistic instincts, or as a product of 'commercial conspiracy'. Another part of the truth, arguably the decisive one, is that the shopping compulsion is part of an uphill struggle against acute, nerve-breaking uncertainty and an overwhelming feeling of insecurity. As T.H. Marshall remarked on another occasion, when crowds of people run in the same direction, two questions need to be asked: what are they running after and what are they running from. In our case, they might be running after pleasures promised by glittering objects in supermarkets or department-stores, or after the deeper, more pleasurable sensations promised by a session with a counselling expert. But they are also trying to find an escape from the agony called insecurity. They want to be, for once, free from the fear of making mistakes, and from neglect or sloppiness. They want to be, for once, sure, confident, self-assured and trusting – and the objects they find when shopping around come complete with the promise of certainty. Whatever else compulsive/addictive shopping may be, it is also a daily ritual which is pursued in the hope of exorcising the terrible night-time apparitions of uncertainty and insecurity.

SEEKING CERTAINTY TOGETHER
We live today in a mobile world. People who live in a mobile world are mobile people. In James Clifford's apt expression, we are all nowadays tending to become 'sedentary in travel'. Or, as Michael Benedikt put it – 'the very significance of geographical location at all scales begins to be questioned. We become nomads – who are always in touch'.[11] Every year 130 million people leave one country to settle in another; 561 million tourists annually cross state boundaries in search of adventure

or business opportunity; in France, 48 per cent of people questioned in 1990 no longer lived in the same place as in 1982. The global figures may be misleading, though. What they hide is the fact that the exact meaning of 'nomadism' varies from one social position to another, and 'mobility' comes to various people in various forms.

Some people, members of the new global elites of finance, trade and information, are mobile in both flesh and mind, and they can choose which one will be the case: distances – space as such – matter to them little, bodily and spiritually. Even at a time when bodily they stay put, distances set no limits to their actions. Dispositions travel instantly, and so it is of no importance whether the places to be reached are close by or far away. Without leaving Chipping Camden, one can as easily run financial operations in Frankfurt as one can in Kuala Lumpur, and one can converse with thought-companions whether they are in Wellington or Santa Barbara. In the life experience of the new global elite, 'borders' hardly ever appear – while in the global web of information there is no room at all for geographical divisions.

Many other people seldom leave home. Physically, they are as immobile as their forefathers. If they try to follow the example of the global elites and take to the road in search of greener or just fresher pastures, they are stopped at the nearest border, rounded up and sent back home. Geographical borders are all too real to them. As Professor Gildas Simon argues, 'on one hand, the world system favours liberation of exchanges, services, images and information; on the other, protectionism is reinforced as far as migration is concerned, in the North as much as in the South, to an extent with no precedent in human history'.[12] While some people have acquired a previously unheard of freedom of movement, others are increasingly tied to the ground. In a mobile world, freedom of mobility is fast becoming a hotly coveted and contested value, and a major factor in new forms of global, as well as inner-societal, stratification.

The fact that they are not allowed to move elsewhere, does not mean, however, that sedentary people strike secure roots in the place where they stay. Nowadays, a person can become cosmopolitan and 'rootless' without ever going outdoors, and without any initiative on his or her part. People may not move an inch, and yet the ground on which their feet rest may move – with pretty similar effects on the roots. The learned elites straddling the new global network of exchanges remind one more and more of the 'absentee landlords' of yore, who communicated little and cared even less about the places where they happened to stay 'in the flesh'. Culturally and spiritually, places are being devalued and disempowered. Localities are losing their meaning-creating and value-selecting capacity. Signals, images, patterns to follow and ideas to believe in come from afar – strictly speaking, from nowhere. This has serious implications for any sense of identity based on location and belonging.

As far as control over one's own identity is concerned, the current process of globalisation means empowerment for some, disempowerment for others. The results seem to be much the same for everyone in the sense that the reliability and durability of identities has been undermined, to become as 'mobile' as the world itself, changeable and elusive, difficult to arrest and hold on to. But the ability to deal with this deeply uncomfortable sense of the brittleness, haziness, temporariness and overall unreliability of identities rebounds in two sharply distinct experiences. For those who can move at will, the experience is joyful and exhilarating. For identities, as for everything else, one may 'shop around': identities may be chosen if they look promising, or discarded if they disappoint, if they run short of their past seductive power or are superseded by new, more attractive offers. But for those who are bound to a place, the experience is threatening and frightening: their identities may be taken away, with or without warning; the habitual and cosily familiar ones may be emptied of their content and made unworkable, while new ones may feel awkward and ill-fitting. To cut a long story short, flexibility and alterability of identities may augur a new, unprecedented, freedom of self assertion, but it may equally portend serfdom to the capricious, distant and invisible master – known only by his indifference to the fate and feelings of his serfs.

The need to construct, remake and update identities is a trait which unites the residents of the mobile world; but the ability to gratify that need to at least a modicum of satisfaction is a dividing, perhaps even polarising, feature. Contemporary social hierarchy stretches from choice to no-choice; from the autonomy of self-identification at the top to the dependency on assigned identities at the bottom. Most residents of the mobile world are located somewhere between these two extremes. Given the intrinsic volatility and un-fixity of all or almost all identities, it is the ability to 'shop around' in the supermarket of identities, the degree of consumer freedom to select one's identity and to hold on to it as long as desired, that becomes the principal measure of social advancement and a successful life.

FREE TO SHOP – OR SO IT SEEMS?

Whether this freedom is genuine or imaginary is a notoriously moot question. It is hardly necessary, for example, to point out the power notoriously exercised by the mass media over the popular – collective and individual – imagination. Powerful images on ubiquitous screens tend to set the standards for reality and its evaluation, as well as stimulating the urge to do something to make the 'lived' reality more palatable. The kind of life desired is life 'as seen on TV'. That other life dwarfs the life lived: it is the lived life which seems unreal – at least for as long as it is not, in its own turn, re-made into screenable images.

Christopher Lasch has argued that the older meaning of identity referred to both persons and things, and that both have lost their solidity in modern society. Lasch's argument implies that in this general 'melting of all solids' the initiative belongs to things; and because things are the symbolic trappings of identities and the tools of identification efforts, people soon followed suit. Referring to Emma Rothschild's famous study of the automobile industry, Lasch suggests that Alfred's Sloane's innovations in marketing – 'the annual model change, constant upgrading of the product, efforts to associate it with social status, the deliberate inculcation of a boundless appetite for change' were the necessary counterpart of Henry Ford's innovation in production: 'Both tended to discourage enterprise and independent thinking and to make the individual distrust his own judgement, even in matters of taste.'[13] Alfred Sloane was a pioneer of what was later to become a universal trend. Commodity production today replaces the world of durable objects with disposable products designed for immediate obsolescence. The consequences of that replacement have been perceptively described by Jeremy Seabrook:

> It is not so much that capitalism has delivered the goods to the people, as that the people have been increasingly delivered to the goods; that is to say, that the very character and sensibility of the people have been re-worked, re-fashioned, in such a way that they assort approximately ... with the commodities, experiences and sensations ... the selling of which alone gives shape and significance to our lives.[14]

In a world in which unstable things are the raw material of unstable identities, one needs to be constantly on the alert; but above all one needs to protect one's own flexibility and speed of readjustment, to be able to follow the pattern of the world 'out there'.

These truths need to be restated again and again, especially at a time when the corpse of the 'romantic concept of the self' – as the inner essence hiding beneath all the external appearances – is being artificially reanimated in some circles. This revival of the notion of a core inner essence is evidenced in what Paul Atkinson and David Silverman have aptly dubbed 'the interview society' ('relying pervasively on face-to-face interview to reveal the personal, the private self of the subject'); it is also evident in the large quantity of current social research aimed at 'getting down to the subjective truth of the self', through provoking and then dissecting personal narratives, in the hope of finding in them the revelation of the inner truth. As Atkinson and Silverman argue:

> we do not in the social sciences reveal selves by collecting narratives, we create selfhood through narratives of biographical work ... The desire for revelation and revelations of desire furnish the appearance of authenticity even when the very possibility of authenticity is under question.[15]

And that possibility is indeed highly questionable. Numerous studies show that personal narratives are largely rehearsals of public rhetoric designed by the public media to 'represent subjective truths'. But this inauthenticity of the allegedly authentic self is covered up by spectacles of sincerity – public rituals of in-depth interviews and public confessions – of which chat shows are the most prominent, but not the only, examples. Ostensibly, these spectacles are meant to give vent to the stirrings of our 'inner selves' which are striving to be let out; in fact, they display and stamp with public acceptability the yarn of emotive expression with which the 'thoroughly personal identities' are to be woven.

Yet the question of authenticity is not the key factor in these 'spectacles of sincerity'. What matters is how the contrived necessity of identity building and re-building feels, how it is lived through. Whether or not representing the genuine choice of the true inner self, the opportunity to 'shop around', to pick and shed one's 'true self', to 'be on the move', has come, in contemporary consumer society, to signify freedom. Consumer choice is now a value in its own right; the activity of choosing matters more than what is being chosen, and situations are praised or condemned, enjoyed or resented, depending on the range of choices on display.

DIVIDED WE SHOP

By no means unexpectedly, the kind of freedom which the mobile society of our times values most – freedom translated above all as a plenitude of consumer choice, and as the ability to treat any life-decision as a consumer choice – has had a much more devastating effect on unwilling bystanders than on those for whom it is ostensibly meant. The lifestyle of the resourceful elite, of the masters of the choosing art, trickles down the social hierarchy as a caricature or monstrous mutant. For those with few resources, the 'trickling down' of the life of consumer choice and risk is stripped of most of its promised pleasures – indeed it is here that its destructive potential is most clearly seen.

In the warehouse world of consumer commodities, the pleasure-generating potential of any commodity tends to be rapidly exhausted. Customers with plentiful resources are, fortunately for them, insured against these unpalatable consequences of commodification – they can discard the possessions they no longer want as easily as they once obtained them. Having resources at one's disposal gives one freedom to pick and choose, but also freedom from bearing the consequences of wrong choices – and thus freedom from the least appetising attributes of the life of choosing.

To take one example: 'plastic sex', 'confluent love', and 'pure relationships' – all aspects of the commodification or consumerisation of human partnership – have been portrayed by Anthony Giddens as vehicles of emancipation, allowing an unprecedented level of individual autonomy and freedom to choose. Whether this is indeed true for the mobile elite of the rich and mighty is debatable. One can support Giddens's assertion whole-heartedly only if one focuses on the stronger and more resourceful individual in any partnership; but partnerships also necessarily include those who are weaker, and who lack the resources they need to attain the freedom to follow their desires – not to mention children, those lasting consequences of partnership, who hardly ever view the breakdown of their parents' relationship as a manifestation of their own freedom. Changing identity may be a private affair, but it always includes cutting off certain bonds and cancelling certain obligations, and those on the receiving side are seldom consulted, let alone given the chance to exercise free choice. But even taking such less fortunate effects of these 'pure relationships' into account, one can still argue that, in the case of the rich and mighty, the customary divorce settlements and financial provisions for children go some way towards alleviating the insecurity endemic to 'until-further-notice' partnerships; or even that whatever insecurity remains is not an excessive price to pay for the right to 'cut one's losses'. All this could be granted. But there is little doubt that when 'trickled down' to the poor and powerless, this new-style partnership, with its fragility of marital contract, and its 'purification' from the union of all but the 'mutual satisfaction' function, engenders a lot of poverty, misery and human suffering, and an ever-growing volume of broken, loveless and prospectless lives.

To sum up: the mobility and flexibility of identification which characterise the 'shopping around' type of life are not so much vehicles of emancipation, as instruments of a redistribution of freedoms. They are for that reason mixed blessings – enticing and desired as much as repelling and feared, and arousing very contradictory sentiments. They are highly ambivalent values, which tend to generate incoherent, quasi-neurotic, reactions. The task of self-identification has sharply disruptive side-effects. It becomes the focus of conflicts, and triggers mutually incompatible drives. Since the task shared by all has to be performed under sharply differentiated conditions, it divides human situations and prompts competition rather than serving to unify the human condition, or to prompt solidarity. Mostly for this reason, finding a universally gratifying discursive resolution of the resulting tensions looks improbable, to say the least.

NOTES

1. See Nigel Thrift, 'The Rise of Soft Capitalism', in *Cultural Values*, 1/1, April 1997, pp29-57. Thrift creatively develops here the concepts coined and defined by Kenneth Jowitt in *New World Disorder*, University of California Press, Berkeley 1992; and Michel Serres in *Genesis*, University of Michigan Press, Ann Arbor 1995.
2. See note 1.
3 . Alain Lipietz, 'The Next Transformation', in *The Milano Papers: Essays in Societal Alternatives*, Michele Cangiani (ed), Black Rose Books, Montreal 1996, pp116-7.
4. Daniel Cohen, *Richesse du monde, pauvretes des nations*, Flammarion, Paris 1997, pp82-3.
5. See Max Weber, *The Theory of Social and Economic Organization*, transl. by A. R. Henderson and Talcott Parsons, Hodge, New York 1947, pp112-4.
6. Gerhard Schulze, 'From Situations to Subjects: Moral Discourse in Transition', in *Constructing the New Consumer Society*, Pekka Sulkunen,

John Holmwood, Hilary Radner and Gerhard Schulze (eds), Macmillan, New York 1997, p49.

7. See Turo-Kirrimo Lehtonen & Pasi Maenpaa, 'Shopping in the East-Central Mall', in *The Shopping Experience*, Pasi Falk & Colin Campbell (eds), Sage, London 1997, p161.

8. See David Miller, *A Theory of Shopping*, Polity Press, Cambridge 1998, p141

9. Hilary Radner, 'Producing the Body: Jane Fonda and the New Public Feminine', in *Constructing the New Consumer Society*, pp116, 117, 122.

10. See Michael Parenti, *Inventing Reality: The Politics of the Mass Media*, St Martin Press, New York 1986, p65. In Parenti's words, the message underlying the massive and ubiquitous commercials, whatever they try to sell, is that '[in] order to live well and properly, consumers need corporate producers to guide them'.

11. Michael Benedikt, 'On Cyberspace and virtual reality', in *Man and Information Technology*, Stockholm, IVA 1995, p42.

12. Quoted after Dominique Dhombres, 'Les paradoxes de la "planete nomade"', in *Le Monde* 9.10.97.

13. Christopher Lasch, *The Minimal Self*, Pan Books, London 1985, pp32, 29, 34.

14. Jeremy Seabrook, *The Leisure Society*, Blackwell, Oxford 1988, p183.

15. Paul Atkinson & David Silverman, 'Kundera's Immortality: The Interview Society and the Invention of the Self', in *Qualitative Inquiry*, 1997/3, pp304-25.

Notes on Contributors

Frances Angela was born in Bolton and now lives in North London. Her poetry has been published in a variety of journals and magazines.

Zygmunt Bauman is Emeritus Professor of Sociology at the University of Leeds and the author of numerous books and essays on philosophy and modernity.

Ulrich Beck is Professor of Sociology at Munich University and the author of books on the risk society, individualisation, globalisation and the reinvention of politics.

Madeleine Bunting is a leader writer on *The Guardian*; she was religious affairs editor on the same paper from 1995 to 1998. She is author of *The Model Occupation*, a history of the Channel Islands in the Second World War.

Bo Carpelan is one of Finland's leading poets. Forest Books has published a selection of his poems *Room Without Walls* (1987), translated by Anne Born.

Nina Cassian was born in 1924 in Romania and is a poet of worldwide reputation. Since 1985 she has lived in New York City. Two books of translated poems Life Sentence (1998) and *Take My Word for It* (1998) are available from Anvil Press.

Suzanne Franks is a writer and journalist. Her latest book, *Having None of it: Women, Men and the Future of Work*, is published in paperback by Granta.

Brian Heaphy is a research fellow on the Economic and Social Research Council funded project 'Families of choice: the structure and meanings of non-heterosexual relationships', based at South Bank University.

Jaan Kaplinski was born in Tartu in Estonia, and is one of Eastern Europe's leading poets. His poetry is published by Harvill Press. His latest book (in translation) is called *Through the Forest* (1996).

Jackie Kay is a poet and novelist. Her latest book of poetry *Off Colour* (1999) is published by Bloodaxe Books.

Mike Kenny is Lecturer in Politics at the University of Sheffield and author of *The First New Left*, Lawrence and Wishart 1995.

Mimi Khalvati lives in Hackney. She runs poetry workshops and courses. Her latest book *Entries on Light* (1997) was published by Carcanet.

Stephen Knight lives in London. His latest book *Dream City Cinema* (1996) is published by Bloodaxe Books.

Roshi Naidoo writes on issues in black cultural politics. She is lecturer in media and cultural studies at Middlesex University.

Ray Pahl is at the Institute for Social and Economic Research at the University of Essex and is Emeritus Professor of Sociology at the University of Kent and Canterbury. He is currently completing a book for Polity Press on friendship.

Brian Patten is one of Britain's best known poets. His latest collection *Armada* (1996) is published by Flamingo.

Adam Phillips is a psychoanalyst and writer. His latest book is *Darwin's Worms* (faber and faber).

Jacek Podsiadlo was born in Szewna in the Kielce region of Poland. A few of his poems have been translated into English by Donald Pirie and are published in *Young Poets of a New Poland* (1993) by Forest Books.

Anna Robinson teaches at Brixton Prison and has had poems published in a variety of magazines.

Jonathan Rutherford is part of the Signs of the Times group. He is a lecturer in media and cultural studies at Middlesex University. His most recent book is *I Am No Longer Myself Without You* (Harper Collins 2000).

Nick Stevenson is a lecturer in Sociology at the University of Sheffield.

Rachel Thomson is a Senior Research Fellow based in the Social Science Research Centre at South Bank University, London. She is a research fellow on the Economic and Social Research Council funded study *Children 5-16: Growing into the 21st Century*. Other researchers include Janet Holland, Sheila Henderson, Sheena McGrellis and Sue Sharpe.

Wendy Wheeler is Reader in English at the University of North London and author of *A New Modernity? Change in Science, Literature and Politics* (Lawrence and Wishart 1999).

ACKNOWLEDGEMENTS

I'd like to thank the Signs of the Times group for providing a space to think and argue, and Frances Angela for her help with the poetry.

The editor and publisher gratefully acknowledge the following for permission to quote copyright material: Carcanet Press Ltd for 'Years Like Leaves' in *Homecoming* (1993) by Bo Carpelan, translated by David McDuff; Anvil Press for 'Youthing' by Nina Cassian in *Take My Word For It* (1998), and 'Temptation' by Nina Cassian in *Life Sentence* (1998), translated by Brenda Walker and Andrea Deletant; Blood Axe Books for 'The Stepfather' in *Flowering Limbs* (1993) by Stephen Knight; Forest Books for 'Don't Leave Me' and 'Grass Accepts' by Jacek Podsiadlo, translated by Donald Pirie in *Young Poets of a New Poland* (1993); Flamingo for 'The Armada' by Brian Patten, in *Armada* (1996). 'My Name is...' by Anna Robinson first appeared in *Prop* magazine; 'A British Summer' by Stephen Knight first appeared in *London Review of Books*.